SAGE was founded in 1965 by Sara Miller McCune to support the dissemination of usable knowledge by publishing innovative and high-quality research and teaching content. Today, we publish over 900 journals, including those of more than 400 learned societies, more than 800 new books per year, and a growing range of library products including archives, data, case studies, reports, and video. SAGE remains majority-owned by our founder, and after Sara's lifetime will become owned by a charitable trust that secures our continued independence.

Los Angeles | London | New Delhi | Singapore | Washington DC | Melbourne

MODERN MEDIA, ELECTIONS AND DEMOCRACY

MODERN MEDIA, ELECTIONS AND DEMOCRACY

BHEEMAIAH KRISHNAN RAVI

Los Angeles | London | New Delhi
Singapore | Washington DC | Melbourne

Copyright © Bheemaiah Krishnan Ravi, 2018

All rights reserved. No part of this book may be reproduced or utilised in any form or by any means, electronic or mechanical, including photocopying, recording, or by any information storage or retrieval system, without permission in writing from the publisher.

First published in 2018 by

SAGE Publications India Pvt Ltd
B1/I-1 Mohan Cooperative Industrial Area
Mathura Road, New Delhi 110 044, India
www.sagepub.in

SAGE Publications Inc
2455 Teller Road
Thousand Oaks, California 91320, USA

SAGE Publications Ltd
1 Oliver's Yard, 55 City Road
London EC1Y 1SP, United Kingdom

SAGE Publications Asia-Pacific Pte Ltd
3 Church Street
#10-04 Samsung Hub
Singapore 049483

Published by Vivek Mehra for SAGE Publications India Pvt Ltd, typeset in 10/12 pt Adobe Garamond by Fidus Design Pvt. Ltd., Chandigarh and printed at Chaman Enterprises, New Delhi.

Library of Congress Cataloging-in-Publication Data Available

ISBN: 978-93-866-0237-4 (HB)

SAGE Team: Rajesh Dey, Guneet Kaur, Syeda Aina Rahat Ali and Rajinder Kaur

To my parents Late N. B. Krishnan and Smt G. N. Rathnamma

Thank you for choosing a SAGE product!
If you have any comment, observation or feedback,
I would like to personally hear from you.

Please write to me at **contactceo@sagepub.in**

Vivek Mehra, Managing Director and CEO, SAGE India.

Bulk Sales

SAGE India offers special discounts
for purchase of books in bulk.
We also make available special imprints
and excerpts from our books on demand.

For orders and enquiries, write to us at

Marketing Department
SAGE Publications India Pvt Ltd
B1/I-1, Mohan Cooperative Industrial Area
Mathura Road, Post Bag 7
New Delhi 110044, India

E-mail us at **marketing@sagepub.in**

Get to know more about SAGE

Be invited to SAGE events, get on our mailing list.
Write today to **marketing@sagepub.in**

This book is also available as an e-book.

Contents

Foreword by Jabbar Al-Obaidi — ix
Preface — xi
Acknowledgements — xv

1. Elections and Media in Democracy — 1
2. Modern Media and Society — 23
3. Media and Elections — 52
4. Media Professionalism and Election Coverage — 63
5. The Media in Political Campaigns — 91
6. The Role of Television — 110
7. Legal Framework for Media and Elections — 129
8. International Case Studies on Media and Elections — 160
9. Media and Elections in India — 177
10. Ethical Considerations in Election Coverage — 199

Bibliography — 209
Index — 216
About the Author — 225

Foreword

Books and materials focused on media and elections in the advanced countries are not rare these days. However, writing about strategic, democratic, vertical and horizontal relations of media and elections from international perspective with illustrative case studies such as India is rare and exceptional. It is thus worth noting this book titled *Modern Media, Elections and Democracy* by Professor (PhD) B. K. Ravi. It distinguished itself by high-quality writing approach and inclusiveness in its analytical discussion and focus. I know Professor Ravi as a friend and colleague, but most importantly, I know him as skilful educator and a researcher of high calibre.

The book is well organized, and its chapters are logically interconnected. It begins with two chapters that cover the nature and relations of elections and media in democracies. Chapter 1 examines the role of media in the democratic processes, the relations between media and politics, the public discourse and the debate about various issues. While Chapter 2 highlights the importance of media in relations to society, media landscape in different countries and media ownership; private and community media, politics, regulations, the Internet and social media in modern society.

Chapters 3 and 4 lay out the concepts and procedures for media and elections, and media coverage. Chapter 3, for example, illustrates the development of communication technologies and the obligations and duties of media prior, during and after elections. Chapter 4 establishes the importance of media professionalism and media responsibility in covering elections.

Chapter 5 offers an elaborative coverage of media and political campaigns and political debate about essential and secondary national, regional and global issues. In addition, this chapter discusses the agenda-setting theory and the forgotten media's social responsibility. Chapter 6 demonstrates the critical role of television in elections. Candidates and the audiences appear to rely heavily on television during elections. Politicians recognize the impact of television political programmes on their audience. For instance, the chapter provides full account of the role and impact of television on voters in India.

The lens of legal and practical experience is the focus of the next two chapters. Chapter 7, 'Legal Framework for Media and Elections', delivers a comprehensive discussion of international law and regulations, polls, pluralism versus individualism and freedom of speech and limitations. Chapter 8, 'International Case Studies on Media and Elections', comparatively, explores numerous international media cases showing the role and impact of media in elections.

Thoughtfully and deliberately, the case of the largest democracy in the world is the subject of the next chapter. Chapter 9, 'Media and Elections in India', argues that 'The survival and success of India's democracy owes great deal to the vigor and vibrancy of the media'. The 2014 election in India is a focal point for this chapter.

Morally and critically, attention focuses on professional codes and ethics in the final chapter. Chapter 10, 'Ethical Considerations in Election Coverage', provides an intellectual opportunity for the reader to reconsider and rethink the role and impact of media in elections and in nurturing true democracies throughout the world. This chapter offers a map for media practitioners, media students and media teacher, and even politicians, along with best practices that apply ethics, responsibilities and duties. The 'First duty of a journalist is to report accurately and without bias'.

Based on more than two-and-a-half decades of professional experience and as journalist, educator and seasoned researcher, Professor B. K. Ravi stood and always stands for free media with social responsibility, media ethicality, morality and media public access. In this book, the author sustains his strong argument to disseminate information and accurate news and analysis to everyone in the society including rural and remote areas. In other words, Professor Ravi promotes the concept of media for all, and not for elites or the capitals and big cities.

In summary, this is a valuable source for college students, educators and media people. It is audience-/reader-friendly, well-structured and focused on the position of media in any elections including his own country India.

Jabbar Al-Obaidi
Professor of Media Studies and Communication Technologies,
Director, The Center for Middle East Studies,
Bridgewater State University, USA

Preface

The history of Indian media is very interesting. We should not forget the fact that India is a multicultural, multilinguistic country with a lot of social disparities. The entry and growth of media in India was unsystematic. The technology was imposed on the dark society, unaware of the scientific temperament or exposure in the other parts of the world. The printed word entered the country when majority were illiterate and unaware and were not able to grasp what was printed. Cinema which was called as the dream factory came as a boon for the mythological content of India, and unfortunately developed itself as the medium of entertainment. The entry of television saw the metamorphosis of Indian media which transformed itself as the Indian media industry. The commercialization and privatization resulted in the modification of the priorities of the Indian media industry. The new media which further resulted in convergence has totally changed the functioning and reach of media. The concepts of boomerang of technology, information pollution and information explosion have changed the total dimension and functioning of media which require redefining the whole communication process. The era of experimentation has begun.

India being one of the largest democracies of the world has a very interesting political history. Although media was at its infancy during the time of Independence, Indian media has gradually played a very important role in moulding public opinion as well as influenced the political behaviour of the people. The greatest strength of media is that it is capable of reminding people about the earlier happenings and developments.

Public memory is always very short. Indian politics had very impressive and colourful personalities. Wooing the voters and convincing them to vote in their favour is not an easy job. There are various factors that decide the results of the elections. The first Prime Minister of India, Pandit Jawaharlal Nehru, won the elections with his message of development. Nehru sowed the seed of development in the minds of the people. The great mass leader Mrs Indira Gandhi was very much oriented towards the message of social justice. Her slogans *Garibi Hatao* (eradicate poverty), *Roti, Kapda aur Makaan* (food, cloth and shelter) and maintaining unity and integrity of our country brought her power every time. She used to get majority in the elections.

Atal Bihari Vajpayee-led Bharatiya Janata Party (BJP) government which lost the government only by one vote in the no-confidence motion later in 1999 campaigned for one vote to BJP and came back to power. Again, in 2004 Lok Sabha elections, BJP had a vigorous campaign, India Shinning, which was rejected by the Indian electorate. In 2013 Karnataka Assembly elections, Congress party campaigned as 'enough is enough' campaign against the BJP Party, which worked out, and Congress came back to power making Siddaramaiah as the chief minister.

The 2014 Lok Sabha elections changed the way India perceived it to be. Termed as 'social media elections', it made the largest democratic election in the world to date and so much of it took place online. While online election activity saw a dramatic increase from early years, the country saw a number of other important election firsts: 150 million between the ages of 18 and 23 were newly eligible to vote, two out of three people in India were under the age of 35 and there was an unprecedented voter turnout at 66.4 per cent. India's Internet penetration is currently estimated to be at 243 million or roughly 19 per cent of India's population. Narendra Modi and Rahul Gandhi, the two prime ministerial candidates, not only campaigned online but also built themselves a brand online.

Meanwhile, the privatization, commercialization and political ownership of media saw the exploitation of Indian media during elections. The competition among the media resulted in sensationalism, exaggeration, sponsorship, advertorials and the concept of paid news. The Election Commission of India took some stringent actions to control the situation.

The role of media in elections is multifaceted. It also involves educating the voters on the election process, convincing them to participate in voting providing a platform to the stakeholders to share their messages and serving as 'watchdog' assessing the fairness of the process. If the media performs these functions with alacrity, it serves the democratic polity well. This compendium is a concise compilation of both theoretical and empirical literature dealing with the relationship between the two, assessing the performance of media in the electoral process.

This book analyses the intricate relationships between modern media and society in general and proceeds to focus the discussion on the role and performance of media in elections. An attempt to review, both historically and geographically, the extensive survey of various elections and the role played by media in influencing the outcomes of those elections are made. The extensive review ranges from the TV magic in Kennedy–Nixon debates in the 1960 in the US presidential elections to the critical role played by social media in Modi's successful campaign for the post of prime minister in India. An important aspect of the delineation of the theme is considerations regarding media pluralism, editorial autonomy and media professionalism vis-à-vis election coverage. The issues have been discussed in detail noting that the absence of these media prerequisites can be detrimental to the election coverage.

Acknowledgements

I offer my heartfelt thanks to Sri Siddaramaiah, Honourable Chief Minister, Government of Karnataka, and the voice of the deprived, for encouraging all my activities. Also, I should remember the support extended to me always by my mentor Sri H. M. Revanna, transport minister, Karnataka, and member, Karnataka Legislative Council, for encouraging me to take up new research projects. I also thank my well-wisher Sri H. Vishwanath, former member of parliament and education minister, Karnataka. My dutiful thanks goes to veteran media educationist and researcher my guru Professor H. S. Eswara for his valuable guidance to me in completing this book. Dr Jabbar Al-Obaidi, Professor of Media Studies and Communication Technologies and Director, the Center for Middle East Studies, Bridgewater State University, Bridgewater, Massachusetts, USA, is an internationally renowned scholar and researcher. In spite of his busy schedule, he has written the Foreward to my book. Professor Jabbar Al-Obaidi is one of my well-wishers and has encouraged all my activities. I am very grateful to him.

I have to thank my student Dr M. R. Sathya Prakash, assistant professor, Department of PG Studies and Research in Journalism and Mass Communication, Kuvempu University, Jnanasahyadri, Shankaraghatta - 577451, Shivamogga district, for supporting me and providing data at every level for completing this book. Without his efforts, I would have not completed this book.

I should thank my family, my mother Smt G. N. Rathnamma, my wife Smt C. Sheela, my daughter K. R. Chaitra Akash and my son K. R. Anoop for having backed me up with unstinted support.

I should dutifully thank Professor B. Thimmegowda, vice-chancellor, Bangalore University, for granting me sabbatical leave to work on this project.

My thanks are due to Professor K. K. Seethamma, registrar, and Sri Lokesh, finance officer, Bangalore University.

I also thank my colleagues Professor Jagdeesh Prakash, Professor H. K. Mariswamy, Dr B. Shailashree and Dr Sanjeev Raj of the Department of Communication, Bangalore University, who co-operated for the completion of this project in their own way.

My sincere thanks is due to SAGE Publications India Pvt Ltd for publishing my book.

1
Elections and Media in Democracy

The role of media as the fourth estate and as a forum of public opinion has been recognized from the late seventeenth century. The press has always been regarded as a critical element in public sphere especially in a modern democracy. However, media has undergone a tremendous change over the years due to various factors. The ownership patterns have changed so as the nature of media and their functions in society. Critics would say that media have taken the downward spiral, which is not helping the public cause. Independent commentators like Noam Chomsky have spoken extensively about the 'manufactured contents' produced by the media. With the onset of global media conglomerates, media have tended to be pro-establishment in nature. Profiteering and aggressive commercialization has led to the deteriorating standards of the media. On one hand, media has benefited immensely by the advances made in information and communication technologies, but on the other hand these technological advances have also created many challenges. People are hardly benefited from the advances seen in the media infrastructure.

Mass media have tended to be bordering on sensationalism and superficiality to survive in the competitive market. Despite this, media is even today regarded as the watchdog and the guardian of the public interest. Given the complex media environment that is prevalent now across the different parts of the world, media role as the fourth estate still remains relevant. However, it should be noted here that under the backdrop of lofty expectations, media have not lived up to the expectations especially in new and restored democracies. Many factors like stringent laws, monopolistic ownership and sometimes the threat of brute force have undermined the power of media. State control is a natural phenomenon, but constraints imposed by the management and market forces have created a situation detrimental to the serious and objective reporting. Sensationalism and shallow reporting and focus on celebrity issues have reduced the media as a mere source of entertainment.

Moreover, the media are sometimes used as proxies in the battle between rival political groups, in the process sowing divisiveness rather than consensus, hate speech instead of dignified debate, and suspicion rather than social trust. In such instances, media contribute to public cynicism and democratic decay. Still, in many democracies, the media has been able to assert its role in strengthening democracy. Investigative reporting, which in some cases has led to the ouster of presidents and the fall of corrupt governments, has made the media an effective and credible watchdog and boosted its credibility among the public. Investigative reporting has also helped accustom officials to an inquisitive press and helped build a culture of openness and disclosure that has made democratically elected governments more accountable (Coronel, 2011).

A true democracy is one in which citizens actively participate in the affairs of the State, especially on issues pertaining to the larger public. Ideally, it is the duty of the media to keep the citizens glued to the affairs of the State by informing and educating and sometimes mobilizing or creating a milieu in which public mobilization takes place spontaneously. For instance, in many democracies radio has become the medium of public choice as it is cheap and easily accessible to all spheres of society. Community and FM radio have been effectively promoting democracy by focusing on grass-roots issues and by acting as alternative and sometimes complementary source of information along with official communication machinery. Radio is a medium that espouses the cause of ethnic and linguistic diversity as the programmes that are aired are invariably about local issues and in the language of the place where it is operating from. Internet can also play a similar role given the interactivity nature of the medium.

Media role in building peace and social consensus is also critical in a democratic system. More often than not, media can act as public platform and provide opposing groups a mechanism for negotiation and dialogue so that they can settle their differences in an amicable and peaceful manner. Unfortunately, as it is being witnessed in television news channels in India, media have been taking sides and reinforcing prejudices or fanning the flames of public discord by displaying the ill-informed or parochial points of views. Trial by the media is another negative trend being witnessed in the national English news channels. Half-truths or prejudiced mindsets have been ruling the roost. Sadly, the journalism for peace, promoted by various NGOs, has suffered big time as high decibel arguments have drowned the objective reportage and have negated the possibility of reconciliation by rightfully providing voice for all the sides of a conflict. Opportunities are given for all the sides, but unfortunately, the nature of argument is replete with incendiary remarks, parochial expressions and tit for tat, to say the least.

It should be noted here with emphasis that the media can play a positive role in democracy only if there is an enabling environment that allows them to do so. Media working in newly established democracies especially need necessary training and skill development in order to carry out in-depth reporting. There should also be mechanisms to ensure that media professionals are held accountable to the public and that ethical and professional standards are met with utmost seriousness. Another important factor in ensuring the media independence is the financial viability of the media organizations. And of course, it should be free from the interference of media moguls and the State. A competitive media environment is also essential in the effective functioning of the media. Competition is in terms of maintaining highest of the professional standards among the media persons especially in serious and objective reportage as mentioned earlier. Media which caters to the elites of the society does not help the public cause. Mainstream media have always shown the tendency to be working for elites of the society. This has to change. The media should also be accessible to as wide a segment of society as possible. Building media capacity and democratization of media accessibility would create a better condition for the society. Efforts should be made to provide the press freedom and at the same time ensure media accountability.

1.1 Media Role in a Democracy

No democracy can survive without a free and fair press. As early as the seventeenth century, enlightenment philosophers have espoused the cause of openness with regard to governance as an essential shield against the tyranny and excesses of arbitrary rule. In the early seventeenth century, the French political philosopher Montesquieu, reacting on a secret accusation delivered by palace courtiers to the French king, prescribed publicity as the cure for the abuse of power. English and American thinkers who have appeared on the scene during the later part of the century would agree with Montesquieu, by recognizing the importance of press in making the administrators aware of the public discontents and allowing the governments to correct their errors and mend their ways.

Since then, the press has been widely recognized as the fourth estate of a democracy providing checks and balances and making all the stakeholders accountable in the effective functioning of administrative mechanisms. It is exactly for this very reason that those who believe in democracy have tended to take the enlightenment philosophy's view of the media (press). Although a staunch critic of the journalistic practices, Thomas Jefferson celebrated the press, arguing that only through the exchange of information and opinion through the press would the truth emerge. Jefferson famously declared: 'Were it left to me to decide whether we should have a government without newspapers or newspapers without government, I should not hesitate to prefer the latter' (Tabassum, 2009).

Contemporary studies on democratic theory and practice appreciated the media role in ensuring accountability of governments. In democracies across the different parts of the world, media has been accepted as the watchdog and not merely as a passive recorder of events that unfolds at their own backyards. It can be argued that the governments cannot be held accountable if the citizens are ill-informed about the functioning of the administrative mechanisms. The press should act as a guardian of the public interest, informing citizens against those who are carrying out wrong or detrimental policies and practices.

A free, fair, fearless and proactive media is essential in democracies where administrative institutions are weak or weighed down by political pressures of incumbent government or powerful lobbies operating from the government as well as outside. For example, when legislatures, judiciaries and other important bodies of the State become ineffective against the mighty and powerful or these very institutions become corrupt, the onus would always be on the media, as it is the only check available against the abuse of power. This implies that the media have to play a kind of heroic role in exposing the excesses of powerful leaders like presidents, prime ministers, legislators, executives, magistrates, despite the risks involved in doing so. Media also act as a medium between administrators and citizens thereby leading to more intelligent and inclusive policy and decision-making. Hence, it can still be argued that the enlightenment tradition of the press as a public forum still remains strong. In new democracies, there is a huge expectation from the media that it would help build a civic culture and a tradition of dialogue and discussion, which was not possible during the period of erstwhile authoritarian rule.

Eminent contemporary thinkers like Nobel laureate Amartya Sen have also ascribed to the press the same responsibility and powers that enlightenment philosophers had envisioned. Sen calls it as 'transparency guarantees'. Free press and the free flow of information and critical public discussion, he said, are 'an inescapably important requirement of good public policy'. These guarantees, he wrote, 'have a clear instrumental role in preventing corruption, financial irresponsibility and underhanded dealings' (Sen, 1999).

Sen sees the media as a watchdog not just against corruption but also against disaster. 'There has never been a famine in a functioning multiparty democracy', he said.

> A free press and the practice of democracy contribute greatly to bringing out information that can have an enormous impact on policies for famine prevention…a free press and an active political opposition constitute the best early-warning system a country threatened by famine could ever have. Stefanick (2011)

The United Nations Development Programme (UNDP) ascribes an exalted position for the media especially in addressing poverty across the world. In order to address poverty, the UNDP says, it is not just enough to transfer the economic resource to the needy. It is more important to provide information to them thereby creating a conducive atmosphere in which they participate more meaningfully in political and social life. Poor people cannot assert their rights if they do not know that they can do so. If they remain outside of the laws and procedures of acquiring entitlement or any other mechanisms they can use to remedy their deprivations, they will always remain poor. It should be noted here that the democracy cannot take root if the poor and powerless are kept out of the public sphere. The argument is that effective media are the key as they can provide the information to all sections of the society, thereby creating a level playing field for the poor people as well to take part in public life.

Ideally, the media should provide voice to these marginalized sections as this would amount to providing space for poverty, gender, ethnic or religious affiliation. By giving these groups a place in the media, their views and their afflictions become part of mainstream public debate, and hopefully this would contribute to a social consensus against injustices meted out to them. In this way, the media also contribute to the easing of social conflicts and to promoting reconciliation among divergent social groups. All these are extrapolations on the media's role as virtual public platform by providing information, media play a catalytic role, making reforms possible through the democratic process and in the end strengthening democratic institutions and making possible public participation, without which democracy is mere good theory on paper.

1.1.1 Media Constraints

Media often have to face many constraints emanating from various sources: ownership pattern, commercial pressure, State control, lack of professional standard and so on. Due to any one of these constrains, media have been found wanting in reporting the issues that matters the most to the public. Unfortunately, public interest has taken a backseat owing to pressures faced by the media. For example, media in new and restored democracies have not lived up to the task. Although, new constitutions are written to provide guarantees of press freedom and the right to information, allowing journalists to report on areas that were previously taboo. In addition, democratically elected legislatures have enacted laws that allow both journalists and ordinary citizens much more access to information on government policy and the actions of politicians than in the past. Despite the availability of these legal provisions, media have not been able to function freely because of the failure of the administration to uphold the values enshrined in their own constitutions.

Today, in most countries that have undergone a democratic transition since the 1980s, the press is considered as an important player on the political arena. Journalists are often feared by politicians because they have been successful in uncovering corruption, the abuse of power and assorted wrong practices. Journalists are also being relentlessly wooed by the leaders of different hue, because a bad press can mean the end of their respective political careers. Media exposures have led to policy changes and reforms as well. Corrupt officials including presidents and prime ministers have been ousted partly because of media exposures. In many new democracies, active press is part of the political process, and it is hard to imagine how governments would function without it.

In Indonesia, hundreds of new newspapers started after the 32-year reign of President Suharto ended in 1998. Indonesians called it the 'euphoria press'. Euphoria is a wonderful thing, but fortunately or unfortunately, it does not always give birth to good journalism. The same is the case for Central and Eastern Europe and the newly independent States of the former Soviet Union, where there were lack of skilled journalists to work in the news organizations created by the media boom. The boom also results in intense competition, which often means racing for the headlines and sacrificing substance and depth.

The competition for the market has meant that the media in most new democracies have succumbed to the global trend of 'dumping down' the news. This is especially true in the case of television, where reports on crime and entertainment occupy more airwaves in comparison to other important news of the day. The importance given to glitzy effects and bite-sized news reports in television have left no time for serious in-depth discussion of the issues that matter the most in a democratic society. As a result, public discourse has suffered, and both officials and citizens have got used to infotainment types of news that they get to see every day on every possible television news channels.

In many news organizations, including European and American countries, budget limitations do not allow reporters to go in pursuit of solid and serious journalism. In many countries, media have become profitable industries. But unfortunately, this does not translate into good journalism as media organizations are putting their money on technological upgradation and glitzy effects in news presentation at the cost of objective reportage. Another important issue is about the professional training required by the journalists in order to do the contextualized reporting needed by democracies. Often, journalists do not have the experience and the training to live up to the professional standard. The miniscule minority of the journalists who manage to get their acts together are undermined by the political or commercial interests of the media owners.

In many countries, ownership of the media is controlled by corporate interests. A 2001 study of 97 countries by the World Bank shows that throughout the world, media monopolies dominate. The study says:

> In our sample of 97 countries, only four percent of media enterprises are widely held. Less than two percent have other ownership structures apart from family or state control, and a mere two percent are employee owned. On an average family controlled newspapers account for 57 percent of our sample, and families control 34 percent of television stations. State ownership is vast. On an average, the state controls approximately 29 percent of newspapers and 60 percent of television stations. The state owns a huge share (72 percent) of radio stations. The media industry is therefore owned overwhelmingly by parties most likely to extract private benefits of control. (Coronel, 2011)

Media owners have unapologetically been extracting such private benefits. For instance, in the new democracies, media magnates have used their newspapers or broadcast stations to promote their commercial interests, to cut down their rivals and in other ways to advance their political or business agenda. State ownership, meanwhile, allows government functionaries to clamp down on critical reporting and disobedient reporters, and enables the government to propagate its unchallenged views among the people. The media owners have always been dictating the terms as per their political and business interests. Media content have often followed this norm and more often than not have allowed it to be manipulated by vested interests. In many cases, the media acts as anti-democratic, contributing to cynicism about government and democratic process. As a result, the public loses confidence in the media and in democratic institutions in general.

1.2 Good Media Practices

In today's politics and society at large, media is essential in safeguarding the transparency of the democratic processes. Transparency here implies various things like access to information, accountability of individuals, institutions and processes, and also rightful participation and public debate. Transparency also means that citizens are provided with necessary and comprehensive information so as to make informed choices as well as be able to hold officials and institutions accountable.

In a modern information society, information is an important factor which ensures healthy democratic practices. Access to legal and operational proceedings as well as information about officials and institutions are essential from the public perspective. So far as elections are concerned, the election commission (EC), for example, is obligated to inform the public on their actions, decisions and plans. Individuals appointed or elected to an EC are public figures who should be working in the interests of the public. As such, information regarding their affiliations, histories and performance while in office is to be freely accessed by the public.

Media should act as an institution that strives towards prevention and investigation of allegations of violations or malpractices of political parties or leaders or officials. This watchdog role of the media extends from holding officials accountable for their actions while in office and also for the entire electoral process. Media presence at voting and counting centres is critical to preventing electoral fraud. However, media should be able to act independently and impartially in order to ensure proper information is disseminated to the public. An election in which pubic is not able to participate cannot be deemed democratic. Media should ensure that the public is involved transparently in electoral debate and discussion. Transparency would also imply that candidates are represented publicly. At the macro level, it is the duty of the media to provide details about the processes of voting, counting, registering candidate nomination, campaigning and so forth in order to enable public participation in them.

In many new democracies, the mass media are challenged by market forces, restrictive states and in some cases hostile or apathetic citizens. Despite the prevalence of such negative trends, some news organizations and media non-governmental organizations (NGOs) in many countries have managed to assert the media's role in strengthening democracy.

> Perhaps the most instructive case is that of Latin America, where it is widely acknowledged that sustained investigative reporting on corruption, human rights violations and other forms of wrongdoing has helped build a culture of accountability in government and strengthened the weakening democracies of the continent. There, media exposure, particularly of corruption in high places, has helped bring down governments. The downfall of four presidents—Fernando Collor de Mello of Brazil in 1992, Carlos Andres Perez of Venezuela

in 1993, Abdala Bucaram of Ecuador in 1997 and Alberto Fujimori in 2000—was due in large measure to investigative reporting on their complicity in corrupt deals. Such reporting has made the press a credible institution in the region's new democracies. Because it has functioned effectively and independently, the media here enjoy the public's support and trust. (Corone, 2011)

In Southeast Asia's new democracies, sustained reporting on corruption in public life has resulted in the ouster of corrupt officials and raised public awareness on the need for reform. For instance, impeachment charges were filed against President Joseph Estrada in 2000 mainly due to investigative reporting that provided the evidences against him. Estrada was ousted from his office in a popular uprising on the streets of Manila in January 2001, mainly due to objective reporting carried out by the media. Similarly, in Thailand also, investigative reports have unearthed evidences about the shadowy business dealings of Prime Minister Thaksin Shinawatra. In Indonesia, the press has been able to uncover wrongdoing that led to the filing of charges against high officials, including the powerful speaker of Parliament Akbar Tanjung in 2001.

However, it should be noted here that this success has come at a great cost. The New York-based Committee to Protect Journalists tallied 117 killings of journalists in Latin America from 1988 to 1998. In the Philippines, 36 journalists have been killed since the restoration of democracy in 1986. In Thailand and Indonesia, journalists have been beaten up, threatened and killed. Worldwide, 15 of the 68 murdered journalists in 2001 were slain because of investigative work related to corruption. Most of the murders have taken place in countries where the rule of law is weak and the judiciary is unable and unwilling to defend press rights.

At the most fundamental level, a free and fair press is possible only in a country where journalists enjoy protection and where their rights are ensured. The constitutional and legal provisions do not always ensure that the media can report without any sort of fear or favour. But it is the responsibility of a democracy to ensure security to journalists working for the betterment of the institutions. The rights of journalists must be upheld by an independent judiciary and protected by the rule of law. In Latin America and Southeast Asia, many of those murdered were the victims of small-town bosses able to terrorize communities because weak States cannot enforce the law and provide protection to their citizens, journalists included.

Press freedom is possible only when other institutions perform their functions properly. But unfortunately due to various factors, these institutions are unable to perform their duties. One of the chief reasons for this failure is that press is threatened and bullied. It is invariably up to crusading journalists to break this impasse despite the risks. In many places, there is no dearth of journalists willing to take on this arduous task of bringing out the truth on to the public domain. However, it should be noted here that many journalists do not have the skills or training to carry out investigative reporting. On top of this, even news organizations may not be willing to put in the investment in time, resources for research and the development of journalistic talent that investigative journalism essentially needs.

One of the dangers of investigative reporting is that it threatens to upset the cordial relationships between media owners and their friends belonging to the upper crust of business and political class. Media owners are wary that the hard-hitting investigative stories would drive away the advertisers from their respective media houses. So, the task of bringing out investigative stories pertaining these very business barons and political heavy weights is indeed an onerous task.

> Given these obstacles, the only way that investigative reports can make any headway in the media free market is to show that they can sell newspapers and news programmes and that there is an audience for serious reporting. The truth is that in many countries, investigative reports do sell. They generate a great deal of public reaction and bring recognition to news organizations. The key is to get newsrooms to initiate and invest in investigations despite the costs and the risks. One way is to convince them of the rewards, in terms of increased audience share, name-brand recognition or professional prestige. Awards for investigative reporting offer one way to encourage this trend. (OECD, 2000)

Carefully researched and high-impact investigative reportage would go a long way in establishing public trust and build media credibility among the public. Hence, the onus is also on journalists to put the hard work against all odds in order to demonstrate that they serve the public interest by unearthing corrupt practices, scams and abuse of power. Such reportage and courageous journalistic practices would always have popular backing. There have been many instances of public standing by such brave journalists by way of subscribing to journals and magazines which carry explosive investigative stories. In India, *Tehelka*, a weekly magazine, and in Karnataka, *Lankesh Patrike*, a Kannada tabloid, are cases in point. *Tehelka* is known for publishing investigative stories and *Lankesh Patrike*, edited by popular Kannada writer P. Lankesh, has unearthed several scams that have rocked the respective governments of the time. *Lankesh Patrike* has always enjoyed popular public support, in spite of not publishing any advertisement as a matter of policy.

> Such support may not be forthcoming if journalists compromise on their freedoms on the superficial and the sensational. Moreover, by constantly

digging for information, by forcing government and the private sector to release documents and by subjecting officials and other powerful individuals to rigorous questioning, investigative journalists expand the boundaries of what is possible to publish. (OECD, 2000)

Such a process would accustom officials to an inquisitive press. They would eventually realize that putting the information on the public domain benefits the government in the long run. Without a free flow of official information, journalists tend to report lies, rumours and speculations, thereby damaging the reputation of the government. Hence, it is in the interest of the government to make available the official document in the public domain. It may take some time, but officials must be convinced that informed citizens make better citizens, even if in the process government takes a beating in the press. On a positive note, it should be recorded here that any government, no matter how corrupt or autocratic, would definitely have reform-minded officials and bureaucrats who understand and appreciate the role of journalists and are willing to co-operate with reporters. In the long run, the constant give and take between journalists and officials helps develop a culture of transparency.

1.2.1 As Peace and Consensus Builder

Democracy would not survive or thrive in a country which is plagued by violence, lawlessness and political instability. Ideally, democracy should guarantee representation for opposing groups so that they can settle their differences in an amiable and peaceful manner. But the constant violence and strife would damage the very fabric of democracy. It should be noted here with a touch of sadness that in many newly formed democracies, this is the situation that prevails. In some countries, even the democratically elected governments have forced to behave and act in an authoritarian manner in order to check the violence and instability.

An overview of the media practices across such democracies has indicated towards a disappointing trend. Contrary to the expectations, media have not played an objective or neutral role during the times of conflict and communal violence. In many cases, media have been accused of sensationalizing violence without getting to the root of the conflict and covering the conflict with objective mindset. By focusing on warmongering, the media have been ignoring peace-building efforts. Sometimes, media organizations have sowed hate speech and encouraged violence.

At the height of the conflict in Rwanda in the 1990s, a radio station that had been supported by international donors became the mouthpiece of extremists who favoured and encouraged genocide. Recognizing the crucial role that the media play in conflict situations, many NGOs have embarked on training journalists in what is called 'peace journalism', which endeavours to promote reconciliation through careful reportage that gives voice to all sides of a conflict and resists explanations for violence in terms of innate enmities or ancient hatreds. Peace journalism avoids giving undue attention to violence, focusing instead on the impact of war on communities on both sides of the divide and their efforts to bridge their differences.

1.3 Media and Elections

Electoral democracy is nearly impossible without an effective and proactive media. Elections are not just about the freedom to vote, it is about a participatory process where the voters actively involve themselves in public debates on key electoral issues. In order to do that, they need to have adequate information about leading political parties in the fray, their policies and of course candidates contesting elections. Apart from these, understanding of election process is a major factor in making informed choices. Media play a significant role in providing information to the voters as well as acting as a watchdog to safeguard the transparency of the electoral process. Any election without a free and fair media is detrimental to democracy.

Independent and pluralistic media acts as catalyst in ensuring transparency, accountability and participation necessitating good governance and human rights-based development. News media is an important factor in paving the way for good governance. It is also vital to increase transparency and accountability on the part of the lawmakers involved in the decision-making process. Media is also essential to communicate the principles of good governance to the society. In a functional democracy, media plays multiple roles. Media acts as a watchdog, a gatekeeper, a whistle-blower, an advocate, a conscience keeper, platform of information and debate, and a catalyst in the process of development and, more importantly, as an agent of change in the society.

In order to fulfil their responsibilities, media needs to maintain a very high level of professionalism, objectivity, accuracy and impartiality in their coverage of news and events. Regulatory frameworks can help ensure high professional standards. Laws and regulations governing media should be able to assure fundamental freedoms essential to democracy, including freedom of information and expression, as well as freedom of participation. Public service broadcasting (PSB) networks funded by the government need to provide fair and equitable coverage to opposition parties in order to ensure appropriate media behaviour during elections (Carver, 2001).

Traditionally, media have been understood to refer to the printed press as well as radio and television broadcasters. However, in recent years, the definition of media has become broader encompassing new media including web journalism and social media. Social media has of late become a major source of news for traditional media players as well as subscribers or users. Citizen journalism is also widely gaining ground, especially in countries where traditional media is either controlled or strictly regulated by either government or private operators. A major concern of media coverage during elections is the right of voters to full and accurate information, and their rights to participate in debates and dialogue on policy matters and with politicians. Pertinent to this task is the entitlement of parties and candidates to use the media as a platform for interaction with the public. Further, the EC needs to communicate information to the electorate and other stakeholders, including the political parties and candidates. The media themselves have a right to report freely and to scrutinize the whole electoral process. And this scrutiny is in itself a significant safeguard against interference or corruption in the management or conduct of the electoral process.

1.3.1 Media Role during Elections

Most of the debates on media's functions within electoral contexts often focus on their watchdog role; by continuous and objective scrutiny and discussion of the successes and failures of candidates, governments and the EC, the media can inform the public of how effectively the candidates have performed and help to hold them to account. Media also have other roles to perform in enabling greater public participation in electoral process in terms of educating voters as to how to exercise their democratic rights; by providing coverage with regard to latest developments on election campaigns; by providing a platform for the major political parties and their respective candidates as well as independent candidates to communicate their message to the public; by providing an interactive platform for the voters to communicate their concerns, opinions and needs to the parties, candidates, the EC, the government and other voters, and to interact on the issues which they feel need to be discussed; by allowing the parties and candidates to debate with each other; by reporting and interpreting results and monitoring counting of votes; by scrutinizing the entire electoral process, including conduct of elections and its management, in order to evaluate its fairness, efficiency and probity; by providing information to the public that is as far as possible avoids inflammatory language to help prevent poll-related violence.

However, it should be noted here that the media are not the sole source of information for voters; but in a world dominated by mass communications, it is increasingly the media that determine the political agenda, even in less technologically developed countries. The media plays a major role in keeping the citizens informed of current events and raising awareness about various issues in a democratic society. Media also makes an extremely significant impact on the public opinion and public agenda. The media is the primary means through which public opinion is created, shaped and most of the times manipulated. If this is the media's role in normal course of events, it becomes even more vital in exceptional times, one of which is electoral process, when the media becomes a one of the all-important primary players. Elections constitute a basic challenge to the media, putting its impartiality and objectivity to the litmus test. The task of the media, especially national media organizations, should not be to function only as a mouthpiece for any government body or particular candidate. Its basic responsibility is to inform and educate the public and act as a neutral and objective platform for the free debate of myriad points of view (Carver, 2001).

It is for this very reason that election observers, for instance, routinely comment on media access and coverage of elections as one of the major criteria for judging whether elections are being held in a free and fair manner. Monitoring the mass media during the election periods has become an increasingly important practice in modern democracies. As new democracies started to mature and attempting to resolve issues pertaining to electoral reforms, they have also been able to measure and monitor the media practices during elections by using a combination of statistical analysis and the techniques of media studies and discourse.

1.4 Media as a Campaign Platform

Candidates and parties have every right to provide the electorate information pertaining to their attributes, political agendas and proposed plans. On the one hand, candidates accomplish this task by directly meeting the members of the electorate, and on the other hand, they also carry out their campaigns through media. It is essential that all candidates and parties are provided with equal access to media for this endeavour. Political parties and candidates invariably use the mass media for campaigning through sponsored direct access spots, paid political advertising, televised debates, use of social media and other mechanisms. Sometimes candidates would get ample coverage by the media due to the newsworthiness of their campaign activities. It is no secret that political parties spend a huge money and human resources on planning and executing the mass media campaigns along with the traditional and time-tested door-to-door campaign that they undertake.

Hence, the media should also create a level playing field for the contestants to rightfully express or campaign about their candidature. An equal access to State broadcasters as well as other State resources should be made available to them.

> Among the most effective, but least analyzed, means of autocratic survival is an uneven playing field. In countries like Botswana, Georgia, Kyrgyzstan, Malaysia, Malawi, Mozambique, Senegal, Singapore, Tanzania, and Venezuela, democratic competition is undermined less by electoral fraud or repression than by unequal access to state institutions, resources, and the media. An uneven playing field is less evident to outside observers than is electoral fraud or repression, but it can have a devastating impact on democratic competition. Levelling the campaign playing field is one of the main justifications for regulation of media during elections. (Carver, 2001)

1.5 Media as a Public Forum

Citizen participation is an important requirement for any democratic society. It is the duty of all citizens to be proactive and participative in the affairs of the society. Media should provide them platform to be engaged in the process of governance and come out with reactions and necessary actions as and when required. Media also acts as a tool of information dissemination thereby helping the public in making informed choices on issues related to electoral process and other important policies of the government. Ideally, newspapers, radio and television news channels should inform, educate and engage the public on issues pertaining to the larger society. But unfortunately, the track record of media so far in newly established democracies have left lot to be desired and inconsistent to say the least. Due to pressures from various quarters like market or the State itself, the media often shy away from the responsibility towards the society, instead toeing the pro-establishment line.

Elections are fundamental element in a democratic set-up. Elections are also major news for media that will have both negative and positive impacts on the minds of the people. Media have also evolved along with societies. Modern societies have also created modern media, which are becoming more and more intrusive and interventionist. Hence, it can be said that the traditional factors and institutions do not wield the influence once it had on the public. Candidates, parties and party leaders are now more comfortable to carry out their campaigns through media. Perhaps this is also one of the reasons as to why the election campaigns are expensive in many countries.

Advertising is a huge exercise. The cost of newspaper and television advertising is quite expensive and eats into the major portions of the campaign costs. That is why in modern societies, well-funded candidates have better chance of getting elected to the office simply because they can buy airtime in television or space in newspapers. In some countries, a new development has taken place. Candidates are buying news columns where news stories are being written about their achievements. Instead of openly advertising about their candidature, candidates have opted for the negative trend of 'paid news'. Journalists and media houses are also allowing themselves to be part of this unethical practice citing commercial reasons. For example, in India, Ashok Chavan, former chief minister of Maharashtra, was involved in 'paid news' controversy. In some countries, candidates also bribe editors and journalists who endorse their candidature in many ways, 'paid news' is one such method adopted by media organizations.

That is exactly why one should understand that media-based campaigns do not necessarily guarantee enlightened and informed electorates. As it could be observed with regard to US presidential elections, which are imitated by many countries, that clearly brings out the fact that television campaigns tend to focus more on sound bites, charisma and glamour rather than on the substance and depth of the candidate. Unfortunately, public choices are made based on how well the candidates have projected themselves before the television screen. This is not a trend to be fit for emulation. Thankfully, in many new democracies media have contributed immensely to educate the public. For instance, some of the programmes pertaining to public affairs have managed to provide in-depth, contextual and critical analysis of the current affairs and electoral politics.

In addition, in countries like the Philippines and Indonesia, TV and radio networks have managed to produce well-researched public service programmes helping voters to choose wisely and warning them of the consequences of selling their vote during the very important exercise of democracy. Candidates who do not have money to buy airtime to put forth their views before the public have been given space by media organizations during the debates organized by them. Similarly, media have also provided time and space to independent thinkers and NGOs campaigning for clean and transparent elections and also attempting to work against money and muscle politics. Despite the prevalence of such instances, financially influential candidates still have the edge over others as they can buy more airtime and newspaper space to occupy the public imagination. Hence, it can be said that the media is not a level playing field as far as elections are concerned.

> In many new democracies, radio has become the medium of choice, taking the place of newspapers in drawing citizens to the town square for discussion and debate. Compared to television, radio is a less expensive and more accessible medium and is especially popular in poor countries where the media infrastructure is not well developed. FM radio with its localized signal can be an instrument for promoting grass-roots democracy. In Nepal, it took five years after the restoration of democracy for the government to give in to demands by civil society and journalists who argued that it was unconstitutional for the government to monopolize control of the airwaves. In 1996, Nepal became the first country in South Asia to license a non-governmental FM station, Radio Sagarmatha 102.4. Today there are 25 FM stations all over the country and many of them are networked for exchanging programmes and news. FM stations in Nepal have emerged as a true alternative source of information to official channels, and because they are local they focus on local issues and reflect Nepal's ethnic and linguistic diversity. (Coronel, 2011)

Although candidate and party campaigns form the course of debate during elections, there are also other voices that should be heard within public forums so as to create a more wide-ranging debate, a necessary requirement for the voters to make informed choices. For example, Nepal's rural broadcasters have displayed that radio can help in providing the people a chance to make informed choices by decentralizing communication process. Such attempts would strengthen the democratic process in the long run. 'Radio Swargadwari in the insurgency-wracked Dang district in western Nepal is such a reliable source of information that it is staple fare for government officials, local citizens and Maoist guerrillas alike' (Coronel, 2011).

The Internet has also emerged as a democratic medium in comparison to newspapers and television as it allows for free exchange of views among the users of online media. Social media has in fact created ripple across the different parts of world during the electoral process. Today it is considered as an integral part of modern-day electoral campaigns. In many countries, civil society groups and NGOs have found the Internet as an effective medium for transmitting information and opinion pertaining to candidates or political parties and also for mobilizing people in favour of a social cause.

> In 2000, in the heat of the mass protest against Philippine President Estrada, the Internet was a hive of activity for Filipino activists who mounted 'cyber-rallies' and online signature campaigns, mobilizing students, the middle class and also overseas Filipinos who could not participate in protests at home. There are some 7.5 million Filipinos working abroad, and it was through the Web that they kept track of events and took part in social protest. (Coronel, 2011, p. 19)

Interactivity, low entry costs and relative freedom from the State control give the Internet an edge over the other media. But there have been attempts by the State to take control of the medium. Thankfully, so far, such attempts have been met with least success due to the nature of the medium itself. Many civil society groups have also managed to create pressure on the governments across different parts of the world to leave the Internet medium alone as it has become peoples' medium over the past decade or so.

More traditional media like newspapers have also played an educational and informational role, filling the knowledge gap that other social institutions cannot breach. Media companies often blame the need to compete in a tight market for their inability to live up to democratic ideals of the press. But recent experiences have shown that this need not always be the case. The Indonesian news magazine *Tempo*, for example, provides a weekly analysis of the news in addition to original reporting on current affairs, proving that good, solid journalism that appeals to readers as citizens sells. *Tempo*, which is one of the most respected and bestselling publications in Indonesia, is seen as a beacon of democracy and has influenced public opinion on issues of governance, human rights and ethnic and religious conflict. Its commercial success has not blunted the edge of its journalism (Coronel, 2011).

1.5.1 As a Platform for Candidates and Voters

The role of media to act as a forum for public debate and discussion is very important. Media at times provides a mechanism for people to convey their opinion and have a say in formulating political agendas, sometimes even influencing fellow voters in making right political choices during elections.

Members of the public, pressure groups, experts with different perspective and candidates should be provided with platform to air their views on certain policies. Interactive programmes, phone-in programmes where public also participate and air their opinion on pertinent issues is desirable especially during the times of elections. Even the new media and Internet-enabled social media platforms like Facebook, Twitter pages of candidates and political parties are important. People can directly participate and provide their opinion to candidates on such pages. News reports of press conferences, protests and election meetings, media surveys of public opinion, citizen journalism and so forth are also significant both for candidates and voters alike.

However, in post-conflict situations, the role of media as a public forum is very complex as the line between debate and conflict is blurred. One needs to be very careful in professionally managing the situation which can go out of hand at any point in time during sensitive situations. Political violence that took place in East Africa during elections is a case in point. When perspectives are being discussed over media platforms, it can lead to polarization and further create more conflicting agendas. Media's ability to serve as a public platform would be a weakness for countries that do not have strong institutional mechanism to manage the conflicts arising out of differences of opinion.

1.6 Media's Educational Role

Media at times acts as a public educator by carrying out its chief function of providing objective information to them. For example, as a medium of objectivity and transparency, media ensures that the people are provided with necessary information so as to enable them to be able to evaluate the conduct of candidates, officials, political parties as well as the electoral process in general. By acting as a campaign platform, media educates the public about the agendas of different political parties and candidates. This helps the voters to make informed choices during elections. Civil society groups, eminent citizens, political leaders and electoral officials often use this open forum to educate ordinary voters.

Media also provides education to the public through dissemination of information pertaining to the voters. The EC, NGOs, political parties and other stakeholders can directly use the media platform to transmit the critical information needed for the voters. It could be in the form of awareness programmes on importance of voting, voting rights, media reports on electoral events, details such as the location of voting sites, the necessity of voter registration, the nature of counting and so forth provided to the people. Perhaps, this is one of the major reasons as to why it is very important for the EC to communicate frequently with all media, providing them with the necessary facts and figures about the elections, constituencies, voter lists, candidates, etc., to ensure accurate reporting.

Media also play another important role of creating the public awareness about the elections. Media does not simply reproduce the press releases or any other significant information provided by the EC. Instead, media process, evaluate and analyse the content made available by the EC so as to make this information relevant to the public. Without the contextual analysis of the press releases in relation the ground realities, or prevalent opinions of opposing groups, information aired or published in media would remain one-sided. Hence, it is the responsibility of the media to ensure that the public has the right kind of information to make informed choices. Media at its disposal has various tools of analysis techniques like opinion polls, policy evaluation, review of reports, investigative journalism, use of expert input and opinion and critical review of candidates or parties' electoral promises.

1.7 Media, Gender and Elections

Gender is an important factor in media reportage. Media tend to treat men and women differently throughout the world. When it comes to elections, men and women have vastly different experiences of participating in electoral processes. As in the case of other spheres of society, men are more visible and dominant in elections, and their presence in media is also more in comparison to women. Wittingly or unwittingly, gender stereotypes often sneak into media portrayal of men and women. And more importantly, these are mutually reinforcing in nature as women get less visibility in the media thereby affecting their chances at the elections. Another important issue is the lack of women candidates and leaders during elections. Political parties tend to favour men over women in providing party tickets to contest elections. Across the world women do not have proper political representation. Very few women political leaders make way up the ladder of governance because very few women are considered winnable candidates. Hence, very few women get chance to contest elections.

Participation of women in political process as political leaders, candidates, civil society activists, voters and other roles are important as it allows them to exercise their fundamental right. And it is also important for a country as it allows involvement of human resources irrespective of gender, available at its disposal, to use for its betterment. Women's need should also be adequately represented in policymaking processes. Media should play the role of catalyst in creating awareness about the need and importance of including women's perspective in policy matters. Society needs to understand that in the long run, gender stereotypes and discrimination are damaging to both men and women. No society can afford to leave out the vast majority of its people in nation building because they belong to a particular gender. This would put the strain on the entire society to put in the extra effort to meet the requirements of its citizenry in which women form an integral part.

The UN's Special Rapporteur on Freedom of Expression acknowledges this problem saying, central to the issues of equal access for women to rights, equal opportunities for the enjoyment of rights and equal treatment in that enjoyment is the actual extent to which women may exercise their rights to opinion, expression and information without discrimination and the degree to which women actually enjoy the right to participation in public life. The Special Rapporteur states that the problem does not lie in the manner in which international human rights standards have been elaborated but rather in the restrictive and traditional interpretations and applications of human rights law. It emphasizes that it is not acceptable for women still to be dependent on men to represent their views and protect their interests nor is it acceptable that women continue to be consistently excluded from decision-making processes that not only affect them but society in general (Carver, 2001).

Women's participation in political processes has improved in most countries in recent decades. The percentage of women in parliament increased fourfold in the half-century to 1995. Nevertheless, in 2012, the percentage of women in parliament even in established democracies was still well below parity (India 11 per cent, the USA 17 per cent and Denmark 39 per cent). Many countries, particularly new democracies, now have policies that directly promote women candidates, often through voluntary or mandatory quota systems. Most democracies now have universal suffrage in which women have the same rights as men even if there are more barriers to exercising them, in many countries, and civic and voter education usually targets both men and women (Carver, 2001).

With all the progress that is seen across the world, even today gender stereotyping and limitations continue to affect political life of women. Although women's participation as members of parliament is growing, women are less likely to get ministerial berths or other such highest offices of the country. If at all women are given ministerial positions, again they are stereotyped in a sense that they are given portfolios like social welfare, women and child welfare rather than ministries like finance, home or defence. Many studies have demonstrated that citizens too do not support women candidates, debunking the explanation given by the political parties that women candidates will have lesser chances of winning elections. Citing such reasons, political parties seldom promote women leadership in their own organizations as well as during competitive elections. Other reasons like cultural conditions that limit them to familial responsibility also stand in the way of their participation.

Gender discrimination is also compounded by the general news media. According to the Global Media Monitoring Project (GMMP), in 2010 men were 79 per cent of news subjects and 'news continue to portray a world in which men outnumber women in almost all occupational categories, the highest disparity being in the professions', with obvious implications for the visibility of women in politics. The media sector has improved in some ways, however, with a growing number of female reporters in all issue areas including 'hard' topics such as security, politics and economics. Women reporters were 6 per cent more likely than male ones to have women as subjects in their stories.

It is increasingly recognized that media have a key role to play in women's participation throughout political life. In 1994, the US Inter-Parliamentary Union stated:

> [The media can] help to instill among the public the idea that women's participation in political life is an essential part of democracy and can also take care to avoid giving negative or minimizing images of women and their determination and capacity to participate in politics, stressing the importance of women's role in economic and social life and in the development process in general. (Nyakweya, 2013)

In most of the countries, electoral competition is often played out in the media. Media therefore acts as an important agenda-setting platform for future policymakers. Media carries out this task by way of coverage as well as debates and discussions. But invariably, women are least represented even on such occasions. Media coverage of women leaders are biased and appear to be stereotypical across the spectrum. Quite a number of studies carried out on media coverage of female candidates have revealed that even when there are a reasonable number of women candidates, they are often neglected by the media. Unfortunately, gender parity is not one of the top agendas of media organizations that still leave a gaping hole in constructing a meaningful democracy.

2
Modern Media and Society

Contemporary media have gained an overbearing presence across the world. On the one hand, there is a presence of a huge print and broadcast media, and on the other hand, growth of the Internet, satellite communication and telecom services has also contributed in the proliferation of the media network. New communication technology-enabled social media services like Facebook, Twitter, Instagram have expanded the very scope and dimension of media per se and its accessibility. We are living in a global village characterized by media diversity, where information is a fundamental aspect of society. Depending on the national and regional contexts, people access and use media differently. National-level media landscape depends on factors like political economy of the country, media literacy, access to electricity, geographic location and culture. The kind of role media play during the electoral process depends on the media landscape. Political orientations, ideological leanings act as determining factors in setting the agendas for political debates in media platforms.

Hence, most stakeholders of electoral politics make it a point to carry out media mapping in order to understand the availability of the kind of media apparatus, to know about the strengths and weakness of these media organizations and also to have knowledge of accessibility of these media networks. Media mapping does not necessarily look only at local media, it also takes into account the vast number of media content that is downlinked from international sources. Mere examination of media landscape and coverage is not enough, a proper analysis should also incorporate factors like ownership pattern, investment and management, political history, legal and ethical framework and cultural dynamics operating in a particular country. Such a comprehensive understanding of the media landscape is paramount in a democratic set-up. According to one analyst, 'access to accurate and objective information is more important than ever for a healthy democracy to flourish. This access is crucial to improve conditions for trust among citizens, media, and state, and to implement and sustain the governance agenda' (Martinsson, 2009).

Political economy of the country is one of the major determining factors affecting media landscape. This not only affects media ownership pattern but also plays a significant role in media reach and accessibility. For instance, a country where there is less opportunity for advertising revenue, it is hard to expect independent local media, unless there is funding from external sources from wealthy donors. More often than not, independent media would invariably concentrate in and around urban areas with very little reach beyond them. Even today, with all the media expansion, public service broadcasting (PSB) or government-owned media is the only media that is available in rural areas. This has led to a phenomenon called as 'digital divide', which refers to inequalities between populations that have access to modern media, including digital media.

Multinational or global media conglomerates such as Star News Corporation and Walt Disney have established their presence throughout the world, except in some of the underdeveloped countries. Despite the matters of economics, the access to multinational media companies is on the rise across the world.

> For example in Afghanistan prior to 2002, access to broadcast media was limited to a network of state owned outlets except for a smattering of multinational AM radio stations such as BBC and Voice of America. Over the course of the next ten years, the landscape had altered dramatically, with a flourish of independent and private national broadcasters. Yet, even in areas where there is still little reach of national media, access to multinational media via satellite has, in varying degrees, altered access to information. (Martinsson, 2009)

However, money and investments are not the only factors that determine media landscape. Political and cultural traditions are also equally important. Most of the European countries, for instance, have a tradition of strong PSB. France legalized private broadcasting as late as in the 1980s. Countries with a history of military or single-party rule have developed their own set of State-controlled media network. During the 1960s and 1970s, private media in South America was often associated with military dictatorships of the day. A country's historical context of media influences the tendencies of the audiences, which in turn affects content reception. This will lead to a situation which either encourages or discourages the emergence of certain typologies of media.

But the most critical aspect in determining the media landscape is the nature of legal framework, political freedom and freedom of expression that exist in a country. Preferably, the media should be operating under the due protection of strong constitutional mandate of freedom of expression and access to information. For example, the extent to which broadcasting frequencies are allocated in a fair and transparent manner will likely to have a significant impact on how the broadcasters discharge their responsibilities during election time. Similarly, media censorship or physical intimidation would act as a constant threat over media professionals during the coverage of elections.

Legal policies of a country would greatly have an impact on the accessibility to international media. The North Korean government, for example, has been successful in remaining almost entirely isolated from the international media scene. There is currently no broadband data network in the country, and the Internet satellite receivers are not permitted except in extremely controlled circumstances or for government and elite use. Countries with economic prosperity, a history of pluralism, freedom of expression and independence will have had the opportunity to cultivate diverse and stable media as well. Professional standards may also be higher, although the sometimes weak ethics of media in advanced democracies show that the correlation is not an exact one (Martinsson, 2009).

In order to understand the media landscape of a given country, one should also need to understand as to how people use media. Along with the factors like media accessibility, other important factors like people's personal preferences, usage pattern, work environment, everyday routine, the overall trust the audiences have on the media and also general media literacy. A study conducted in 2012 in Nigeria found that while radio usage was generally the same in rural and urban areas, and that 4 out of every 10 respondents said they listened to the radio on their mobile phones within the week prior to the survey, more urban residents watched TV in a given week than rural residents. These differences distinguish one country's media usage patterns from another and affect media usage during elections. In addition to, and in some instances instead of, electronic or print media, direct personal communication remains greatly important in election campaigns and processes (BBG, 2012).

Yet, even in these instances, the media still have an important role in communicating political information. Even when rural communities do not have direct access to independent media, the information generated by the press will still go into general circulation and may reach the rural voters at some stage. 'Information gatekeepers' may themselves rely on media as a source of news and will therefore pass on what they glean from the press. Therefore, although word of mouth may be the direct source of political information in some instances, the media will likely contribute importantly to the mass of information in circulation (BBG, 2012).

Audience analysis is often quickly outdated, however, as preferences and access change so rapidly in today's media environment. A study by the Pew Research Center in the USA in 2008, for example, found that there was an almost twofold jump in the Internet news consumption, from 24 per cent to 40 per cent, in just one year (2008). General news consumption does not translate cleanly into election-related news consumption. For example, a report issued in 2006 exploring global audience reaction and affinity for political campaign ads found that 'political advertising is the most derided form of political communication' (Scammell, 2007).

The popularity of political advertising appears to be very low, but there are indications that people turn to specific kind of media for the general information pertaining to elections. Of late, there have been many studies on the impact of social media on voters and voting behaviour. In fact, the 2014 general elections in India were characterized by the extensive use of social media by all leading political outfits in the country. Just like the US presidential elections of 2012, in which Obama returned to the office for the second time with the help of social media along with other factors, India too witnessed similar trend in 2014.

2.1 Types of Media Funding

In order to understand the media functioning in a given country, it is essential to understand the types of ownership that is in place. The following paragraphs will throw light on this very important aspect. The State, specific governments, or the public, own a large proportion of the world's media—especially radio and television. The term 'public media' is often used to refer to these forms of media ownership. There are important distinctions between these forms however.

2.1.1 Public Media

PSB is funded by the public money and serves the public interest. These broadcasting units are often established by law, and are ideally expected to be non-partisan, that is, not supporting any political party or incumbent ruling party also. They are non-profit organizations. These media networks funded by public money are directly controlled by the respective governments of the day. PSB units are expected to perform public service function. But more often than not, it may be used as a propaganda instrument of the state or the government. These media may be financed out of one or all of these following sources: license fee paid by television viewers, the government budget, programming fee paid by production house, public subscriptions and commercial advertising. These different revenue sources obviously will have impact on the day-to-day functioning of the broadcasters.

UNESCO (2015) defines PSB as:

> [B]roadcasting made, financed and controlled by the public, for the public. PSBs are neither commercial nor state-owned; they are free from political interference and pressure from commercial forces. Through PSBs, citizens are informed, educated and also entertained. When guaranteed with pluralism, programming diversity, editorial independence, appropriate funding, accountability and transparency, public service broadcasting can serve as a cornerstone of democracy.

Widely accepted principles for PSBs include universal accessibility, universal appeal, particular attention to minorities, contribution to sense of national identity and community, distance from vested interests, direct funding and universality of payment, competition in good programming rather than numbers, guidelines that liberate rather than restrict programme-makers. PSBs may be mainly funded by television license fees, as is the case for the British Broadcasting Corporation (BBC); directly by the government, for example, the Australian Broadcasting Corporation; by individual subscribers, grants and programming fees, as is the case for National Public Radio (NPR) in the USA or at least partially from commercial sources, as is the case with the Australian Special Broadcasting Service (SBS). What PSBs have in common in terms of funding is that they are not dependent on advertising.

PSBs are often established by government through acts of parliament, and while some are subject to broad control by the State, most also have strict guarantees of independence incorporated in their guidelines. The Swedish PSB *SvT*, for example, is kept at an arm's length from the State by being owned by a foundation, not the State, and by directly collecting license fees from the public, not via the government. However, it is subject to broad oversight by a parliamentary committee as a check-and-balance mechanism. In transitional democracies, there have been some bold attempts to rapidly retrieve and modernize the public service ideal after a history of heavy-handed State control. In South Africa, since 1993, the public broadcaster has statutory independence and even, at one stage, had its board members appointed after public hearings. State- and government-owned broadcasters, directly controlled by the State, were a common model in the Soviet Union and later in many countries that followed its lead. In the post-Soviet era, these broadcasters have often proven difficult and slow to reform. In Latvia, for example, two decades since independence, the distinction between PSB and State broadcasting remains unclear to many parliamentarians (Horwitz, 2001).

British and French colonizers took their model of public broadcasting wherever they set foot in, but with less success as the colonial broadcasters and media professionals did not enjoy freedom. However, after independence, most of the post-colonial governments carried on with the same tradition of broadcasting paradigm. PSB was established on a sound belief that the private media alone cannot guarantee pluralism in broadcasting. But contrary to the expectations, the public media have not been able to deliver on that count. In some countries, the private media have created a situation where in the governments have become more determined to hold on to the editorial control of the PSB units.

Across the world, broadcasting units are usually owned by public, the State or the government. Newspapers are hardly owned by the State. There are exceptions to this rule, as is seen in Uganda. The largest newspaper in Uganda is called as *New Vision*, in which the government holds the controlling stakes. But unlike government-owned newspapers in other parts of the world, this paper is known to enjoy editorial freedom, media professionalism. However, at times, this newspaper was also accused of pro-government bias during elections. But thankfully, there is also presence of quite a number of independent private media in Uganda providing space for alternative point of views.

2.1.2 Private Media

Unlike public sector media, private media operate distinctly for profit. Private media is usually supported by commercial revenue. And the corporate media is nothing but the private mass media that is controlled by a corporation. For example, in the 1980s, approximately around 50 different corporations controlled the vast majority of private media in the USA, in 2012, this had consolidated to six mega corporations: Time Warner, Walt Disney, NBC Universal, CBS Corporation, Viacom and Rupert Murdoch's News Corp. Another company called as Clear Channel owned over 1,000 radio stations. In 2012, India's Mukesh Ambani's Reliance Industries Ltd (RIL) invested ₹17 billion in Network 18 Group, which owns channels such as *CNN-IBN, CNBC 18* and *CNBC Awaaz*. Although technically, ownership still rests with Network 18, RIL controls the media house because of its heavy funding.

The multilayered deal involves the TV18 broadcast shelling out ₹21 billion to buy out ETV's Hindi news channels in Uttar Pradesh (UP), Madhya Pradesh, Rajasthan and Bihar, and ETV Urdu, as well as a 50 per cent stake in ETV's Marathi, Kannada, Bangla, Gujarati and Odiya regional channels and a 24.5 per cent stake in ETV Telugu and ETV Telugu News. The Reliance group firm already owns a 50 per cent stake in ETV's Telugu channels and a 100 per cent stake in the other ETV channels with an investment of ₹26 billion. With this major deal, the Reliance, controlled by billionaire businessman Mukesh Ambani, will have a major stake in a cross-media enterprise, spanning digital divides to encompass print publications, news and entertainment broadcasting, consumer Internet, film production and e-commerce.

Private broadcasters range from huge multinational corporations run by some of the richest and most politically powerful people in the world to small, local FM stations. In most of the cases, broadcasting will be under the terms of a license granted on a periodic basis by the State. These licenses will lay down the terms and conditions under which news or current affairs programmes can be broadcast. Sometimes this will also include prescriptions as to what kind of election coverage should be carried out. There may also be an explicit public service component to the license, for example, obliging to carry voter education programmes on their media platforms.

Private print media is also extremely diverse, ranging from daily to weekly newspapers and magazines to special-interest publications and journals, relying heavily on advertising, sales and subscription for revenue. Even in situations where the State retains a large stake in broadcasting, the print media are usually in private hands. Even in authoritarian contexts, at least some newspapers in any country are likely to conduct serious news investigations and to comment in a reasonably sophisticated manner on political developments. But private newspapers often have their own political agendas, which may not necessarily be a democratic one. A notorious example was the Chilean newspaper *El Mercurio*, which, aided by the CIA, campaigned against the elected government in 1973 and in favour of a military coup—a clear case where the press dismally failed to promote political pluralism (ACE Project).

In mature democracies of the world, invariably newspapers are more likely to endorse political party or a political candidate openly than broadcasting studios depending on the political culture of a country. In some of the countries, open editorial endorsement of a political candidate is unthinkable, but in some, it is considered as a normal thing. However, when it comes to journalistic ethics, it should be strictly separated from the editorial expressions. With all said and done, one cannot rule out political agenda creeping into the news columns. The presence of wide number of newspapers reflecting varied ideological positions would ensure a well-informed public, who are fed with political ideas of different hues.

With the emergence of media convergence, the concepts of separate print, broadcast and online media are starting to become outdated. Many media outlets which were traditionally operating with one medium or another are now operating across a range of media. Last few decades have witnessed the emergence and expansion of large media conglomerates owning a wide range of media as well as other business units. And non-media conglomerates are also getting into the media industry by purchasing huge stakes. As a result, media landscape has undergone a tremendous change, as it is no longer the ideal 'fourth estate', but subject to ideological and political orientations. Big media moguls have their own set of political agendas just like any other industry leaders will have. Therefore, in a way, the line between State-owned media and private or independent media is blurred. Not all private media are monopolized by large conglomerates, particularly in the developing world. Those that are owned by large conglomerates also exercise independence and objectivity at least on some occasions.

2.1.3 Community Media

Community media are a rapidly growing phenomenon around the world in recent times. Community media usually have the following characteristics: community ownership and control, community service, community participation and a non-profit business model. Community media can be book or broadcast, as able-bodied as online and may broadcast in local languages. Community radio stations now breed as an archetype for announcements of local-level development. Community television stations are also increasing in number. In some countries, national public broadcasters also play a community role by carrying out the content produced by local communities.

The definition of 'community' is often questioned when discussing community media. What exactly is a community? Traditionally, it has been assumed to refer to a geographical community. However, in South Africa, for instance, with one of the widest networks of community radio within the world, the term is additionally used to refer to a community of interest, particularly among underprivileged sectors of society. So, there could be a 'women's community', a 'gay community' or a 'community of individuals with disabilities'.

Online or virtual communities additionally challenge the definition of community. They are social media-based and transcend geographical boundaries, nonetheless count as communities of sorts. As long as they adhere to the broad principles of community media, some uses of social media also can be thought about to be community-oriented. The significance of this for elections is straight away apparent. Community media, virtually by definition, have a restricted but loyal audience. For the purposes of educating the citizens, community media is extremely vital, particularly as they will reach sections of society that is bypassed by traditional media. The terms of community broadcasting licenses often prohibit explicit political campaigning. It is significantly vital for a regulatory authority to watch compliance with the terms of a license throughout the periods of election.

2.1.4 Party- and Politician-owned Media

Basically, political party media makes up one among three categories, and it is for regulatory agencies to determine which publicity sheets, that may not be considered as a media regulator, however, could be watched if, for instance, they represent campaign spending, which can be restricted by law—typical private media that simply happen to be closely held by a party. In that case, they will need to change to the prevailing standards or laws for alternative private media; and also government media, in a scenario within which the ruling party and government are tangled. In that case, media using public funds ought to change to the same standards as the other public media which in practice most likely means that they cannot campaign for the party at any respect.

Political parties usually own newspaper in comparison to broadcasting stations. In several countries, political parties are not allowed to have their own broadcasting stations, since this can be deemed to be an unfair allocation of a national resource—for example, the allocation of frequency spectrum—to a slender political interest. In Turkey, for instance, the 2011 Law on Establishment of Radio and Television Enterprises and their Media Services states that 'A broadcasting license cannot be granted to political parties and a range of other entities' and that they cannot be 'direct or indirect shareholders of media service providers'.

Another type of media nearly blurs the distinction between party and private media; owned by individual politicians or business leaders with political stakeholds, it seems to be regular outlets. Politician-owned media has become common practice in Ukraine, for example, where advocates for freedom of expression are gravely worried about pluralism in media ownership and the control of key broadcasters by wealthy political leaders and their families. In Italy, Silvio Berlusconi's broadcasting stations usually promoted his ambition to become his country's leader. These politician-owned media are conventional private media that are subject to the same laws and regulations as any other; however, the potential conflict of interest and the questions of pluralism in major media are causes for concern.

2.2 Media Literacy and Election Coverage

Media literacy is essential in ensuring that media coverage of elections is effective in informing citizens, and that the media itself is held accountable. Media literacy is a twenty-first-century method to education. It provides a framework to access, analyse, evaluate, create and participate with messages in a varied number of forms—from print to video to the Internet. Media literacy builds a knowhow of the role played by the media in society as well as imparting important competencies of inquiry and self-expression necessary for people in a democracy.

Media literacy development goes beyond just increasing the abilities and skills of media audiences. It also includes focusing on information holders, such as government officials, and, more specifically, to elections—electoral officials, candidates and political parties, so as to have a better understanding of the electoral process and relationship with media. These bodies and people are usually liable to withholding information out of suspicion towards the media's intentions or fear of negative repercussions. However, this fear or suspicion is usually a result of absence of training and experience in handling media. Media literacy is an alternative to censorship and is instrumental in fostering democratic practices.

The survival of free and independent media also depends on media-literate audiences and information providers. Media literacy includes understanding how to use the rapidly changing media landscape. This is essentially relevant in present-day era of social media and ever-evolving media technology. Media literacy also involves understanding the use of subtext in media messages. Subtext is the context or background of the primary message and may include images, background audio and framing, each of which conveys specific messages, associations and embedded meanings. In short, media literacy is about developing critical thinking abilities and overall awareness and also the ability to understand the media content based on the critical awareness. This in turn encourages pluralistic media as well as media that foster professionalism.

Media literacy gives rise to set of audience who understand the media landscape as a whole, including the impacts of legal frameworks.

It is clear that much of the aforementioned critical thinking is important to citizens in making informed choices. Additionally, media literacy is also vital in conflict and post-conflict situations as an insurance against hate speech in otherwise volatile circumstances. An audience that is educated within the tenants of media professionalism more often than not demand for high-quality media content. Media literacy is also significant for emerging democracies. In these circumstances, legal frameworks can greatly impact the long-term status of independent and free media. Additionally, audiences may also experience a rather sharp explosion of news sources and media formats after decades of controlled media. The greater the media literacy, the more prepared audiences will be in understanding the messages and recognizing the value and credibility. However, while there have been considerable concerted development efforts across the different parts of the world to encourage media professionalism and foster media independence, the same cannot necessarily be said for efforts to improve upon media literacy.

2.3 Traditional Media and Elections

The functioning of democracy in a way is determined by the role played by traditional media during elections. That is exactly why it is very important to understand the different set of media that form the generic concept of traditional media, namely radio, print media and television before embarking on measuring influence wielded by them.

2.3.1 Radio

While the media landscape is ever-increasing and diversifying, radio remains the foremost prevailing and accessible form of media worldwide. Wherever FM radio is scarcely available or non-existent, AM radio is still accessible to audiences. By the early 2002, 95 per cent of the world's population was covered by analogue radio signals. The emergence of satellite radio has also greatly expanded the variety of radio programming available to audiences across the world. Although satellite radio remains comparatively expensive, traditional radio is quite popular among the audience because of its relative cheapness. However, a handheld radio will still need batteries, but these costs are a fraction of those associated with other forms of media. Furthermore, a lack of electricity is not necessarily a limiting factor for radio. Radio also transcends limitations of media literacy. This makes it essentially an important source of information for rural areas where women are less likely to be literate than men.

A Gallup poll conducted in 23 countries in Sub-Saharan Africa in 2008 disclosed that 59 per cent of respondents claimed national radio to be their most vital source of information about national events, while further 9 per cent turned to international radio over other forms of media for this information. Combined, this contrasts starkly to the 3 per cent who are dependent on newspapers, or the 1 per cent who used the Internet, as their most important source of news on national events.

Although radio prevails as the most easily accessible source of information on a global level, individual countries show variations when it comes to radio consumption despite the general lack of consistent statistics in many countries. For example, in the USA, where in 2012 an estimated 96.7 per cent of households owned a television set—a number comparable to the percentage of Americans tuning into radio every week (93 per cent), the average amount of time an American spent watching TV as opposed to listening to radio was nearly twofold (Neilson estimates).

2.3.2 Television

In places where it is both affordable and accessible, television continues to be the most popular form of media. According to the International Telecommunications Union (ITU) in 2009, there were significant regional differences with regard to television ownership. Europe, the USA and the Commonwealth of Independent States all showed household ownership as 95 per cent or more. Arab States and Asia and the Pacific showed lower statistics of 82 per cent and 75 per cent respectively. Estimates for Africa were well below those of other regions with only 28 per cent ownership (ITU, 2010).

Categorization of television ownership per region can be misleading, however, as statistics for countries within the regions can vary dramatically. A comparison of 2007 and 2008 radio and television ownership clearly shows that ownership of the former far surpasses that of the latter for the majority of 50 of the world's 'least developed countries'. Yet, many of these countries fall into the general regions listed earlier which show overall high television ownership. Some countries which did not demonstrate this trend were Bangladesh, Cambodia, Laos and Myanmar, where television ownership was near equivalent to radio ownership or indeed surpassed it. Furthermore, individual statistics demonstrate that significant proportions of these countries' population do not own either a radio or a television set; in many cases, television ownership was well below 30 per cent (ITU, 2010).

Nevertheless, television remains one of the most dynamic and ever-expanding forms of media in the world. In addition to terrestrial television programming, there is now satellite programming available to viewers. Satellite television has made television truly 'global' in characteristic, in that satellites cover large regions of the world. This has had a dramatic effect on how international news and general programming are produced and consumed. It also plays an important role in opening up access to information in otherwise relatively closed countries, with limited media freedom. 'For example, in 2009 in Egypt, satellite television penetration was 43 per cent, allowing residents access to non-state media, as well as to independent media that was not indirectly controlled by way of self-censorship and fear' (ITU, 2010). Similarly, in 2009, 74 per cent of the population in Syria had access to satellite television.

Terrestrial television is also diversified. Analogue television, transmitted through electromagnetic waves, is slowly paving the way to digital terrestrial programming, a process that began early in the 1990s. Digital programming allows for transmitted content to be converted into code and that needs to be compressed, which in turn allows for a greater number of channels to be broadcast within one bandwidth. Not only has this change made a sizable increase in programming available to viewers but it has also allowed for diversification of how television programming is transmitted; on a computer through the Internet, on a mobile phone or at home over a regular television set.

Due to extremely high costs that are involved, countries have staged switchover to digital broadcasting. The Netherlands was one of the first countries to fully switch off analogue broadcasting, followed shortly by Finland, Sweden and Switzerland. The United States made a complete switch in 2009 after a process that took almost 10 years. At an ITU conference in 2006, nations of Europe, Africa and the Middle East agreed to phase in digital broadcasting. A statement released by the conference stressed that digitization of broadcasting in Europe, Africa, the Middle East and the Islamic Republic of Iran by 2015 represents a major landmark towards establishing a more equitable, just and people-centred information society. The digital switchover will leapfrog existing technologies to connect the unconnected in underserved and remote communities and close the digital divide. As of mid-2012, roughly 25 European countries, including Estonia, France, Malta, Slovenia and Spain, had made the switch. European countries such as Greece and Ireland had not yet made the change (ITU, 2010).

2.3.3 Print Media

Within traditional media, print and electronic media, print media reflects the greatest diversity of all, in both ownership as well as content. Print media ranges from daily to weekly newspapers and from news magazines to a range of special-interest magazines. Print media also includes one-off publications such as pamphlets, fliers and leaflets. Out of all of the mass media formats, print media is also the oldest.

In present-day world, print has a relatively smaller audience compared to other forms of mass media. This could be due to literacy levels, accessibility and economic conditions. For example, in China, where earliest known print media originated, one calculation in 2009 determined that 81.5 per cent of the population was literate. Total circulations of daily and non-daily print publications were 202 per 1,000 citizens, roughly 20 per cent, while radio and television sets were around 32 and 31 per cent respectively. Another calculation placed the number of radios and televisions sets as more than double the number of daily and non-daily circulations. What calculations like these do not account for of course is the number of people who read one print publication, or the numbers of people who listen to one radio set or watch one television set. However, it is clear from the various angles of statistics around the world, one can safely assume that more people listen to the radio or watch television than do those who read a publication (Nation Master, 2013).

However, this in no way make print media any less valuable nor less necessary to the overall pluralism of the media landscape in a country. Print media has a history of being privately owned rather than State–owned, and is therefore may be less likely to be considered biased depending on individual country contexts. Moreover, print media in a sense has more longevity, as it is existing for longer periods of time in comparison to electronic media. Readers of print media also select only what they want to read, unlike radio or television, for example, where the audience who do not have control over the content aired in television.

Information that is accessed and used out of personal interest may be more easily remembered than information which is not desired for by the audience. Additionally, a number of studies have revealed that in numerous contexts, even if readership is less than television viewership, newspapers invariably set the agendas in terms of topics and debates for other media, and for politicians, to follow. This is due to the fact that print media can afford to more in-depth stories compared to television which thrives on breaking news and audio visuals. It is also due to print media's more 'serious' profile compared to other forms of media, and also habits of political leaders in terms of media use and their assumptions about the power of newspapers. Although, of late, this influence may be changing with the new media revolution, it still remains true to some extent.

2.4 New Media

New media is comprised of the Internet, mobile phones, social media like blogs and microblogs such as Twitter and Sina Weibo, social networking websites like Facebook, video-sharing sites such as YouTube and others. In other words, new media is a generic term that describes a range of media that are used for basically socializing purposes. Some of the factors that make new media different from traditional media are as follows: new media are basically interactive; they employ digital, online and mobile technology; unlike traditional media, content in new media are often audience-created and user-driven; they function in real time; more often than not, they are usually borderless; but the information has a short shelf life; one of the most interesting thing about new media is that they are hard to regulate and to censor; very significantly, infrastructure for producing and publishing is usually cheaper for individuals to access and lastly, new media do not necessarily adhere to journalistic standards and ethics.

However, the difference between traditional media and social media is often not much, with most 'traditional' journalists also using the Internet as an important source of information for their stories and most of the traditional publications also creating their own online editions or transforming themselves into fully multimedia outlets. Traditional media also uses the new trend known as 'citizen journalism' stories—for instance, CNN's *iReport* invites viewers to contribute stories. Traditional media at times depends on personal mobile phone images and video to cover stories that are hard to cover such as military violence against people. Big media organizations like the BBC expect most of their correspondents to possess professional skills of traditional as well as online and interactive media. Almost all major news media outlets today have their own online versions, some of them are interactive.

There are varied opinions and points of views about the overall impact of new media, but very few question the fact that it has fostered further globalization that has paved way for communities of varied interest, political and otherwise, to organize themselves in a better manner and communicate among them despite separated by geographical distances. It has changed the face of traditional journalism and blurred the lines between published media content and personal communication. Additionally, new media has created a situation for individuals, groups and smaller companies to challenge the monopolies of traditional media—that have become a big concern of democracy throughout the world—by using the borderless and relatively inexpensive infrastructure of the Internet to communicate alternative views. New media also provides new opportunities for elections stakeholders. However, like any other technology, it also has certain limitations and challenges. This section reviews the impact and relevance of new media to each of the key roles mass media play in elections.

2.4.1 New Media as Fourth Estate

New media have started to play an important role in reinforcing transparency in democratic processes that obviously includes elections. Short Message Service (SMS), that is, text messaging, is presently being used around the world by many election-monitoring groups for quick collection and transmission of information pertaining to election irregularities, voter statistics on time-to-time basis and other such purposes. For instance, in Montenegro in 2005, an SMS-based quick-count process helped control the tensions prevailing there about the integrity of the referendum election count, and thereby helped influence the voters to trust the official referendum result.

Citizens utilize new media to watch electoral fraud. In the 2012 elections in Mexico, social media sites were employed to reveal vote-buying, including video posted across social media websites of a warehouse filled with grocery, allegedly meant to bribe voters. Additionally, 'at least three groups ... set up sophisticated websites where citizens could upload complaints and videos or other material to document irregularities. There were also social media sites for reporting alleged fraud in real time'. As a further example, in the 2012 presidential elections in Russia, activists created a new social media platform 'Citizen Control' specifically designed to bring all social groups together to monitor the elections (*The Guardian*, 2012).

Social media is also used to improve candidate behaviour and candidate–voter interaction. In Malaysia in 2012, Transparency International (TI) asked all elections candidates to sign a voluntary 'Election Pledge'. TI stated:

> [T]he purpose of the pledge is to recognize that it is the responsibility of every candidate to fight corruption, practice good governance and uphold the rule of law. The pledge also emphasizes the crucial role citizens play in monitoring their politicians by providing a platform where the public can monitor and comment on candidates' performances. (Ong, 2012)

What was unusual about this pledge was that it actually required candidates to open Facebook and Twitter accounts and to interact with voters on them (Ong, 2012).

Traditional media's watchdog role is significantly improved upon by its use of new media as both a source of information and also as a mouthpiece for elections reporting. By watching social media content, observing citizen journalism publications and by creating new media of their own through blogs and microblogs on official media websites, traditional media's elections' investigations have become quicker, more varied and more interactive.

Social media has also been used extensively to overhaul hate speech, as well as social media 'buzz' that might lead to or encourage elections violence. It has also been used to monitor and map ongoing elections-related conflicts. Many tools have been created especially for this purpose. For example, the *Ushahidi* cloud-sourcing software gathers data from SMS, Twitter and email and combines it on a map using Google maps to show the geographical spread and scale of violence. Similarly, in Zimbabwe, *Sokwanale* digitally mapped reports of election violence and intimidation (Ushahidi, 2012).

2.4.1.1 CASE OF 'ARAB SPRING'

The term 'Arab Spring' refers to the democratic protests that erupted independently and spread throughout the Arab world and North Africa in 2011. The movement started in Tunisia in December 2010 and quickly spread to countries like Egypt, Libya, Syria, Yemen, Bahrain, Saudi Arabia and Jordan. The term was used in March 2005 by many media writers and commentators to suggest that a corollary benefit of the invasion of Iraq would be the emergence of Western-friendly Middle East democracies.

2.4.1.2 TUNISIA

The Tunisian Revolution, also known as Jasmine Revolution, started in December 2010 after Mohammed Bouazizi, a 26-year-old Tunisian man, set himself on fire in front of a local municipal office. According to *Al Jazeera*, earlier that day, Tunisian police confiscated his cart and beat him because he did not have a permit. He went to the municipal office to file a complaint, where workers there ignored him. Bouazizi then set himself on fire.

Small-scale demonstrations then began in Sidi Bouzid, Bouazizi's hometown, and spread throughout the country. According to *Al Jazeera English*, 'Bouazizi's act of desperation highlights the public's boiling frustration over living standards, police violence, rampant unemployment, and a lack of human rights'.

Zine el-Abidine Ben Ali became the president of Tunisia in 1987 and 'tried to calm the situation by promising more freedoms, including a right to demonstrate, and announcing that he would not seek re-election when his term would end in 2014.' In previous elections, he had received 90 per cent votes. According to *Al Jazeera English*, 'A UN investigative panel reports that at least 219 people were killed during the uprising against Ben Ali, a figure it says is likely to rise'.

On 24 October 2011, the moderate Islamist party Ennahda emerged as the victor in elections for a constitutional assembly. Ennahda began to engage in talks with liberals in hopes of forming a unity government. The party claims to have 'a greater commitment to the principles of Western-style liberal democracy than any other Islamist party in the region', and has 'repeatedly pledged to promote equal opportunities in employment and education as well as the freedom to choose or reject Islamic dress like the head scarf'. Since their election, the Islamist party Ennahda has tightened censorship, being accused of clamping down on national media. The arrests of two Tunisian artists reignited protests. Human Rights Watch has called on Tunisian authorities to drop all charges on the artists.

2.4.1.3 EGYPT

Close on the heels of the Jasmine Revolution in Tunisia, Egyptian activists organized a demonstration on 25 January, Egypt's Police Day, to protest the Emergency Law, unemployment, poverty and Hosni Mubarak's government. Police day, a national Egyptian holiday, celebrates the 50 officers killed on

25 January 1952 by the British in Ismailia, Egypt. This sparked anti-British protest leading to the Free Officers taking power in Egypt.

The protests began in Cairo, Egypt and spread throughout the country. According to *Al Jazeera*, the protests gained more strength when widespread protests were held across the country. Jack Shenker, writing for *The Guardian*, described downtown Cairo as a 'war zone' filled 'with running street battles'. According to Wikipedia, pro-Mubarak supporters escalated the violence when they rode on camels and horses into Tahrir Square. The Mubarak government attempted to thwart protest with armed forces, and when those tactics failed, State media started to portray the protesters as foreign agents. The government also targeted foreign journalists and human rights workers. However, during the protests, Muslims and Christian Egyptians demonstrated unity, and, according to Wikipedia, Muslims protected Christian demonstrators during Sunday service.

Protests in Egypt portrayed more than political will, *Al Jazeera* Correspondent Fatima Naib said:

> Egyptian women, just like men, took up the call to 'hope'. Here they describe the spirit of Tahrir—the camaraderie and equality they experienced—and their hope that the model of democracy established there will be carried forward as Egyptians shape a new political and social landscape.

On 11 February 2011, Hosni Mubarak resigned his presidency and handed power to the army. *The New York Times* described Hosni Mubarak as 'Egypt's modern pharaoh', spending almost 30 years in office. He was sentenced to life in prison on 2 June 2012 by an Egyptian court for his role in the killing of unarmed protestors. Human Rights Watch reported that '302 people have been killed since the start of Egypt's pro-democracy uprising. Based on visits to a number of hospitals in Egypt, the organization says that records show the death toll has reached 232 in Cairo, 52 in Alexandria and 18 in Suez' (Abdelfattah Mohsen, 2011).

Social media role: Facebook pages, Twitter, BlackBerry Messenger and blogs were platforms people in Egypt used to exchange information globally. According to *Al Jazeera English*, in 27 January 2011, people complained of disruptions to their Facebook, Twitter and BlackBerry Messenger services. The disruption to the Internet service lasted until 2 February, but the Internet services were 'partially restored in Cairo after a five-day blackout aimed at stymieing protests'. The use of social media to intensify the protests is a contested one. Mary Botarri, writing for *PRWatch* says:

> In the end, we may discover that the old-fashioned Friday prayer service was the critical vehicle for educating and mobilizing the great unwired. But

Facebook appears to have played an important role in mobilizing the younger, more urban and wired classes, giving them the comfort of an online community and making it safer to take collective action.

2.4.1.4 LIBYA

The protests in Libya instantly turned violent when the Libyan government reacted harshly towards peaceful protests. On 18 February, three days after the protests began, the country erupted into an armed conflict when protesters executed policemen and men loyal to Colonel Muammar Gaddafi for killing protesters. According to *Al Jazeera English*, the Libyan government, on 19 February used artillery, helicopter gunships and anti-aircraft missile launchers to kill protesters. The government's forces also opened fire on people attending a funeral for those killed in the protests. *Al Jazeera* reported 15 people killed in the incident. Social media sites were used to organize people; however, on 18 February, the Libyan government imposed restrictions on the Internet.

Colonel Qaddafi was in power since 1969, making him the longest-serving ruler in Africa and the Middle East. Throughout the recent protests, Gaddafi continued to hold onto power. According to *Al Jazeera English*, 'critics dismissed his leadership as a military dictatorship, accusing him of repressing civil society and ruthlessly crushing dissident'. The move to attack civilians costed Gaddafi many of his close advisors and military. *Reuters* reported soldiers defecting to support protesters and because they refused to shoot on their own people.

On 20 October 2011, Qaddafi was killed by rebel fighters in his hometown of Surt. He was found in a 'large drainage pipe after a NATO air assault destroyed part of his convoy'. Rebels were shown 'manhandling' Qaddafi following his capture in video footage subsequently released. In response to demands from the international community, a 'commission of inquiry' has been created by the interim government to inquire into the circumstances surrounding Qaddafi's death. Anti-Qaddafi fighters have been accused of perpetrating 'arbitrary arrests and torture' as well as 'extralegal killings'. Although rebel leaders have promised to prevent atrocities by their soldiers, the interim government may be limited in its ability to carry out a thorough investigation.

2.4.2 New Media as Public Educator

The decentralized and interactive nature of new media has unleashed its potential as a public education platform. For instance, ECs, international democracy promotion organizations, civil society groups and others have made extensive use of YouTube and other video sites to communicate civic and voter education videos. Electoral commissions have Facebook profiles to attract new voters and provide information to existing ones, as well as to get feedback. *Elections New Zealand*, for example, has an active Facebook page, and the Jamaica elections commission is also considerably active. The UK Electoral Commission puts out almost daily tweets on Twitter with announcements of key dates, guidelines, highlights from reports and so on. There are also a few independent websites that promote voter registration such as *Rock the Vote* in the United States.

2.4.3 New Media as Campaign Platform

Creative use of new media for political campaigning continues to grow, and candidates and parties now use a full range of tools to woo voters. Many political parties and candidates of course have their own sophisticated websites. British Prime Minister David Cameron used the 'Webcameron', an Internet video diary, to appeal to voters in the 2010 UK elections. All the UK parties used 'viral' advertisements, which spread through online social media, as an important part of their campaigns in the same elections. Barack Obama famously used social media to raise funds and spread campaign messages for his successful 2008 US presidential campaign, which some commentators term the first 'Facebook election'. According to a news article, 60 per cent of people preparing to vote in the 2012 US presidential elections said that they expected candidates to have an online presence. In addition, in some contexts, the fact that new media is relatively cheaper for campaigning than traditional media means that smaller parties can also have better campaign exposure. However, it has yet to be seen whether this advantage leads to better electoral performance.

Online campaign techniques are totally different from ground-level campaigns, not only in medium but also in message, tone and timeframe. It looks as though that it is not so much the quantity of new media usage by candidates that appeals most to voters but the quality and interactivity of their respective campaigns. This suggests that new media have triggered greater expectations of political parties and candidates for direct online interaction. There is greater pressure from audiences for online media to be succinct particularly with regard to microblogs. Also, campaigning using social media can take a long time, in that candidates need to build social media profiles, a process which takes weeks or months. New media campaigning often requires the 'long campaign' model in which politicians maintain social media presence in pseudo-campaigning modes between elections. According to some analysts, this suggests that new media campaigning might privilege incumbents, depending on the regulatory environment and the extent to which candidates and potential candidates are proactive online.

New media activity can be an accurate predictor of electoral outcomes. The losing candidate in the Egyptian run-off presidential election received almost triple the number of Twitter mentions as the winning candidate, so in this case, Twitter mentions clearly did not convert into electoral victory. However, in the 2010 elections in the United Kingdom, social media monitors such as Tweetminster's analysis fairly, accurately predicted the winners and losers in the electoral debates. Election campaign managers now use monitoring of social media called sentiment analysis, extensively to understand voter opinion patterns. Social media can also pose risks for candidates. There have been cases of candidates posting comments on social media forums that have backfired.

2.4.3.1 NARENDRA MODI AND SOCIAL MEDIA

In India, in the general elections of 2014 conducted in the months of April and May, BJP won a landslide victory. India held its 16th general elections for the 543 parliamentary constituencies in nine phases stretching over a period of over a month. Nearly 814.5 million of the 1.2 billion people of India were eligible to vote in the general elections, making it the largest elections ever conducted in the world. The two main coalitions of the country's parties, the Indian National Congress (INC)-led United Progressive Alliance (UPA) and the BJP-led National Democratic Alliance (NDA) competed with each other to form the government. In fact, days earlier, Modi's election victory tweet 'India has won! *Acche din ayenge* (Good days will come)' went on to become the most retweeted tweet of all time from India. Just before the election results were declared, Modi said in a blog post, 'This is the first election where social media has assumed an important role and the importance of this medium will only increase in the years to come. It became a direct means of information and gave us the much-needed local pulse'. Narendra Modi with his team was quite active on social media since 2009, but when BJP declared him as the Prime Ministerial candidate, upsurge use of digital media was seen. In the 16th general elections, nearly 814 million of 1.25 billion populace were eligible to vote. In order to reach out to huge mass or potential voters, all the channels of digital media as well as offline medium were used so that could be accomplished to more voters.

Through social media, Narendra Modi's opponents could know how much support he has of public, and this support infused positive energy and gusto amongst his cohorts. Advertising Gurus like Sam Balsara, Piyush Pandey and Prasoon Joshi were the ones who created catchy slogans like *Janta Maaf Nahi Karegi* (public will not forgive), *Ache Din Anne Wale hai* (good days are about to come). These catch phrases became viral on social media as well. And *Ab ki Baar Modi Sarkar* (it is the time for Modi government) had become a tag line of BJP as well. The Facebook page 'I support Narendra Modi' got about 8 million likes, and the slogan *Har Har Modi Ghar Ghar Modi* (all hail Modi, omnipresent Modi) went viral across social media platforms.

Through social media, he not only disclosed the bad doings of Congress government but also made voters aware about their voting rights. And through digital media, he made people aware about the development that was done in Gujarat. Moreover, as digital media is a two-way communication, so as to keep public engaged he used to reply on their comments. However, Narendra Modi has been considered a progressive man, who wishes to bring in latest technology in India. That is why he was supported by the urban-class population.

An urban population which uses technology the most extended support to him. And support and love was seen in terms of likes, shares, comments, retweet, etc. He understood very early that these elections were hugely influenced by youth and, therefore, the whole of his strategy was accordingly planned and implemented. And youth who was seeking such a kind of leader could connect with each other through social media as well as engage with ease. This is for the first time that Indian elections were fought as presidential election of United States of America. Narendra Modi's marketing strategy not only created a synergy but also amazed pre-eminent marketing Gurus and pundits of across the world. Most imperative thing about Modi's campaign is that his team maintained consistency throughout elections, whereas competitors of Narendra Modi surrendered amid election campaigns. #Namo has become a household name or a name for which people wanted to make him win.

2.4.4 New Media as a Forum for Dialogue

In many countries, new media has become one of the most dynamic platforms for people to voice their views, share information, interact with leaders and debate on important electoral issues. New media offers the advantages of being 'democratic', allowing anyone to post their opinions on blogs and microblogs, share links, send and forward emails, create websites and so on. It also has the advantage of working in real time, thereby allowing people to keep up with dynamic and ever-changing developments. Finally, new media is also much more difficult to censor or silence as governments cannot easily suspend blogger 'licenses', raid offices of Twitter users or prosecute someone for posting links on Facebook.

The use of new media in the Arab Spring uprisings is an example of the contribution of these new tools to political change. As some analysts writing in mid-2011 put it, seeing what has unfolded so far in the Middle East and North Africa, one can say more than simply that the Internet has changed the way in which political actors communicate with one another. Since the beginning of 2011, social protests in the Arab world have cascaded from country to country, largely because digital media have allowed communities to unite around shared grievances and nurture transportable strategies for mobilizing against dictators. In each country, people have used digital media to build a political response to a local experience of unjust rule. They were inspired by the real tragedies documented on Facebook. Social media have become the public sphere upon which civil society can build, and new information technologies give activists things that they did not have before.

Uncensored debate on new media has started to impact electoral outcomes. The *Malaysiakini*, an online journal in Malaysia, is an example of new media which provided an alternative voice and has had a significant electoral impact.

> In March 2008, the ruling party made its worst showing at the polls in half a century, losing its two-thirds parliamentary majority for the first time since independence. Facilitating this was the growing prominence of online journalism, which diminished the massive BN advantage in media access and 'shocked the country' by documenting gross police abuse of demonstrators, particularly those of Indian descent. (Larry and Marc, 2012)

New media has also allowed traditional media to dodge censorship. According to an article in the *Journal of Democracy*, for example, 'when Venezuelan president Hugo Chávez forced *Radio Caracas Television* off the air in May 2007, it continued its broadcasts via YouTube'. New media lends itself to informal and ironic opposition too. For example, during the UK 2010 general election campaign, one of the most successful independent sites was a satire of a major party's election billboards. Using what was felt to be an overly 'airbrushed' photograph of the party leader, visitors to mydavidcameron.com could create and publish their own digital versions of real posters, complete with amusing slogans.

2.4.5 Regulation of New Media

Are the regulatory practices and styles of reporting that have developed over the years for conventional media equally applicable to new media as well? When it comes to regulating the behaviour of new media, many of the assumptions that underlie the regulation of conventional media simply do not apply. For example, the space to publish material on the Internet is literally unlimited, compared with the assumption behind broadcasting regulation that the frequency spectrum is a finite resource that must therefore be shared. The convergence of traditional and new media also means that governments face the challenge of where and how to draw the line with regulation.

Certainly there is growing international consensus about rights to freedom of expression and information in new media. In 2011, the United Nations Human Rights Committee (UNHRC) recommended:

> [T]he states take all necessary steps to foster independence of ... new media and ensure access of individuals to them ... and specifically indicated that 'operation of websites, blogs or other internet-based, or other information dissemination system, including systems to support such communication, such as internet service providers or search engines', need to be compatible with paragraph 3 of Article 19 of the Covenant. (United Nations Human Rights, 2011)

Paragraph 3 covers the very limited circumstances under which freedom of expression may be restricted, namely to protect the rights of others and for national security reasons. Like other advances in media technology in the past, new media are seen as a threat by some governments. As United Nations (UN) Human Rights Commissioner Navi Pillay stated in 2012, the Internet has transformed human rights movements. States can no longer exercise control by claiming a monopoly over information. This has resulted in a backlash effect and intensified attempts to unduly restrict access to online content or Internet as such ... there is also a real concern that methods to identify and track down criminals may be used to crack down on human rights defenders and suppress dissenting voices.

Ultimately, the Internet and other new technologies are carried on media such as telephone lines that are owned by governments or large corporate owners, and that often require some kind of licensing to operate. For example, in Turkey, according to an Open Society Foundations report, the most significant threat to news diversity and quality remains the repressive legal restrictions under which journalists operate. If anything, this has intensified in response to the rise of digital media. Article 301 of the Turkish Penal Code makes it illegal to insult Turkey and national identity and has been used as a cover for Internet censorship.

The regulatory challenge posed by new media so far has been the following: old media can be regulated in a way that does not constitute censorship and enhances, rather than restricts, freedom of expression. Such regulation of new media has proven impossible. New media can be regulated, but the content of the Internet, for example, is so diverse and widespread that regulation has been heavy-handed and has amounted to censorship: interception of emails, closure of websites and pressure or legal action against Internet service providers.

The Internet poses a challenge to traditional views of media conduct in elections. Pre-polling blackouts on campaign coverage, for example, are difficult to police because of unregulated websites. Meanwhile, in the 2012 French elections, an embargo on reporting results was ignored by online media in neighbouring Switzerland and Belgium, which published results 90 minutes early, thereby making that clause in French law almost impossible to enforce. A characteristic of the Internet that makes it difficult to regulate is its international nature. Attempts by national regulators to close down websites are met by the creation of mirror sites beyond the country's borders. Self-regulation by new media users is also more difficult if not impossible, and new media has sometimes ignored conventions that have been widely accepted by 'traditional' media.

It is generally currently accepted that it is difficult to do anything specific to regulate new media around elections. The law defines what is and is not acceptable in terms of campaigning and other media-related activities. Therefore, all media, traditional and new, as well as political actors need to abide by that law. In New Zealand, an attempt was made to specifically regulate third-party blogs during the pre-campaign period. New Zealand attempted to keep a tight rein on third-party online activity that resulted in protest from the mass media and freedom of speech advocates, and the law was eventually changed. While it is impossible to regulate for all possibilities, registered candidates, political parties and third parties can be held to campaign rules for online campaigns as much as possible.

2.5 Shreya Singhal Case

In India, the Supreme Court of India, in what is sure to go down as an historic decision in *Shreya Singhal v. Union of India* has struck down the notorious Section 66A of the Information Technology (IT) Act, 2000 as being violative of the right to freedom of speech and expression enshrined in Article 19(1)(a) of the Constitution of India. Much praise has been heaped on India's apex court, and the decision has been lauded as being a step in the right direction towards preserving the Internet freedom of the citizens of India.

2.5.1 Section 66A of the IT Act and the Challenge

Section 66A of the IT Act reads, 'Punishment for sending offensive messages through communication service, etc.' and provides that any person who uses a computer device to send information that is offensive, menacing, knowingly causing annoyance, inconvenience, danger, obstruction, insult, injury, criminal intimidation, enmity, hatred or ill will shall be punished with imprisonment for a term which may extend to three years along with a fine.

At the ground level, this translates into the power to arrest and imprison members of the public for freely expressing and discussing ideas and opinions which according to the government are offensive under one of the many categories set out in Section 66A of the IT Act. The primary contention of the Petitioners was that Section 66A of the IT Act infringes the fundamental right to free speech and expression under Article 19(1)(a) of the Constitution and is not saved by any of the eight restrictive subjects mentioned in Article 19(2) of the Constitution which provides for valid and permitted restrictions to the right to freedom of speech and expression.

2.5.2 Restrictions on the Freedom of Speech

After analysing and discussing at length the trail of judgements that have established the contours of the right to freedom of speech and expression in India, the court broke down the right to freedom of speech and expression into its three fundamentals—discussion, advocacy and incitement. The court observed that mere discussion or advocacy of a particular cause, howsoever unpopular it is, is at the heart of the rights under Article 19(1)(a) of the Constitution. It is only when such discussion or advocacy reaches the level of incitement that the permitted restrictions to the freedom of speech and expression set out in Article 19(2) of the Constitution kick in. Of the many heads under Article 19(2) of the Constitution, the State claimed before the court that Section 66A of the IT Act can be supported under the heads of public order, defamation, incitement to an offence and decency or morality, and accordingly the restrictions imposed by Section 66A of the IT Act are reasonable restrictions.

2.5.3 The Court's Rationale

The court took up each limb of the State's case that Section 66A of the IT Act falls within the contours of the restrictions permitted by Article 19(2) of the Constitution and on each count found the said Section to be unconstitutional and not saved by Article 19(2) of the Constitution.

Public order: The court observed that the eventual touchstone on which this restriction is to be applied is whether or not the exercise of one's right to freedom of speech and expression over the Internet has a 'proximate relationship' to disturbing public order. The court held that the acts contemplated by Section 66A of the IT Act are not intrinsically and necessarily those which disturb and affect tranquillity in the current life of the community, and for such reasons the court held that the Section has no proximate relationship to public order. The court also observed that expression of personal views over the Internet are not necessarily aimed at the public at large and may even be aimed at individuals.

Defamation, incitement to an offence and decency or morality: On all counts, the apex court held that Section 66A of the IT Act cannot be sustained. The court observed that Section 66A of the IT Act is not by itself concerned with injury to reputation since something which may be grossly offensive may annoy or be inconvenient to another without at all affecting his reputation. Likewise, the mere causing of annoyance, inconvenience, danger, etc. or an act being grossly offensive or menacing are not by themselves offences under the Indian Penal Code (IPC), 1860, India's principal legislation with respect to criminal liability, and accordingly no question arises of Section 66A of the IT Act nurturing acts that may be termed an incitement to an offence. By application of the same rationale, the court held that what may be grossly offensive or annoying under Section 66A of the Act need not be obscene, indecent or immoral at all. In fact, the word 'obscene' is conspicuously absent from Section 66A of the Act, and accordingly, the court held that the restriction under Article 19(2) of the Constitution cannot be relied upon on this count too.

Vagueness: In addition to holding that Section 66A of the IT Act is not saved by Article 19(2) of the Constitution, the court also held that Section 66A of the IT Act suffers from the vice of vagueness. The court observed that while similar offences as those contemplated by Section 66A of the IT Act are narrowly and closely defined under the IPC, the language used in Section 66A of the IT Act in stark contrast is open-ended, undefined and vague. The court noted that the IT Act does not incorporate the offences defined under the IPC as being applicable to the IT Act.

2.5.4 Verdict and Public Relief

While Section 66A of the IT Act has long been criticized and termed as draconian, the decision of the top court in striking it down as unconstitutional cannot be underestimated or belittled. Had the decision gone any other way, the way we use the Internet would have been forced to undergo a sea change. To the relief of over a hundred million users of the Internet in India and at a time when State-controlled Internet censorship is a growing concern the world over, this decision of the Supreme Court of India goes a long way in backing the Internet freedom.

3

Media and Elections

Elections are important exercises of democracy. Periodic elections that are transparent keep the democratic institutions thriving. Present-day elections without mass media are unimaginable. As mentioned in earlier chapters, mass media provides the platform for the people to express their opinion. Thus, it can be safely said that it is the mass media that provides opportunity to exercise freedom of expression and share information among the larger masses. However, the exercise of freedom of expression will have little meaning if it can only be done so at an individual level. Freedom of expression is not just about what you are able to share with your friend or neighbour; it is more about the expression of ideas and opinions through media and also receiving information from it.

The European Court of Human Rights has concluded that media freedom is crucial for keeping people informed of the affairs of the State. Media freedom provides the public with one of the best opportunities of discovering and forming opinion about the ideas and attitudes of the leaders belonging to different political parties. At the same time, a free and fair media will also provide opportunity for the politicians to understand and reflect upon the wavering trend of public opinion. Thus, media enables the sides, public as well as public servants to participate in the free political debate which is a vital part of a democratic society.

It is a known fact that media provides information pertaining to the matters of public interest and act as a watchdog over issues related to governance. Media is expected to disseminate information, ideas and opinion on matters of public interest. On its part, media have the onerous task of transmitting information; on the other hand, the public also has the right to receive information from the media. Without the participation of the public and public interest, media would find it hard to play its role of 'watchdog'.

According to the European Court, there are two important aspects to this democratic role of the media—First, to inform the public about the matters of public interest, and second, to act as a watchdog of government. However, it should be noted here that this role does not impose particular duties on any particular newspaper or television station as such. Rather it is expected from the governments to ensure that the media are able to perform these functions during elections as well. Governments may regulate the technical aspects of broadcasting. But these duties should also be performed in a fair manner. Frequencies should be allocated in a fair and non-discriminatory manner. Just like any other industry, the media are also subject to the law of the land, but governments rarely restrict the contents of the media citing reasons like defamation, sedition, etc.

3.1 Media Pluralism during Elections

The media play an important role in an election, not only as a means of examining government actions but also making it sure that the voters have all the necessary information at its disposal to make an informed and democratic choice. Governments have vital obligation not to impede the media in performing these functions. Additionally, governments also have a positive obligation to facilitate media pluralism in order to provide exposure to the public to the widest variety of information sources. The obligation contained in Article 19 of the International Covenant on Civil and Political Rights (ICCPR), guaranteeing freedom of expression and freedom of information, applies only to governments and definitely not to individual media houses.

As mass media has made tremendous advances in terms of use of new communication technologies, effective measures to prevent control of the media by government or other agencies is all the more important in order to provide everyone their right to freedom of expression. The UNHRC has elaborated on freedom of expression. It has stated that the State should not have media monopoly nor should it try to control media. The State should always promote plurality of the media. Political parties, leaders and also policies should be consistent with this principle in order to prevent undue media dominance or concentration by privately controlled media groups in monopolistic situations that may be harmful to a diversity of sources and views.

The UN Rapporteur for Freedom of Expression has identified both commercial pressures and government regulation as major threats to media pluralism and content of public interest. Some of the important challenges to free and fair media in 2010 that the Rapporteur listed included increasing concentration of media ownership, cost-cutting measures taken up by private owners and existing broadcasters acquiring access to new digital frequencies during the digital changeover, thereby strengthening concentration and political interference in the media.

Jurisprudence from countries like Ghana, Sri Lanka, Belize, Trinidad and Tobago, Zambia and India underlines the two important points that media monopolies negatively impact freedom of expression. It should be remembered that publicly funded media have an obligation to convey opinions other than that of the incumbent government. A number of those judgements are related to the right of political opponents of the government to have their views heard in the public media. This right to express extends to other types of minorities also. Members of various groups should have the right to participate, on the basis of their own culture and language, in the cultural life of the community to produce and enjoy arts and science, to safeguard their cultural heritage and traditions, to own their own media and other means of communication and to have access on the basis of equality to State-owned media.

It is necessary to understand that the role of media is not just limited to acting as a platform for expression in a limited sense. The media are far more important in terms of enabling the public to exercise their right to freedom of information as well. This right is closely related to media pluralism because without such a guarantee the public cannot access a diversity of information. Reflecting upon best international practice on pluralism and access to the media, the UN has provided detailed guidelines in this regard. The guidelines state that an independent and free media should have diversity of ownership, and it should promote and protect democracy while providing opportunities and means for economic, social and cultural development.

One of the most definitive statements from a UN authority, the UN Special Rapporteur on Freedom of Opinion and Expression, has come from Abid Hussein, who has said in his 1999 annual report:

> There are several fundamental principles that, if promoted and respected, enhance the right to seek, receive and impart information. These principles are: a monopoly or excessive concentration of ownership of media in the hands of a few is to be avoided in the interest of developing a plurality of viewpoints and voices; State-owned media have a responsibility to report on all aspects of national life and to provide access to a diversity of viewpoints; State-owned media must not be used as a communication or propaganda organ for one political party or as an advocate for the Government to the exclusion of all other parties and groups.

The Special Rapporteur then went on to list a series of obligations on the State to ensure 'that the media are given the widest possible latitude' in order to achieve 'the most fully informed electorate possible': There should not be bias or discrimination in media coverage, censorship of election programmes should not be allowed, media should be exempt from legal liability for provocative statements and a right of reply should be provided, there should be a clear distinction between news coverage of functions of government office and functions as a party candidate, airtime for direct access programmes should be granted on a fair and non-discriminatory basis, programmes should provide an opportunity for candidates to debate each other and for journalists to question them, media should engage in voter education, programmes should target traditionally disadvantaged groups, which may include women and ethnic and religious minorities (Hussain, 1999).

3.2 Media Ownership and Elections

Media ownership will have tremendous impact on the nature of media coverage of elections. It is also true of any political coverage for that matter. Government-owned media are under the direct control of the incumbent government and therefore tend to favour parties and candidates who are in power. Although financially supported by the State, PSB must act independently of any political party or leaders. Privately owned media, corporate or otherwise may be independent but may also serve the political interests of their proprietors. In some countries, these proprietors might belong to political parties, and sometimes they are the candidates themselves. Economics and historical context also contribute to the dynamics of differently owned media organizations. Nevertheless, the establishment of the right kind of diversity and balance within the media ownership landscape are key factors in fostering democratic processes in a given country.

A particular country's portfolio of media ownership is likely to have a significant impact on a range of electoral issues such as the extent to which political advertising is allowed in media, peoples' access to civic and electoral education as well as campaign material and the extent to which elections are covered in a balanced and fair manner. In the USA, where private media is predominantly owned by big corporate houses, access to media by parties and candidates is allowed by way of paid advertising. Similarly, Finland, where commercial broadcasting evolved much earlier than in most parts of Europe, has a far free approach to paid political advertising than most European countries. Unlike its neighbours, Finland does not provide free airtime on public media, but allows contestants to purchase unlimited private airtime. However, countries such as Britain and Denmark, with a strong tradition of public-funded media, do not allow paid political advertising at all. Instead have a system of free direct access broadcasts on private broadcasters.

Broadcast licensing is one of the means in which governments try to manage media ownership and promote media pluralism. Most of the countries have some form of regulation in place especially in relation to media pluralism. For example, in Australia, the cross-media ownership law introduced by the Labor Government in 1987 was the beginning of modern media change. The laws strictly prohibited the control of more than one commercial television license or newspaper or commercial radio license in the same market, thus reducing the undue media concentration.

However, it should be noted here that such regulations are not easy to implement in a fair manner as it can be used to corner political competition. In Australia, 'these changes also led to increased concentration in some markets, and were widely seen as rewarding Labor allies', and were later rolled back when the other major party gained power, which then led to further concentration of ownership. In addition, due to their influence and reach, broadcasting licenses for private radio and television often include clauses with various requirements related to elections. For example, the Equal Time rule in the US Communications Act (1934) requires broadcasters to provide an equivalent opportunity to any opposing political candidates who request it; and forbids broadcasters to censor campaign advertisements. Other regulations require private broadcasters carry paid political advertising (Smith, 2011).

Media ownership will have a direct impact on media's ability to perform its watchdog role during elections. State and government media are sometimes conspicuously biased in favour of the incumbent government leaders, parties and candidates. This is particularly true in newer or transitional democracies. During the 2012 Russia elections, the fact that most broadcast media were owned by either the government or by powerful pro-Putin business leaders, it translated into overwhelming bias in election coverage in favour of Putin. The discussions about 'regulation' of the media in elections should in fact be addressing this problem. It is the duty of the incumbent government to ensure that publicly funded media operate with due independence of the government of the day, rather than trying to restrict the operations of media that enjoy complete editorial independence.

Media ownership also affects the right to information of the voters. Voters' access to information related to elections is very limited in some countries because of poor diversity of media ownership and also because of lack of policymaking and investment in media sector so as to ensure that media reaches majority of the population. Lack of diversified media infrastructure and lack of public trust on the existing media networks would lead to insufficient information pertaining to elections. This is another major impact of concentration of media ownership.

3.3 Global Media Ownership

It is often wrongly assumed that the proportion of government or privately owned media reflects a particular country's political and social freedom. It also analysed as dictatorship or authoritarian regimes with controlled media versus democracies which fostered pluralism of media ownership. But the ground reality is far more complex. Numerous factors are responsible in determining the degree of media freedom in a given country, including legal, economic, political and cultural environments that exist there. Ownership also varies from country to county depending on economic and democratic development environment.

However, there are some discernible recent trends. In the developed world, 'the restructuring of telecommunications "markets" exploded in the 1990s' with an 'unprecedented number of international mergers and acquisitions among transnational media corporations, which aggressively pursued the opportunities that privatization provided'. As a result, in some of the most developed democracies, including Australia and the USA, a few large companies own the vast majority of private media. In middle-income countries, these are mirrored by 'the national and regional dominance of some of the world's most powerful 'second-tier media firms' of newly industrialized nations such as Brazil's Globo, Mexico's Televisa, Argentina's Clarín and Venezuela's Cisneros Group—Latin American firms that have 'extensive ties and joint ventures with the largest media TNCs, as well as with Wall Street investment banks' (Murphy, 2007).

Newly emerging democracies have experienced their own dynamics in terms of media ownership: regional trends, such as those in Sub-Saharan Africa, Eastern Europe, parts of Asia and even to some extent in the Middle East, bear testimony to a transition into democracies that have also resulted in dismantling of national broadcasting systems and the reformation of the role of the press connected to authoritarian regimes, the promotion of private independent and pluralistic media and the proliferation of new media channels. Despite a push to privatization above all else, mass media have served remarkably well as a means to globalize the democratic exchange of ideas and issues capable of challenging authority and of fostering an atmosphere of optimism. And while the degree to which civic discourses have found a way to take root differs, when it does emerge, it is often in conjunction with citizen-based media (Murphy, 2007).

Most Western European democracies had, until recent times, State monopolies of broadcasting. Britain legalized private commercial broadcasting as recently as the 1950s. The establishment of the BBC in the 1920s was perhaps a stepping stone towards this privatization, arguably the world's first form of 'PSB'. Although BBC is subsidized by the State, it is independent of the government and acting at the behest of the public. France, Germany and Denmark did not allow privatization of media until the 1980s. Britain and France are particularly significant examples due to their extensive colonial legacy that influenced the organization of broadcasting and media in countries across the world. In Britain and France, there is a strong distinction between broadcasting, with its strong public service history, and print media, which has a distinctly 'privately owned' history. However, in some long-standing democracies—for instance in Sweden and Norway—there is a tradition of State funding of the print media as well. According to the Swedish government, subsidies to secondary newspapers are 'important for the diversity of media at local and regional levels' (Swedish govt. data, 2012).

In Latin America, private media were often closely associated with those in power—especially the military dictatorships of the 1960s and 1970s. Similarly, under the Suharto dictatorship in Indonesia until 1998, private media were closely controlled, while the State owned a large media apparatus in its own right. In addition, the Suharto family bought directly into major media businesses. Far from facilitating pluralism, these private media advocated suppression of media. Indeed, many would argue that the large corporations dominating the US media are not conducive to the expression of alternative political opinions. Whatever the truth of such contentions, it is clear that there is no dependable correlation between the extent of private ownership and media pluralism.

Economics also play a significant role in determining the structure of media ownership. Public versus private broadcasting is sometimes more indicative of national financial resources rather than measures of media freedom. Public media, be it State, government or PSB, has been particularly strong in the early stages for many emerging democracies due to economic conditions that make it more difficult for private broadcasters to start up operations.

> The size of the advertising 'cake' varies according to economic conditions. Most private and some public media are dependent upon advertising to make their business sustainable. The public sector is often important in media in poorer countries for two reasons: the small advertising cake often means less private media, and a dominant public broadcaster; and where there is advertising revenue for private media, it is often from government agencies, or donors working with government. In wealthier countries, companies now use the Internet to advertise their goods and services. This has led to further drops in advertising revenues for traditional media. (Smith, 2011)

In many countries in Africa, for instance, and also parts of Asia and Latin America, this explains why until recently national radio stations, broadcasting on medium- and long-wave frequencies, were almost entirely a State-owned phenomenon. Even where broadcasting regulations permitted, neither private broadcasters nor advertisers had much interest in broadcasting to the entire nation. Instead, private advertisers were primarily interested in reaching an urban audience with disposable income—the type of audience served by private FM stations, most of which primarily broadcast music. The fast growth of private and new media in these countries is now changing the public versus private paradigm, however. Nonetheless, State-owned broadcasters are still important and in some cases remain the only choice for listeners.

Technological developments like satellite and cable television and the Internet complicate the already complex media ownership landscape further. Economic factors are still at play. Factors like those who can afford to subscribe to a pay channel or use the Internet will generally belong to upper class. Local cable and satellite providers are subject to the same political and economic constraints as those broadcasting on terrestrial channels, in that they are dependent on advertising and subscriber revenues to survive and grow. Mass media using the Internet and other new media platforms can often publish or broadcast more cheaply than in the past, and they are free from some of the regulatory constraints that are imposed on traditional mediums. Along with such alternative media, multinational broadcasters such as *Al Jazeera*, Cable News Network (CNN) and the BBC can also play an important role in breaching broadcasting monopolies. That is why some countries have prohibited ownership of satellite dishes. Internet news sites also help to challenge broadcasting monopolies, though caution should be exercised in celebrating pluralism on the Internet. In Australia, for example, 'all but one of the 12 news sites in Australia's top 100 most visited sites are owned by major existing media outlets' (Moehler & Singh, 2009).

Cultural and attitudinal factors will also have an impact on media ownership. For example, according to a report published in the *Political Research Quarterly* in 2009, 'in post authoritarian African democracies audiences trust government-owned broadcast media more than they trust private broadcasters despite the public media's lack of independence as well as a history of state propaganda'. The report suggests that this credibility gap is due to a number of factors such as audiences' levels of political understanding, support base enjoyed by the incumbent leaderships and illiberal attitudes. The study also found that audiences also tended to prefer public broadcasters in countries with lower corruption and greater press freedom.

This trust gap no doubt impedes, to a certain extent, the growth of private media (Moehler & Singh, 2009).

3.4 Freedom of Political Debate during Elections

Freedom of political debate has been recognized by international courts, other international bodies and national tribunals as a fundamental right. The European Court of Human Rights noted in 1978: 'freedom of political debate is at the very core of the concept of a democratic society'. Freedom of political debate means the ability to openly discuss political matters in public or in the media, based on the fullest possible access to information about political issues. It is an expression of a range of fundamental freedoms (*Lingens v/s Austria*, Judgement of July 08, 1986, Series A No. 103, at Para. 42).

In 1992, the European Court of Human Rights elaborated on freedom of political debate, indicating that not only is expressing opinions and receiving information important but so is media as a public platform for interaction between politicians and the public. Freedom of the press allows the public one of the best ways of accessing, understanding and forming an opinion of the ideas and attitudes of their political leaders. Particularly, it provides politicians the opportunity to reflect and comment on the preoccupations of public opinion; it thus enables all the stakeholders to participate in the free political debate which is at the very core of the concept of a democratic society (UN, 1992).

One of the advantages of political debate is that it is a way of giving the electorate information that allows it to exercise its political choice. The UN Technical Team on the Malawi Referendum of 1993, which chose between a single and multiparty system, stated: 'If voters are to make an informed choice at the polling station, then an active exercise of the freedom of expression is essential'. A High Court in Nigeria has also made a similar observation. Freedom of speech is, no doubt, the very foundation of every democratic society, for without free discussion, particularly on political issues, no public education or enlightenment, essential for the proper functioning and execution of the processes of responsible government, is possible, it said.

The Israeli Supreme Court also stated that real democracy and freedom of speech are related to each other. Freedom of speech enables each individual in a society to crystallize his or her own opinion in the decision-making process which is vital in a democratic State. The essence of democratic elections is based on informed opinions, evaluating such opinions and also exposing them to open debate.

3.5 Guidelines for Media during Elections

Elections are hugely significant in a democratic process of any country and especially for countries which are in the early stages of democratic transition. The successful organization of elections often makes or breaks democratic progress. Successful elections can move the democratization forward emphatically, while contested or problematical elections can significantly retard its progress. Within the wider sphere of elections, the mass media, print, broadcast and online have a very important role to play. For most voters, the media is the basic source of information with regard to voting, elections and the different parties and candidates contesting the election.

If the media fails to inform voters properly, there can be widespread confusion and even disenfranchisement. The media also play an important role in preventing political corruption and other activities which dent the electoral process. If the media are strongly biased towards or against certain parties and candidates, it can substantially disrupt the fundamental principle of providing level playing field during elections. It goes without saying both that the right to freedom of expression applies with particular force during elections, including in relation to the media, and that any existing codes of conduct for the media, including of a self-regulatory nature, remain applicable at all times.

Media houses have obligations to be balanced, impartial and fair in the coverage, treatment of news and current affairs. Media organizations should offer a prompt correction and right of reply for significant inaccurate, misleading or distorted statements. Media outlets should reflect the range of political opinions in society and enable free and open debate on matters of public concern. Coverage given to political parties should broadly reflect the support base these parties enjoy in society. The media is the primary source of information about the election for most voters. As part of their general role as sources of information in society, the media also have a duty to inform the public about elections, candidates and party activities during elections.

Informing voters about why it is important to vote and the general role of elections in a democracy is a vital function of media. It provides voters with technical information about how to register to vote and about how, when and where to cast one's ballot, including about advance voting. Media should also keep voters in conflict areas informed about the election situation in their areas. It should also inform voters about the secrecy of the ballot and why it is important to inform voters about the role of the upcoming elections or the positions which are up for election.

The power of those offices wields in terms of governing the country, the right of the public to vote for parties and candidates they trust and whose ideas they support, and to focus on voters living in areas where media access is low is also important for media organizations. It is imperative on the part of media to inform voters about what the different parties and candidates stand for; this goes beyond political advertising and should be done through news and current affairs.

Rules on balance, impartiality and fairness are important at all times, but they assume special significance during elections due to the sensitivity and potentially serious implications of media bias at such times. In some countries, the fairness of elections has been seriously undermined by strong media bias towards one or another political party or candidate. It also undermines the level of playing field all parties and candidates are supposed to enjoy during elections. However, media does not vouch for legality of statements made by political parties and candidates during elections nor does it act as intermediaries between them. Media role is strictly limited to providing balanced coverage of elections and to act as a public platform for political debates during elections.

4
Media Professionalism and Election Coverage

The performance of media during election campaigns is a topic of great importance. When it comes to the performance part of the media, editorial independence and professional integrity are the cornerstones of sound election coverage. A lack of journalistic autonomy or responsibility can, in combination with an unbearably huge media landscape, affect the results of elections. Therefore, it is imperative to have media diversity, which caters to various stakeholders. However, this also creates competition, and the proliferation of television channels and the increased competitiveness in the broadcast market are also matters of particular concern. Does the battle for the viewer negatively affect the election coverage? This is an important question that needs to be addressed.

Should editorial bias in the print media be curtailed? How do different countries monitor the media coverage of elections? Should there be free or paid political advertisements in the newspapers? Do private television channels also have to follow the principles of fair and balanced coverage, or does this obligation only rest upon public broadcasting channels? How can this be implemented? Is it through self-regulation and responsibility, or statutory regulation and further control? Should infotainment and debates be regulated to ensure balance? How should free political advertising on television be allocated? Should paid political advertising be aired? If so, how to tackle the advantages enjoyed by those with big wallets? Which body should monitor all this? How can its independence be guaranteed?

Media pluralism, editorial autonomy and professionalism are canons of journalism recognized by all. At the same time, there is broad consensus about limitations to the freedom of the press—not only general guidelines pertaining to transgressions of civil and criminal laws on racist publications, defamation, etc., but also concerning coverage of elections. For instance, reporting about exit polls is not desirable as it may affect the ensuing electoral results. Legal provisions alone cannot guarantee objectivity and fairness. Experience from many countries and media outlets have indicated that the values of self-regulation, internal guidelines and editorial statutes are also important in achieving this ideal journalistic practice.

In many countries, the PSB media have certain statutory obligations. Technically speaking, there may not be any justification for treating the electronic media differently from print, but examples do suggest that there is broad consensus and acceptance regarding this dual approach to electronic and print media. So far as self-regulation is concerned, it has often been stated that preparing the campaign codes of ethics and editorial practice should be done with the participation and acceptance of journalists and media houses. After all, a code of ethics is useless if it is not accepted by the people to whom it applies. Ideally, the framing of suitable clauses of the electoral law and of regulations with regard to the media coverage of elections should also be the outcome of consultation between the media, the regulatory body and the government. The journalists must at least be involved in the framing of the rules that apply to them.

Quality of media coverage and professionalism in reporting act as important factors during election periods in conflict and post-conflict situation and countries in transition. Free and fair elections are fundamental for democratic consolidation and prevention of conflicts. In order to promote free and fair, safe and professional coverage during elections, UNESCO advocates about fair and efficient disclosure of information to journalists covering the elections. Training to enhance professional skills during elections, training on the safety of journalists and their right to work without threat, production and distribution of election guidelines containing principles of professional reporting during elections, electoral processes and safety information, as well as briefing notes on international human rights law with emphasis on freedom of expression, are to be provided to the journalists.

The UN Plan of Action on the Safety of Journalists and the Issue of Impunity was endorsed by the UN Chief Executives Board on 12 April 2012. The Plan was prepared during the 1st UN Inter-Agency Meeting on this issue, convened in September 2011 by the Director General of UNESCO at the request of the Intergovernmental Council of the International Programme for the Development of Communication (IPDC). A second UN Inter-Agency Meeting was held in Vienna in November 2012, convened by UNESCO and co-hosted by the Office of the High Commissioner for Human Rights, the UN Office on Drugs and Crime and the UNDP (UNESCO, 2015).

The meeting brought together representatives from 15 UN bodies and more than 40 non-governmental and intergovernmental organizations, independent experts, media groups and professional associations. The purpose of the meeting was to formulate a concrete implementation strategy by outlining more than 100 areas of work by UN bodies and civil society groups to secure the safety of journalists. As the strategy is now being operationalized at the national level in first-phase countries where it will be implemented in 2013–14 and regionally in Latin America, it will serve as a key platform to galvanize efforts to ensure journalists safety (UNESCO, 2015).

Considering that during electoral periods, journalists can either become victims of violence or a key factor in preventing the further escalation of social conflict, support to media in electoral contexts is an aspect to be naturally considered in the process of implementing the strategy in this regard. In fact, the strategy document explicitly includes, as a foreseen action line, the integration of elements related to the safety of journalists and the issue of impunity in the reports prepared for and after electoral observation missions.

4.1 Freedom of Expression

The freedom of expression is a fundamental human right. It is fundamental in terms of its central importance to human life and dignity, and also because it is an essential foundation of all human rights—including the right to participate in political life—due to its intermediary nature as well as its role in ensuring effective protection of rights. The right to freedom of expression is recognized in all the important international and regional human rights treaties. It was universally declared to be a right of the highest importance in the Universal Declaration of Human Rights, adopted unanimously by the UN General Assembly in 1948, just three years after the UN was first created. Article 19 of the Universal Declaration states that everyone has the right to freedom of opinion and expression, and this right includes freedom to hold opinions without interference and to seek, receive and impart information and ideas through any media and regardless of frontiers.

This right has also been included in the ICCPR. Three regional human rights treaties in Africa, Europe and Latin America also protect this fundamental human right. Guarantees of freedom of expression are found in majority of national constitutions. The right to freedom of expression, guaranteed under international law, that includes the right to seek, receive and impart information and ideas, is very broad in scope. In terms of imparting information and ideas, it includes the right to express verbally, by word of mouth, and also by writing, by electronic means or through any other means of communication. Importantly, it also includes the right to express controversial opinions in public. Just because an idea is unpopular, it cannot justify preventing a person from expressing it.

However, freedom of expression is not limited to the right to express oneself. It also includes the right to seek and to receive information from others, including the right to obtain and read newspapers, to listen to broadcasts, to surf the Internet and to participate in discussions in public and private as a listener. It is also being recognized that the right also includes the right to access information held by public authorities. As such, it places a duty on these bodies to both disseminate information of key public importance and to respond to request for access to publicly held information.

The right is also fully guaranteed notwithstanding a person's level of education or his or her race, colour, sex, language, religion, political or other opinion, national or social origin, property or birth or other status. Significantly, the right to freedom of expression includes not only negative obligations on the State not to interfere with the flow of information but also positive obligations, for instance, to create an environment in which a free and independent media can do well. During elections, these positive obligations imply that the State is under a duty to ensure that voters are properly informed as to how to vote and other election issues. But the right to freedom of expression, unlike the right to hold opinions, is not absolute. It is universally recognized that a few number of important public and private interests may justify restrictions on this all-important right. These include the right to one's reputation and privacy, and the need to maintain public order and national security. However, international law sets out a strict test which any restrictions on freedom of expression must meet in order to be valid.

Although freedom of expression is universally recognized, such recognition has not always been accompanied by governmental back up and respect. Administrations throughout the world have resorted to illegal censorship, repressive restrictions on what could be published or broadcast, often accompanied by the threat of imprisonment for breach, and direct State control over the media. Even in matured democracies, there is usually some sort of tension between the right to freedom of expression, and the media in particular, and the authorities, who often dislike being criticized. For this reason, the right must be strictly protected and defended, not the least, by journalists and others working in the media. In transitional democracies, laws from erstwhile repressive administrations, which breach the right to freedom of expression, are often still in force. There is an urgent need to reform of these laws. Leaders belonging to these transitional democracies should take initiatives regarding this. This should be an important priority as part of the move towards a democratic form of government is concerned.

4.1.1 Restrictions on Freedom of Expression

Although the right to freedom of expression is universally recognized as one of fundamental rights, it is also accepted that the right is not absolute. Certain overriding public and private interests may justify restricting this right. But important question here is under what circumstances this right is to be restricted? International law, as enshrined in international treaties and their interpretation by international courts and others, have recognized that interference with freedom of expression is an extremely serious issue; therefore, such interference is permissible only in few narrow instances.

Freedom of expression therefore should be subject to certain restrictions, but these shall only be such as are provided by law and are absolutely necessary. It is subject to respect of the rights or reputations of others, for the protection of national security or of public order, or of public health or morals. However, it should be noted here that the interference must be in accordance with a law, legally sanctioned restriction should also protect or promote aims deemed legitimate in international law and, more importantly, restrictions must be necessary for the protection or promotion of the legitimate objective.

The interference cannot be merely the result of the whims and fancies of an official. It must actually be an enacted law or regulation which the official is applying. In other words, only restrictions which have been officially and formally recognized by lawmakers are legitimate. Additionally, the law must meet certain standards of clarity and precision so that it is clear in advance exactly what expressions are restricted. Vaguely worded regulations with potentially very broad application will not meet this standard, and are thus illegitimate prohibitions on freedom of expression. For instance, restriction on 'displeasing the government' would often fail the test on account of vagueness.

The list of legitimate aims provided in Article 19(3) of the ICCPR is exclusive, and governments may not add to these. This includes restrictions on freedom of expression following legitimate aims; respect for the rights and reputations of others; and protection of national security, public order, public health or morals. Finally, even if a restriction is in accordance with an acceptably clear law and if it is in the service of a legitimate aim, it will breach the right to freedom of expression unless it is necessary for the protection of that legitimate aim. This has a number of implications. First, if another measure which is less intrusive to a person's right to free expression would accomplish the same goal, the restriction is not in fact necessary (Universal Declaration of Human Rights, 1948).

For example, shutting down a newspaper for defamation is excessive; a retraction, or perhaps a combination of a retraction and a warning or a modest fine, would adequately protect the defamed person's reputation. Second, the restriction must impair the right as little as possible and, in particular, not restrict legitimate speech. In protecting national security, for example, it is not acceptable to ban all discussion about a country's military forces. In applying this, courts have recognized that there may be practical limits on how finely honed and precise a legal measure can be. But subject only to such practical limits, restrictions must not be overbroad. Third, the impact of restrictions must be proportionate in the sense that the harm to freedom of expression must not outweigh the benefits in terms of the interest protected.

A restriction which provided limited protection to reputation but which seriously undermined freedom of expression would not pass muster. This again is uncontroversial. A democratic society depends on the free flow of information and ideas, and it is only when the overall public interest is served by limiting that flow that such a limitation can be justified. This implies that the benefits of any restriction must outweigh the costs for it to be justified. In applying this test and, in particular, the third part on necessity, courts and others should take into account all of the circumstances at the time the restriction is applied. A restriction in favour of national security, for example, which is justifiable in times of war, may not be legitimate in peacetime (Universal Declaration of Human Rights, 1948).

4.1.2 Freedom of Expression and the Media

It is recognized throughout the world that the media play a significant role in protecting democracy and its allied institutions. The media are in the best position to investigate and report on issues of public interest, particularly those issues related to political process, the public conduct of government officials; the positions taken by government with respect to international issues, corruption, mismanagement or dishonesty in government; human rights issues. Indeed, it is fair to say that a large majority of individuals gain almost all of their knowledge about the society and its day-to-day affairs from the media.

This role of the media is as important during elections as at other times. People depend heavily on information conveyed by the media to know about the contesting candidates, the major electoral issues being debated and the platforms of the various parties. Without the media, providing the most fundamental information related to the democratic process, for instance, making a decision to vote for a particular candidate during elections, it would be difficult for the people to have informed choices.

Therefore, it is of paramount importance that the freedom of expression of the media be guaranteed and protected at all cost. Media professionals, like journalists and editors, should be able to exercise their own right to freedom of expression during and after elections. Even more important is the right of common public to seek and to receive information, a key component of freedom of expression, which depends upon respect for the media freedom.

The significance of freedom of the media has been stressed by international courts. The UN Human Rights Committee, the official body responsible for overseeing compliance by States with their obligations under the ICCPR, has reiterated the importance of a free media to the political process. The free communication of information and ideas about public and political issues between citizens, candidates and elected representatives is essential especially during elections. This implies that media is able to report and comment on public issues without censorship or restraint and to inform public opinion.

The Inter-American Court of Human Rights has stated: 'It is the mass media that make the exercise of freedom of expression a reality'. And, as the European Court of Human Rights has noted, the media as a whole 3: Freedom of Expression and the Media merit special protection, in part because of their role in making public 'information and ideas on matters of public interest.' Not only does media have the task of imparting such information and ideas: the public also has a right to receive them. Were it otherwise, the press would be unable to play its vital role of 'public watchdog' (Mendel, 2000).

It follows from these general principles that the government and public figures must tolerate a great degree of criticism from the media. The media's role as watchdog in a democratic society implies that it has a duty to scrutinize the actions of those in power, as well as those up for election and, where the media themselves consider this appropriate, to criticize them. It is illegitimate for governments to clamp down on media because they criticize or because the government does not like the particular form in which the media choose to express their criticism, for example, through satirical cartoons. Governments must also expect and accept the use of strong language and a degree of exaggeration, particularly in relation to topics of acute public interest.

In a strong democracy, the media should themselves play an important role in protecting freedom of expression. If the media are not active in this regard, freedom of expression will be very much at risk. The media can do this in a number of ways. These include a strong commitment to publishing material of public interest, highlighting instances where freedom of expression has been restricted, and challenging laws restricting freedom of expression in solidarity with others.

4.1.3 Freedom of Expression during Elections

In a democracy, people elect the government of their choice by voting for their preferred leaders during elections held at periodic times. In order to exercise this power freely and wisely, the voters needs accurate information about the various candidates, belonging to different political parties, their programmes and backgrounds and also about important issues being debated during the election.

The UN Human Rights Committee has stressed upon the free flow of information and ideas about public and political issues between voters, candidates and elected representatives is of utmost significance. It implies that the media is able to comment on public issues without censorship or restraint and to inform public opinion. It also implies that people in particular should have wide access to information and the opportunity to disseminate information and opinions about the activities of elected bodies and their members through the media. The provision of such information in the run-up to elections includes rights and duties for three groups, namely the political parties and candidates contesting elections, the news media and, more importantly, the electorate.

4.1.4 Political Parties and Freedom of Expression

The right to freedom of expression, as guaranteed, among others, in the ICCPR, protects the right of all political parties to convey their messages to the public through any media of their liking. The ability of political parties to communicate with voters is important for the proper functioning of a democracy. Voters will be reluctant to vote for a party if they are not sure what it stands for. Although voters may formally be able to vote for the party of their choice, such choice is illusory in the absence of adequate information about the competing parties and candidates. If only one or two parties have been able to communicate their views, they will inevitably dominate the election.

Some political parties will obviously be in a better position to spread their message than others; a party founded by a well-known person or funded by rich industrialists will more easily attract attention than a party which lacks funds or fame. However, such natural advantages are simply part of politics. Under the ICCPR, the State is under an obligation to ensure that all parties have at least some access to means of communicating with the public. Any hurdles other than the natural disadvantages which flow from being a small party should be removed. For instance, conditions such as having a certain number of members should not be required before parties may spread leaflets or hold public meetings. Additionally, the State must take certain positive measures to ensure that these parties have some access to the means of mass communication. Typically, a publicly owned or funded broadcaster is under an obligation to provide a measure of free airtime to all competing parties.

4.1.5 The News Media and Freedom of Expression

As the principal means through which the public gathers information, the news media play a vital role in the electoral process. News media provides potential voters the opportunity to know about the various parties and their programmes and influences the outcome of elections by exposing hidden flaws and strengths of the candidates. Given their importance, there is always a risk that news journalists are subjected in order to report in a certain way. To assist them in the task of reporting as objectively and honestly as possible, journalists enjoy rights protected under the ICCPR.

Particularly journalists have a right to freely seek, receive and impart information in any way they deem fit, without interference from the government, subject only to legitimate restrictions, for instance, appropriate defamation laws. The authorities should not harass, intimidate or otherwise obstruct journalists in their work, or impose censorship or offer rewards for reporting in a biased way. Journalists should be permitted to cover all political parties, including those considered most hostile to the government and they should not suffer any adverse consequences for publishing material which places the government in a negative light.

4.1.6 The Voters' Right to Freedom of Information

The ICCPR confers on the general public the right to receive information. Combined with the right to participate in public affairs, also guaranteed under the ICCPR, this means that the public has a right to receive complete and unbiased information about the contending parties. The main responsibility to ensure that this right is respected lies with the State, which has an obligation to create an environment within which the media—who are the primary source of information—are freely able to go about their job of informing the public. Publicly owned or funded media also have an important role to play in informing the public, and are under an obligation to do so, and without political bias.

At the same time, the media are under a professional obligation to inform the public fully and truthfully about all matters relevant to the elections. This implies that the journalists have the difficult task of reporting on all the parties in a neutral way, however laudable or repugnant a particular candidate may seem to the journalist in question. However, in a democracy, the power belongs to the whole population, not just the educated or informed elite. It is imperative that journalists do not substitute their own judgement for that of the electorate by reporting more extensively and favourably on one party than another.

4.2 Media Regulation and Pluralism

The concept of pluralism is fundamental to both democracy and to the protection of the right to freedom of expression. A society where only a privileged few can exercise their right to freedom of expression effectively is not a free society. Such a situation would breach not only the rights of those who are denied the ability to exercise their right to freedom of expression through the media but also the right of society as a whole to be well informed and to receive information from a variety of sources. Indeed, the right of the public to receive a diversity of information and ideas is central to the right of freedom of expression.

For these reasons, international human rights law strongly not only promotes the idea of pluralism in relation to the right to freedom of expression but also requires States to take positive steps to safeguard it. In an often-repeated statement, the European Court of Human Rights has stated: The

Court has frequently stressed the fundamental role of freedom of expression in a democratic society, in particular where, through the press, it serves to impart information and ideas of general interest, which the public is moreover entitled to receive. Such an undertaking cannot be successfully accomplished unless it is grounded in the principle of pluralism, of which the State is the ultimate guarantor (FNJ, 2008).

The protection of pluralism provides one of the main justifications for media regulation, particularly in relationship to the broadcast media. It is internationally accepted that States should regulate the airwaves to provide for a plurality of voices. State monopolies are incompatible with the right of the public to receive information from a variety of sources. Simply allowing private broadcasters, however, is not enough. States should take steps to avoid excessive concentration of media ownership and to ensure that licensing systems for broadcasters promote a diversity of content on the airwaves. Indeed, contribution to diversity should be an explicit licensing criterion.

With regard to the print media, it is internationally accepted that the best way to encourage pluralism is by abolishing legal and administrative measures that inhibit the establishment of newspapers and magazines. In particular, there should be no licensing systems and, where a registration scheme exists, it should not impose onerous obligations on applicants. These differences from broadcast regulation are justified by a number of considerations including public ownership of the airwaves, the dominant and intrusive nature of broadcasting and the relatively low cost of setting up print media outlets.

Regulatory measures may not be sufficient to ensure pluralism in the media and, where this is the case, States should also consider providing support measures. These may include general measures aimed at the media sector as a whole such as the abolition of taxes on print paper and other materials necessary for operating media outlets, as well as direct support for certain types of media outlets, for example, those that serve small or minority sections of the audience. If direct support measures are provided, States should take care to ensure that this takes place on the basis of objective and non-partisan criteria, within a framework of transparent procedures and subject to independent control (FNJ, 2008).

4.2.1 Guaranteeing Safety of Journalists

The guarantee of freedom of expression places a strong obligation on States to protect the safety of all media workers within their jurisdiction, as well as providing equipments necessary for their work. States are under a general duty to protect all of their citizens, but the special duty in relation to journalists is due to the fact that violence is sometimes used as a tactic to silence critical voices.

In 2000, the special mandates for protecting freedom of expression of the UN, the Organization of American States and the Organization on Security and Cooperation in Europe adopted a Joint Declaration stating: Censorship by killing attacks such as the murder, kidnapping, harassment of or threats to journalists and others exercising their right to freedom of expression, as well as the material destruction of communications facilities, pose a very significant threat to independent and investigative journalism, to freedom of expression and to the free flow of information to the public. States are under an obligation to take adequate measures to end the climate of impunity, and such measures should include devoting sufficient resources and attention to preventing attacks on journalists and others exercising their right to freedom of expression, investigating such attacks when they do occur, bringing those responsible to justice and compensating victims.

States are under three important duties. Never to take part in, or to sanction or condone attacks against the media or media facilities; to take effective action to prevent violent attacks from taking place; where violations have taken place, to investigate the attack, to bring the guilty parties to justice and to provide an effective remedy to the victim. The first duty not only means that States have to refrain from taking part in attacks, it also means that they should never condone attacks, even indirectly. Indirect support may, for example, be provided where senior political figures make excessively critical statements about the media or make serious and unfounded allegations against the media. Indeed, in certain circumstances, the authorities might even have an obligation to speak out publicly in response, for example, to particularly egregious attacks on the media (ACM, 2005).

The second duty implies that the States should take necessary measures to prevent violent attacks, particularly when these are foreseeable. Adequate security measures should be taken to protect the media, and States would have to send extra police or security forces, and implement protective measures, when they become aware of a real and immediate threat. During demonstrations or riots, for instance, both events which the media are under a professional duty to report on, police and other security forces should see it as part of their role to protect media professionals. On the other hand, because of their role in reporting events to the public, the State should never curtail access of journalists to a specific area for their own safety. Such measures are often abused to close troubled areas off from the outside world.

The third duty is to investigate any occurrences of violence and is clear-cut under international law. Failure by the State to take any measures in the face of attacks is a serious issue. The Inter-American Commission on Human Rights, in the context of frequent and serious attacks against journalists in the Americas, has stated that a State's refusal to conduct a full investigation of the murder of a journalist is particularly serious because of its impact on society. The impunity of any of the parties responsible for an act of aggression against a reporter, the most serious of which is assuredly deprivation of the right to life, or against any person engaged in the activity of public expression of information or ideas, constitutes an incentive for all violators of human rights. At the same time, the murder of a journalist clearly will have a chilling effect, on other journalists and also on ordinary citizens, as it instils the fear of denouncing all kinds of offences, abuses or illegal acts. Finally, where journalists go missing, States are under an obligation to take measures to trace them, ascertain their fate, provide appropriate assistance and, wherever possible, facilitate their return to their families.

4.2.2 Regulation of Broadcasting

It is almost universally recognized that some regulation of broadcasters is very much required. Such regulation is justified on a number of grounds, including the need to ensure order as well as pluralism in broadcasting, the fact that the airwaves are a limited public resource, the dominant and intrusive nature of broadcasting and the prohibitive costs of establishing a major broadcast outlet. At the same time, it is essential that regulation should not be abused to silence those critical of the government or who otherwise attract official censure. This would seriously undermine freedom of expression as well as free and fair elections.

The primary means used to balance these competing demands is to allocate regulatory powers in relation to broadcasting to an administrative body which is independent of government. Further protection for freedom of expression is achieved by circumscribing the powers of this body very carefully, so that it may not abuse those powers, and by subjecting its decisions to judicial review. Perfect independence is difficult to achieve, but a number of measures can help prevent political or other interference in the work of the regulatory body. At the very minimum, it is essential that it is not part of a ministry or government department but that it is a separately constituted body, answerable to the public through an independent governing board.

Appointments to the governing board of the regulatory body should be made in a manner that promotes its independence. The process for appointments should be transparent and fair, and allow for participation by civil society and the general public. Appointments should not be made by a single person or party but rather in a manner which ensures a broad range of input. Once appointed, members should be protected against removal outside of certain extreme circumstances (UNESCO, 2006).

In most democratic countries, broadcast regulators undertake two important functions. First, broadcasters are required to obtain a license to operate and the regulator is responsible for overseeing the licensing process. Second, regulators are normally responsible for taking the lead in developing, and for applying, codes of broadcasting conduct which normally deal with a range of content and broadcast practice issues. Licensing is a complex issue, and regulators are required to take a variety of factors into consideration as part of licensing processes. In many countries, broadcast regulators work with those responsible for general telecommunications to develop an overall plan for the use of the radio spectrum. Such plans should include allocation of frequencies to broadcasting to different broadcasting uses such as radio, television, national and local stations, public, commercial and community broadcasting. The idea is to ensure that frequency allocation takes place on a planned manner, not just to the highest bidder.

An important goal of licensing should be to ensure diversity in the airwaves, in terms of both ownership and content. This should therefore be an explicit licensing criterion. The licensing process should be fair and transparent. In most of the countries, calls for license applications are issued from time to time and interested parties can compete for the licenses being offered. Anyone who has been refused a license should be able to apply to the courts for judicial review of this decision. Broadcasters should not be subject to special criminal or civil restrictions relating to programme content, over and above rules of general application. At the same time, it is common for regulators to develop administrative guidelines of conduct governing broadcast content and practice. Such guidelines should be developed in close consultation with broadcasters and other interested stakeholders and should be clear and detailed.

Broadcasting guidelines normally deal with a wide range of issues like accuracy, privacy, treatment of sensitive themes such as bereavement, sex and violence, and the like. They may also address practice issues such as using evasive tactics to obtain information, the conduct of interviews and payment for information. Such guidelines may well set out rules of some relevance to elections, including the requirement of balance and impartiality, and perhaps also the rules relating to direct access programming. Finally, such guidelines may deal with issues relating to advertisements. The primary goal of the system should be to set standards rather than to punish broadcasters for breach. In line with this, sanctions, at least in the first instance, should normally aim at reforming behaviour, and so consist of a warning or requirement to broadcast a message recognizing the breach. More serious sanctions, such as fines or suspensions, should be applied only in the context of repeated and serious breaches, where other sanctions have failed to address the problem.

4.3.3 Regulation of the Print Media

It is generally recognized that specific regulatory measure which govern the print media is not necessary. Unlike broadcasters, who make use of a limited public resource, there are no natural constraints on the number of print media outlets in operation and so no need for particular regulation. However, media are subject to same laws that apply to everyone—for instance, defamation laws and, if they have been set up as corporations, or as non-profit bodies, then they are subject to the same rules that apply to other corporations or non-profit bodies. Under international law, a licensing system for the print media, which involves the possibility of being refused a license and thereby being prohibited from publishing, is not legitimate. The right to freedom of expression includes the right to establish a print media outlet, and, as noted, natural constraints cannot justify limiting this right.

On the other hand, technical registration requirements for the print media, properly defined as mass circulation, periodical publications, do not, per se, breach the guarantee of freedom of expression as long as they meet the certain conditions. Once the requisite information has been provided, there is no discretion to refuse registration. The system does not impose substantive conditions upon the media, and it is administered by a body which is independent of government. However, registration of the print media is unnecessary and may be abused, and, as a result, many countries do not require it.

Imposing special registration requirements on the print media is unnecessary and may be abused and should be avoided. Registration systems which allow for discretion to refuse registration, which impose substantive conditions on the print media or which are overseen by bodies which are not independent of government are particularly problematic. In many democratic countries, the print media has instituted its own self-regulatory systems for promoting better professional standards. Such systems can help promote better standards and rebuff attempts to regulate these matters by law.

4.2.4 Regulation of Journalists

The right to freedom of expression applies to everyone and through any media. As such, it clearly protects the right of everyone to engage in journalism. As regards regulation of journalists, a main issue is that of licensing of journalists, addressed further. Accreditation, which raises rather different issues, is also addressed here. Licensing systems for journalists, whereby individuals are prohibited from practicing as journalists unless they are licensed, are, therefore, illegitimate. In this respect, journalism is unlike other professions, such as the medical profession, for which licensing is accepted. The Inter-American Court of Human Rights dealt extensively with these issues in a reference to it regarding a law from Costa Rica that required journalists to meet certain professional standards and be a member of a professional association.

Journalism is the primary and principal manifestation of freedom of expression and thought. Exactly for this reason, journalism cannot be equated to a profession that is merely granting a service to the public through the application of some knowledge or training acquired in a university, or through those who are enrolled in a certain professional association. International law also establishes that general conditions on who may practice journalism, such as the requirement of a university degree or a certain age, are not legitimate. Such conditions place unjustifiable restrictions on the right of everyone to express themselves through the print media, regardless of age or any other status. Furthermore, experience in many countries demonstrates that such conditions do not promote any useful social goal; in particular, they are not effective in promoting more professional journalism.

It is similarly illegitimate to require journalists to be members of a certain professional body. In many cases, this is simply an indirect way of limiting access to the profession, and is hence just as illegitimate as more direct forms of this prohibition. In other cases, this is a way of seeking to control journalists and to censure those who have in some way annoyed the authorities. All journalists enjoy the right to freedom of association which means that they have the right to join associations of their own choosing, or not to join associations if they do not wish to.

It may be noted that accreditation of journalists raises very different issues from licensing, although the two are sometimes confused. Accreditation refers to a system whereby certain journalists are given privileged access to certain functions or locations which are not otherwise fully open to the public, normally due to space limitations but sometimes also for security or other reasons. A classic example is accreditation to Parliament, where journalists are often guaranteed access and sometimes even granted special privileges or even offices. The rationale for such privileged treatment is that the media are the eyes and ears of the public, ensuring that everyone hears about matters of public interest (UNESCO, 2006).

Accreditation schemes should not be able to be used as a means to interfere with or influence the work of journalists, or to exclude journalists known to be critical. Therefore, they should be overseen by an independent body, and accreditation decisions should be based on objective criteria. The overall aim of any accreditation scheme should be to accredit as broad a range of journalists as possible, subject only to space constraints. Where space is an issue, considerations such as the number of journalists from a particular media that already have been granted accreditation may be a consideration. Accreditation schemes should never impose substantive restrictions on journalists (UNESCO, 2006).

4.3 Political Participation

In a democracy, it is the will of the people that is the basis of the government's authority. But in a modern State, which will have millions of citizens, it is not practically possible to consult people on an individual basis about each and every decision. The solution is for the people to appoint, through elections, a government to take decisions on their behalf, in accordance with its election promises. Elections must be regular, so that the people would be able to replace representatives who are not performing as expected. It is the responsibility of the State to organize the elections and to ensure that every citizen has a chance to cast their votes. It is also the responsibility of the State to ensure that the elections are free and fair, in the sense that citizens are free and able to make informed electoral choices.

4.3.1 The Right to Political Participation

In order for a democracy to be effective, the electorate should have a free and broad choice of candidates to vote for at elections. Therefore, the ICCPR prohibits all unreasonable restrictions on the right to contest for election. The permissible restrictions on the right to contest for election are similar, though not identical, to those on the right to vote. The law may, for instance, set a minimum age for candidates in the election. No candidates should be excluded by reason of their education, residence, descent or political affiliation. However, individuals holding certain positions may be restricted from running for offices if their election would lead to a conflict of interest.

For instance, a judge may be prevented from running for an office if part of his or her task as a judge is to decide disputes involving the office to which he or she aspires to be elected. International law permits the State to require registration of candidates in the elections. However, the registration procedure should not entail conditions, deadlines or fees which are unduly difficult to meet or which give some candidates an unfair advantage over others. Moreover, individuals who decide to stand for office should not suffer any disadvantage or discrimination as a result.

4.4 Types of Coverage in Media

As part of their duty to inform the public, broadcasters normally offer different types of programming during elections. Broadly speaking, these may be classified into three different categories: news and current affairs programming, interviews, debates and other 'special information' programming and direct access programming. These programmes serve different purposes and require distinct approaches. The important aim for broadcasters should be to ensure that the public receive sufficient information, from a variety of sources and perspectives, to enable them to cast an informed ballot.

4.4.1 News and Current Affairs

News and current affairs programmes are an essential means by which the general public receives political information, during, as well as outside of, election periods. During elections, this form of programming assumes a particular importance. Broadcasters in many established democracies are under a strict obligation to be balanced and impartial in their coverage of election events, and may not express a particular preference for one candidate or party or discriminate against a particular party or candidate.

Although the principle of balance is a simple one, its implementation in the context of news reporting during elections can be problematic, given that the governing party normally receives considerable attention by virtue of its role in running the country. The Article 19 Guidelines suggest that measures should be taken to counterbalance this, for example, by granting a right of reply to opposing parties or implementing an 'equal time' rule to ensure that coverage is also provided to parties outside of government. Furthermore, given the potential for editorial opinions to be confused with news, the Article 19 Guidelines recommend that publicly owned or funded media should not broadcast any editorial opinions at all in relation to the elections. Indeed, where a private broadcaster presents his or her views, these should be clearly identified as such and should not be aired during news programmes.

4.4.2 Special Information Programmes

News and current affairs programmes are rarely enough, by themselves, to inform the public sufficiently about electoral issues. The media should therefore broadcast additional programming, which focuses specifically on the policies and programmes under discussion during the election. Such programming should provide an opportunity for party leaders and other candidates to be questioned directly, and for candidates to debate with each other. A number of formats including candidate debates, panels of candidates and interviews may be used for this purpose.

Taking into account general obligations of balance and impartiality, broadcasters have a degree of editorial discretion in deciding how to structure such programmes. A fair and transparent formula must be used in deciding whom to invite, and non-candidate participants should be carefully selected so as to ensure balance. Special information programmes should be aired, among other times, during prime viewing or listening hours.

4.4.3 Direct Access Programmes

So-called 'direct access' programming includes the allocation of airtime to political parties and candidates to broadcast short clips produced by themselves, as well as paid advertising. Direct access programming is important as it is one of the very few ways political parties and candidates can present themselves directly to the public. Public service broadcasters are often required to provide free airtime and production support to facilitate these programmes. Given that broadcasters have no editorial control over the content of direct access slots, their liability for such programmes should be limited. A number of other rules govern the allocation and timing of these programmes.

4.4.4 Balance and Impartiality in News

News and current affairs programming has been identified by a range of actors, including international courts and tribunals, as one of the most important forms of broadcast programming. Even outside of election periods, news and current affairs programmes are the key way in which most people receive political, as well as other, information.

During elections, this form of programming assumes particular importance. Publicly owned or funded media are under a strict obligation to be neutral and impartial in their coverage of election events, and should never express a particular preference for one candidate or party, discriminate against a particular party or candidate or in any other way be biased. In many countries, private broadcasters are also placed under an obligation to be politically neutral, and such obligations may be a legitimate restriction on freedom of expression. It may be noted, however, that a similar restriction on the print media would be very hard to justify given the different nature of this medium.

While the principle is a simple one, its implementation can be problematic. The experience of broadcasting in transitional democracies, and indeed of certain established democracies, shows that news programmes are the broadcast category where the principles of balance and fairness are most often breached. The reality is that politicians belonging to a ruling party or coalition often receive considerable attention by virtue of their role in running the country. This role not only naturally generates news stories but also allows them more scope to manoeuvre themselves into situations where they are likely to receive news coverage (Article 19, 2015).

Because of the importance of the broadcast media during elections, and because of the high credibility the public attaches to news and current affairs programmes, broadcasters should make every effort to ensure that they meet their obligations of balance and impartiality. In particular, an effort should be made to counterbalance disproportionate coverage of incumbent candidates. The Article 19 Guidelines suggest that measures that could be taken include granting a right of reply to other candidates where an incumbent has received news coverage or implementing an 'equal time' rule, whereby the main competing parties get equal news and current affairs coverage during the election period.

Given the potential for editorial opinions to be confused with news, the Article 19 Guidelines recommend that publicly owned or funded media should not broadcast any editorial opinions at all in relation to the elections. Private broadcasters should make a commitment to clearly identify any editorial opinions and not to broadcast them during news programmes. Some form of direct access to the media is essential for parties and candidates in elections to get their message across. While news and other programming should provide voters with information about parties' policies and platforms, direct access to the media allows them to speak in their own voices. Providing direct access to the media thus makes an invaluable contribution to the ability of parties and candidates to communicate their messages to the public. In practice, direct access of some sort is available to parties and candidates in all established democracies.

Direct access refers broadly to two unique types of media content: a system of entitlement to short slots in the broadcast media allocated among the various competing political parties and candidates and paid advertising, in both print and broadcast media. The vast majority of the matured democracies have instituted systems in which a set amount of direct access slots is allocated among the various competing parties and candidates. The idea is to allow parties to speak directly to the electorate. Publicly owned or funded broadcasters are normally the main means for disseminating these slots, but private broadcasters are also required to provide them in some countries.

The exact allocation of airtime among the parties and candidates may be calculated in different ways. In most countries with an established track record of elections, airtime is allocated in proportion to the previous performance of the party in question, as determined, for example, by the number of votes obtained in the last election. In other countries, free airtime is distributed evenly among all political parties and candidates. Broadcasters have no editorial control over the content of direct access slots and, as a result, should not normally be held liable for their content. They may, however, be held liable where the media outlet concerned has taken specific steps to adopt or endorse the statements (Article 19, 2007).

Furthermore, this waiver of liability may not extend to extreme cases where the statements constitute clear and direct incitement to violence and the media outlet had an adequate opportunity to prevent their dissemination. This departure from the normal rules of liability is justified by the short duration of campaign periods and the fundamental importance to free and fair elections of unfettered political debate. This limitation of liability does not, however, relieve political parties and other speakers themselves from liability for their statements.

Provision of these slots for free is recommended as it helps promote a level playing field during elections, paid political advertising, discussed further, is available only in the measure that parties and candidates can afford it. In any country, public service, or publicly owned or funded, broadcasters are required not only to provide airtime free of charge but also to make available production facilities to assist political parties and candidates to prepare their clips.

It is important that the amount of time allocated for direct access slots is sufficient for parties and candidates to communicate their messages and for the public to be informed about the issues, party positions and the qualifications and characters of the candidates. The timing of the slots should be designed to maximize the number of viewers/listeners; wherever possible, slots should be broadcast during prime time, and they should never be broadcast at times when it is inconvenient for large segments of the population to view or hear them, for example, past midnight (Article 19, 2007).

4.4.5 Advertising

Paid political advertising is another way parties and candidates can gain direct access to the electorate. Political advertising in the broadcast media is controversial. Many European countries ban political advertising in the broadcast media, while others place stringent fetters on it on the grounds that it benefits richer parties and candidates. A recommendation calls on European States to consider introducing limitations on political advertising. In the USA, on the other hand, a ban, or even restrictions, on political advertising would be deemed contrary to the right of freedom of expression. Under international law, a ban on advertising in the broadcast media is considered to be legitimate. A complete ban in the print media would probably breach the right to freedom of expression, although some restrictions may be acceptable (Article 19, 2015).

4.4.6 Opinion Polls

Both the contenders for election and the general public are inevitably curious to know in advance what the outcome of the elections is likely to be. Various organizations and individuals may conduct opinion polls, where they question a substantial number of people in order to assess the popularity of the competing candidates. The results of such opinion polls are of interest to journalists, who may wish to publish them for the benefit of their audience. However, opinion polls can have a distorting impact on voting patterns, especially if they are not properly understood by the public. As part of their duty to inform voters, journalists should make sure that reporting on poll results is accompanied by an explanation of their significance.

Opinion polls may be conducted or commissioned by all sorts of different actors including academic institutes, commercial businesses, political parties, NGOs, government agencies and the news media. Polls may be conducted either during an election campaign or at the end of the campaign in the form of exit polls of voters on Election Day. The main methods used for conducting polls are face-to-face interviews or interviews by email, telephone or over the Internet.

4.4.7 Interpreting Opinion Polls

Not all opinion polls results are equally reliable. An opinion poll conducted by an impartial organization will in many cases be more trustworthy than, for example, a poll conducted by the government or a political party. But even a poll conducted by a disinterested organization should be treated with caution and can be substantially wrong or misleading. There are three main factors affecting the reliability of opinion poll results.

The first factor is the wording of the question posed to the public. For example, the question: 'Who do you plan to vote for?' may not be answered by all people in the same way as 'Who do you think should win the elections?' The former question would probably lead to a more reliable prediction of the election outcome. The second factor affecting the reliability of polls is what is known as the 'margin of error'. If you ask only three people about their voting intentions, it is fairly obvious that the result will be extremely unreliable. Asking a hundred people will generate a better result and asking a thousand an even better one. There is, in other words, a positive relationship between the number of people interviewed and the reliability of the opinion poll. This can be calculated mathematically and expressed as a percentage called the margin of error. The lower the margin of error, the better, as it is a measurement of the unreliability of the poll.

The third source of error in opinion polls is the selection of respondents. Although questioning more people reduces the margin of error, it does not always guarantee an accurate result because there may be skews in the sample of people interviewed. For example, an opinion poll conducted by the Internet may be distorted because poor people are less likely to have Internet access than rich people. If poor people tend to vote for different parties than rich people, an Internet poll will overstate the popularity of the party favoured by rich people.

The publication of opinion poll results can have a significant impact on voting patterns. For example, voters may conclude that their favoured party is going to lose the elections anyway and decide not to bother to vote. Or, voters may assume that a favoured party is already doing well in the polls and decide instead to vote for another party, which they would also like to see represented. To avoid a situation where people change their voting intentions on the basis of potentially wrong information, journalists who publish opinion poll results should explain their significance, and the risk of error, to the public.

4.5 Public Media Role during Elections

It is internationally recognized that publicly owned or funded media have a special role to play during elections and have certain obligations over and above those that can be imposed on other media. This is particularly the case for public broadcasters. As publicly funded entities, public broadcasters should observe strict requirements of neutrality and should never endorse any particular candidate, party or programme. If they do carry political advertisements, these should be offered to all parties or candidates on a strictly equal basis.

Additionally, because of their legal obligation to inform and educate the public, public broadcasters have a duty to ensure that the public is informed about the election. This includes practical matters such as where and how to vote, to register to vote and to verify proper registration, the secrecy of the ballot, the importance of voting and the functions of the offices that are under contention. It also includes important political issues and the political programmes and viewpoints of the various parties and candidates up for election. In broadcasting this material, it is crucial that public broadcasters not voice any opinions of their own, nor endorse the ideas of any particular candidate.

The extent of this duty depends on a number of factors, including the level of awareness of the electorate as well as the availability of this information through other sources such as private media and other public initiatives. The duty flows from the need to inform the public; where other sources of information do not adequately inform or reach the public, public broadcasters will need to step in and provide this information.

One way to discharge this duty is to provide airtime for direct access programming to enable those up for election to present short 'clips' on themselves and their political views to the public. Public broadcasters are often required to provide this airtime free of charge and at an hour when a large audience will be reached, and to allocate studio time and technical resources, within the limits of their capacity, to facilitate the production of these clips. The rules relating to this programming, for example, concerning the length and timing of clips, should apply fairly to all candidates.

A second way to discharge this duty is through news and current affairs programmes, as well as special information programmes, such as political debates and political discussion programmes. These are of particular importance where sufficient information on election issues is not forthcoming from other sources. Such programmes should involve all political parties or candidates up for election in the station's geographic area of coverage. The rules and regulations governing this programming, for example, regarding the length of the contribution of each participant, should be applied fairly and equally so as to avoid granting privileged treatment to any one participant. The host of a discussion programme or debate should ensure that the questions asked are balanced and should not extend privileged treatment to anyone.

Finally, also pursuant to the duty to inform, public broadcasters have a particular obligation to ensure that their programming reaches all groups in society, including ethnic, religious or linguistic minorities. This is of particular relevance to those public broadcasting stations whose geographic coverage includes such groups.

4.5.1 Public Newspapers

Publicly owned or funded newspapers are, like their broadcasting counterparts, also covered by a strict obligation of neutrality. Like public broadcasters, they should never endorse any particular candidate, party or programme, and they should provide access to advertising on a strictly equal basis. These newspapers also have an important role to play in voter education. While they are not normally required to provide free space in their columns for political parties and candidates, they should provide relevant information to ensure that the public is informed about practical matters and all political issues of relevance to the election.

4.5.2 Media Network Regulating Bodies

The existence of an oversight body to monitor and regulate the media during elections is crucial to the integrity of the elections process and to respect in practice the rules relating to election media coverage. The jurisdiction and powers of such a body should be clearly delineated and, where a self-regulatory mechanism exists, efforts should be made to ensure that the two mechanisms play a supportive, as opposed to conflicting, role. In particular, an official oversight body should not seek to duplicate or replace functions already being provided in an effective manner by a self-regulatory body.

Both the guarantee of freedom of expression and the need to safeguard the integrity of the elections process dictate that any oversight body with powers over the media be independent. The independence of the body should be formally guaranteed and, at least as importantly, should be protected through the manner in which members are appointed. The appointments process should be fair and transparent, should allow for input and participation by civil society and should not be dominated by any particular political party. Once appointed, the tenure of members should be protected and any reimbursement should be according to set schedules and criteria.

In different countries, different bodies perform the role of ensuring implementation of the rules relating to media election coverage. In many countries, it is the general broadcast regulator which performs this function. An official oversight body is particularly important in relation to the broadcast media, given the detailed rules that govern election coverage by broadcasters. The body should undertake a range of monitoring and regulatory functions in relation to broadcasters, including by playing a general role in monitoring broadcasts to assess their compliance with laws and regulations. These should include allocating time for direct access programmes, making sure broadcast election coverage respects obligations of balance and impartiality and ensuring that publicly owned or funded broadcasters adequately satisfy the public's right to be informed about election-related matters. The official oversight body should also have the power to hear and decide on complaints from media outlets, the public and political parties and candidates regarding breach of election-related rules. In particular, it should have the power to order a right of reply if it finds that rights have been harmed by the publication of inaccurate or misleading information, given the relatively brief duration of an election campaign.

4.5.3 Election Campaigns in India

India's 16th national general election which was held during April and May 2014 was probably one of the most awaited elections in the recent times. According to observers, social media would play a vital role in deciding which party wins the most seats. A report published in April 2013 by the Internet and Mobile Association of India (IAMAI) and the Mumbai-based Iris Knowledge Foundation states that Facebook users will have a tremendous impact on the results of the polls in 160 of India's 543 constituencies, and the reason for this is the youth of India (Wani & Alone, 2014).

The youth is tech-savvy and loves being connected with updated trends and topics which is possible by using laptops, desktops or the most favourite a network-connected mobiles. Even though politicians for their campaign still use posters, cut-outs, fliers, graffiti and personal rallies to reach and win over voters, but with the social media changing the picture of urban India, political parties are becoming tech-savvy and realizing that social media is the only way to reach out to this young youth. For 2009 general election, social media usage in India was little. Today, however, Facebook has 93 million users and Twitter has an estimated 33 million accounts in the country.

As per the IAMAI report 2013, this change for the presence of social media could be observed as every political party participating in 2014 general election has set a 2 to 5 per cent of its election budget for spending on social media. The report says that the leading parties BJP and national Congress party has set this at 5 and 4 billion respectively. From the very beginning, the BJP has the biggest presence in social media. The BJP started using the social medium even before the 2009 general election. Mr Narendra Modi who was the Prime Minister candidate of BJP and all other members of the party had very high popularity and a reach to general public using social media as compared to any other parties. Narendra Modi has highest follower on Twitter and Facebook (Wani & Alone, 2014).

Aam Aadmi Party (AAP) which is a newly formed political party has quite high popularity as compared to the two old major parties—Congress and BJP. AAP is very active on social media channels. It was observed that even though AAP and BJP were fighting against each other on social media, the

Congress party realized its importance quite late. Indian Election is a major Event not only for India but for the whole world. With the changing trends, it is estimated that now the youth following social sites will decide the future of candidates. The urban development rate is growing day by day, which increases the number of Facebook followers. It is said that Facebook will provide a new voter bank for politician. Candidate and a party which could leave its impression on Facebook have definitely seen the positive results. This explains the need for well-defined strategy specially designed for social media to make their campaigns more effective. Twitter had its own 'tweeter election' for election 2014. Fifty-six million election-related tweets were gathered till when election ended. Each of the poll days saw between 54,000 and 82,000 million election-related tweets. The tweeter results showed that the most popular parties and candidates were AAP's Arvind Kejriwal, BJP's Narendra Modi and Rahul Gandhi from Congress party.

As it could be understood from the aforementioned observations, media, be it traditional or new, play a significant role during the electoral process. Given the changing dynamics of journalism and keeping the UN's mandate pertaining to freedom of expression, even the common men or women, not necessarily journalists, have equal right to express their ideas and opinion towards political parties or candidates. This poses additional challenges for the professionals who are involved in journalism as voters themselves are playing dual role of information seekers and providers. Media professionalism could suffer in this paradoxical situation, where ordinary people write about elections.

But this situation also provides added opportunity for professional journalists and media houses to reach out to the larger audience through multiple means of communication along with traditional media. For, example, they can use social media to drag the audiences into reading their own newspapers. Most of the media houses are now actively using social media sites like Twitter, Facebook to get the tech-savvy audiences to their media platforms. Therefore, it could be safely said that the information pertaining biggest democratic exercise like elections are provided by professional journalists as well as common social media users, thereby fulfilling the ideal situation envisioned by the UN. This ensures that the information becomes a shared experience rather than a commodity sold by media organizations. At times, professionalism and felicity of reporting could take a back seat, but objective and plain narration of common readers would definitely compensate because of the availability of wide range of posts or messages pertaining to a single electoral event.

5

The Media in Political Campaigns

Media have their own set of values to determine what is newsworthy, and these stories usually include a certain amount of conflict and emotion believed to be appealing to their audience. Because of this, such emotional stories get more news coverage than other stories. Media attempt to portray stories about the candidate or campaign because it considers such stories as more valuable, whether or not the campaign wants this. The media has enough control over the general population that candidates also feel like they have to respond to such media coverage. The role of the media in campaigns, however, remains unclear. There is no evidence that the media has an effect on the long-term opinions of the people or an effect on the outcome of an election.

The mass media includes all types of communication system designed to reach out to large audiences. It includes music, movies and entertainment, but also news media which is most likely to affect an election or campaign. Traditional media sources such as television, radio and newspapers still remain prominent, but the growth in prominence of new media which is based on the Internet has changed the way campaigns are carried over now. Some types of media such as newspapers or radio are helpful to reach specific audiences, though newspaper use as a source of information has declined, while the Internet has seen a definite increase in the recent past. So far as the television medium is concerned, both traditional news and cable news programmes hold on to their place among the audience.

5.1 Role of Mass Media in Political Campaigns

The mass media are the most fundamental source for information with regard to election campaigns in democracies and societies in democratic transition around the world. In terms of the sheer amount of information available to people through the media on various issues, political parties and leaders, election campaigns are often considered as a vital part of political communications. However, there are concerns about political bias in the mass media. In fact, these concerns form the crux of the debates going on around the roles and responsibilities of the media at election time. Behind these concerns there are assumptions that there may be intended or unintended impact on public opinion and political behaviour and, more importantly, electoral outcomes.

In every election campaign, people must not only decide upon the party or candidate they wish to support, they must also make a decision whether they will vote for those respective candidates at all. In democracies that do not mandate compulsory voting, most political observers would agree that participation in an election is a measure of success where the higher the turnout, the better for democracy. In most instances, parties and candidates use all possible ways to encourage electoral turnout and motivate supporters to go to the polls. In some instances, parties and political groups aim to try to avert the turnout to accomplish their narrow goals. It is the larger context of political party strategies and tactics, and the structure of the mass media environment, that one needs to consider when we try to address questions about balance during election campaigns.

As is well known, elections are the central activity determining the fate of any democracy. By casting their ballots, people can convey their opinions, express their hopes and aspirations, discipline their leaders and ultimately control destiny of their country. According to a democratic theory, elections are the public's major source of power, but in order to use its power effectively, the public need to understand where candidates and parties stand on vital public policy issues.

Those contesting for elections must clearly state their positions. Otherwise, there will be no real choice, and elections would lose its meaning. However, the responsibility does not lie only with the candidates for the success of the system. The mass media also have an important duty to perform in terms of reporting thoroughly and accurately as to what these contestants stand for. This is one of the major roles a media organization has to play. All news is important, but campaign coverage is more crucial because of its capacity to empower the voters. What voters know about campaigns comes to them almost entirely from newspapers, television and magazines. Therefore, in assessing how well the political system works, it is necessary to inspect the media coverage of elections.

In reporting about political campaigns, the news media bring in their usual procedures and tendencies to the campaign trail as well. In other words, far from simply mirroring all that politicians say and do, journalists carefully select the information to be reported from the public interest perspective. Because time and space restrictions do not allow speeches and rallies to be explained in its entirety, some interesting parts are mentioned, others ignored. Thus, once again the basic question is not whether the media are selective but what they include and exclude, and how these choices affect voters' behaviour and electoral outcome.

5.1.1 Coverage of Campaigns

Instead of inspecting electoral issues in a holistic manner, reporters tend to describe campaign drams, the size of crowds, surges and declines in the polls, organizational triumphs and failures, endorsements won and lost and above all the ebb and flow of momentum for political parties. Elections are compared to horse races in which attention centres on who is ahead, who is behind, who is gaining and who has dropped out. What gets lost in the excitement is why the race is being run at all.

Political coverage has become too much like a sports show, equated to the colour and drama of a sporting event. The action-packed attractiveness of a sport, its drama, tension, unexpected twists and uncertainty of outcomes are likened to electoral coverage also. Media houses tend to treat elections as athletic contest, thereby making it seem more interesting and appealing to the viewer.

But this kind of coverage would sometimes feed the electorate with the wrong kind of information. Many a time media coverage does not enlighten voters but leave them mystified about complex issues. The following anecdote illustrates the preoccupation with campaign hoopla. In 1976, Jimmy Carter, the Democratic nominee for president, granted an interview to Robert Scheer, who was writing for the *Playboy* magazine. At the end of the session, as the two men walked out Carter's front door, the candidate delivered a spontaneous monologue during which he said, 'I've looked on a lot of women with lust. I've committed adultery in my heart many times. This is something that God recognize and God forgives me for it' (*New York Times*, 1976).

Needless to say, this offhand remark created an instant sensation. Carried by every wire service and network in the country, it stirred up a week-long political storm that nearly destroyed Carter's candidacy. It was one of the more memorable incidents of the election period and is, in fact, about all that most people remember about the *Playboy* interview. It is debatable whether this confession deserved all the fuss it received. Carter did, however, say something else in the course of the interview that was at least as significant and, ironically, touched on the media's priorities.

Carter probably did not realize how close to the truth he was. For students of American government, this last statement is more informative than the furore over 'lust in the heart' because it underscores the press's propensity to give not the whole truth but of necessity only a portion of it. What it chooses to present are frequently the surface elements of election campaigns—the personal and sporting aspects—while it downplays candidates and parties' stands on major public disputes (Patterson, 1980).

5.1.2 Candidates and the Media

It is not entirely fair to blame news organizations for avoiding certain important issues. Candidates themselves are often all too eager to go after controversies and showcase their personalities and images instead. Many of these candidates and also some members of the media do not believe that voters are knowledgeable or interested enough to care about specific policy questions. Candidates prefer to speak in easily understood symbols than to deal with complexities of the economy. They also downplay their positions on contentious issues because of their fear of losing out potential voters.

In fact, many candidates and their teams believe that the media should be used mainly to promote and advertise their political campaigns and not to inform or educate the electorate about the important issues of governance. They very well understand that unmanaged news is the politician's worst enemy. Electoral campaign strategists work with a set of principles in mind: First, because they know that people heavily rely on television to know about candidates, television exposure outranks substance in prioritization. Second, due to space and time constraints, television news airs stories that can be told in one or two minutes and invariably in such short stories portray people doing something visually exciting. And third, news anchors also avoid leaders who are seriously talking about some complex issues. What they are looking for are short interesting statements or sound bites that can be aired in 30 to 45 seconds.

Integrating this knowledge into their electoral campaign strategies, candidates often try to manipulate media coverage to serve their own purposes. Surprisingly, candidates are very successful in achieving these purposes. By carefully orchestrating the location, timing and context of their appearances, candidates can virtually dictate how they will be reported in the media. Former President Reagan was the master of this art, but his successors quickly caught on. Perhaps, Bush's most brilliant effort to manoeuver the media to his advantage came early in the 1988 campaign.

Although Bush's advisers may have been superstars in this game, they are certainly not its only players. Pseudo-events, staged visits to nursing homes, polluted beaches, orphanages, slums, drug rehabilitation centres, factory gates and toxic waste dumps are the lifeblood of electoral politics. They are popular with candidates precisely because everything is supposedly under their control; the 'image' is not disturbed by placard-waving protestors or tricky questions from hostile reporters. This is how the game is played, and the press knows it.

In an article titled How Television Failed the American Voter, David Halberstam summed up the media's acquiescence: If they covered professional football ... in the same way it would go something like this: During the season, they would not cover any games live but would instead give 75-second reports on the previous day's game. This would continue right through to the Super Bowl. Nor would they deign to cover the Super Bowl itself. After the game, however, they would cover the three-hour champagne celebration in the winner's locker room (Halberstam, 1981).

5.1.3 Campaign Debates

Electoral debates are commonplace these days, and on paper they serve democracy by placing candidates and their programmes in the spotlight. Every election season, for instance, there are various debates. Yet, appearance does not always match reality, since these affairs are not as spontaneous and freewheeling as they seem. In the US Presidential elections held in 1988, both the Bush senior and Dukakis camps laid down the ground rules, specifying the number of debates, the format for questioning and the length of time for answers and rebuttals. No direct exchanges between the men were allowed instead a panel of reporters interviewed each man. Hence, the candidates controlled the planning, and they had the final say on the timing and positioning of the candidates.

Many observers are convinced that candidates participating in debates deliver prepared speeches that have nothing to do with the questions they are asked. They deal in platitudes, symbols and images, and evade controversies. They frequently contradict their earlier statements and that interviewers seldom have a chance to point out these evasions or inconsistencies. The overriding objective is always to sell oneself. Whatever issues and polices discussed in debates, the media tends to downplay them in favour of discussions of 'winners and losers'. Instead of focusing on such trivial issues related to candidates, journalists are more apt to analyse how each side prepared, how it came across in the heat of the battle and especially how its future chances were affected. The media are encouraged in this post-mortem analysis by media spin doctors, campaign leaders tend to appear in interviews and press conferences after the debates to clarify or emphasize certain points.

With all this said and done, few voters seem to be influenced by such political debates. The most common impact is to reinforce initial preferences they had about candidates. Formation of new opinions among those who were previously undecided is less likely to happen. Voters rarely get influenced by such debates and switch sides. For example, 77 per cent of the people interviewed by a Gallup poll after the first Bush–Dukakis debate in 1988 claimed that the debate did not change their voting plans. Still, the small portion of the electorate that does switch can be decisive in a close election. This possibility explains why candidates invest so much time and energy preparing for debates (Gallup report, 1988).

The mass media have always been an important factor in the political sphere in democracy. During election, the mass media, especially the broadcast media, provide a link between the political party or candidate and the voters. It serves as a platform for political parties to campaign for votes. Through coverage of electoral campaigns and promotion of political advertisements, the electronic media influences voters' behaviour either in favour or against a given political party or candidate.

5.2 Political Campaigns and Media Coverage

The rule that will have an impact on the media is the right to equal time, which states that basic television and radio stations should provide equal time to all candidates contesting elections, and this includes advertising. The incumbent leader's actions during the course of his job are exempt from this rule. This undoubtedly gives them a distinct advantage. The right to equal time does not require that news media organizations cover election events such as debates or speeches. In some cases, some networks choose not to air the political events in order to keep to the original programming.

5.2.1 What Gets Covered, and How

Generally, the media covers races that are competitive, and the more competitive the race, the better the chances are for more coverage. The media is also more likely to cover races where there is an important or well-known office at stake such as that of a president, a governor or a mayor of a large city. When other races appeal to the audience in other ways such as elections in which celebrities are running for office, there is a greater chance of media coverage as well. Fortunately for State and local campaigns, local news outlets will be more likely to cover smaller elections as well as the larger ones (Norton, 2011).

The majority of the campaign events covered by the news are specific events that occur during the election such as debates or the national conventions. The media values new ideas or stories for their novelty, as well as valuing personality, or the level on which candidates especially can engage the viewers—they will go so far as to analyse candidates' personalities and end up shaping much of their public persona. News media also values conflict, which viewers find interesting, as well as scepticism, which leads to a certain level of analysis and interpretation of what candidates do and say. Perhaps, what is most covered by news media is the strategy of the campaigns and the results of that strategy—which candidate is ahead in certain states, and where other candidates are gaining ground in others. The topic of strategy is relatively inexhaustible, providing ample resource for coverage, from using polls of voters to the amount of funds raised (Norton, 2011).

It also provides most suitable subject for news media to provide contextual analysis and interpretation, a critical part of professional journalism. Campaign coverage can be biased in that media coverage tends to favour those who are in power or those who support the editorial agenda. A television channel can be biased towards a certain political ideology, but this is as much a reflection of the viewer preferences as the media choices. In general, however, studies have shown that there is little evidence to show that coverage of the news is biased towards one party as a whole, though it has been shown that news media tend to be biased for those candidates ahead in the polls during an election.

5.2.2 Profits and the Norm of Objectivity

News organizations have practical limitations, such as time and personnel, and so cannot cover everything related to elections. One of the objectives that motivate them to cover some stories during an election over others is called the profit motive. As a business outfit, media organizations are also expected to generate revenue and keep costs down. Maintaining a business as a media outlet can be difficult when television and newspapers are losing viewers and money from advertising, and when attempting to cover campaigns, many of which would like around-the-clock news coverage. Because of this reason, many television studios have less number of reporters covering very less amount of campaigns, preferring to use interesting clips of candidates obtained from handheld cameras rather than maintaining special team to cover the entire campaign. The media organizations can also look to cable television and Internet media to disseminate information cheaply. The other important norm that media organizations follow is that of objectivity. News media were very partisan until the second half of the twentieth century, but currently most of the press values the principle of impartiality in reporting. This type of news reporting is still preferred by many citizens, though the rise of non-neutral news outlets, especially on television, provides an alternative that is growing in popularity.

5.2.3 Interaction between Candidates and Voters

The main goal of the candidates is to spread their message to as many potential voters as possible, and so they employ the media to both clarify and articulate their message as well as to reach many more homes than they would be able to alone. Hence, candidates spend a lot of time interacting in many ways with the media, keeping it as much on their terms as possible. The news media also chooses what stories to publish and how often to publish them. Reporters also sometimes will not report the information that the candidates are trying to get across, and they will choose to cover other aspects of the race that are more interesting. In general, the relationship between the news media and the candidate is one of compromise and conflict, in which both sides depend on each other to meet their goals.

5.2.4 The Effects of Media Coverage on Citizens

Regardless of their basic objectives, most media outlets do not work in persuading viewers to change their opinions about an election—most potential voters pay little attention to elections and would have already made up their mind politically. Because of this, media works to reinforce existing notions, and does not change how people think about something but what they are thinking about. When the media covers one topic more than others, it is not only considered more frequently but also considered more important by viewers—whether or not the campaigns or elections are mentioned.

The media also assist people by providing them information about subjects and candidates that they may have been previously unaware of thereby increasing recognition of the names and faces of candidates that are covered in elections. However, the rapid growth of the Internet and satellite television has made it easier for viewers to select information they want and ignore information on elections and candidates that they are not actively interested in. This makes voters in general less susceptible to the political messages being floated in the news media.

5.2.5 Media Coverage and Campaign Awareness

Regardless of its exposure to the news, media does influence public awareness of elections. In a study of the 1988 Southern Super Tuesday regional primary, researchers found exposure to all media to be positively and significantly related to voter awareness of the campaign, as well as to voter perceptions of increased campaign activity and perceptions of increased Southern political prominence. Exposure to partisan political information was found to be significantly related only to perceptions of increased campaign activity (Gottlieb, 1992).

Educators need more information about the role of television in elections, and particularly how television influences young voters. Among future voters, television appears to affect their political attitudes. A study examined the political views of 10- to 17-year olds and their parents before and after the 1988 election. While parents' attitudes seemed to be the greatest influence upon the political socialization of the younger children, television appeared to be the greatest influence upon the older ones (Gottlieb, 1992).

The effect of media coverage of elections is visible on the local level as well. Newspaper stories and advertisements can raise public awareness of municipal and school board elections, to the extent that voter turnout increases as a result. Interestingly, a study of Philadelphia voters suggests that media reliance is unrelated to campaign knowledge and activity. Between 1972 and 1988, there was an increasing tendency among the major news outlets to report on the content of the political advertisements themselves. By presenting segments of negative ads during newscasts, such news reports may have had the effect of promoting the candidates whose commercials were being discussed and legitimizing political advertising as a basis for political decision-making (Gottlieb, 1992).

5.3 Evaluating the News Media Role in Campaigns

The news media helps to meet the standards of free choice, generally, because they pass on the information to citizens about their choices during an election, although the coverage is not designed for this purpose. At the same time, there are many smaller, less competitive and non-national races that receive little coverage by the news media because they are not considered 'news worthy' by the business, although whether this is the fault of the business or the audience that demands sensational stories is difficult to tell.

This same logic applies to the idea of equality—that information via the news, especially via the Internet, is available to those that desire it, but that broadcast news in general caters to a larger audience more interested in topics like sports or entertainment. The media allows a level of deliberation to occur that would not otherwise be possible in such a large country, providing information that clarifies the points of each side and usually making specific note about the differences between candidates. Conversation among citizens can also be facilitated to an extent through media, like blogs and the Internet, though these types of media are self-segregating and do not reach all types of citizens equally (Anetwesonga, 2015).

Much is written about the effect that the mass media have upon the presentation, and the outcome, of political campaigns. Frequently, critics have charged that news reporting focuses on the superficial and personal characteristics of candidates and ignore the issues underlying elections. Observers of the process also target advertising, which they say distorts positions and trivializes important issues. At the same time, it is suggested that the predominance of polling by news outlets turns elections into popularity contests and causes candidates to follow rather than lead voter opinion on contemporary issues (Anetwesonga, 2015).

Advertising, by its nature, takes positions. Commercials suggest that the advertiser's product is better than a competitor's or is important to the viewer's well-being. Such a claim may or may not be true, and the question is not always so easy for the reader, viewer or listener to evaluate. While the results of a bad choice about which brand of soap to buy may be inconsequential, a wrong decision about whom to elect to a position of public trust can have far-reaching consequences. The ramifications of advertising in politics are not all negative. Advertisements can help the public become aware of political candidates and issues and educate would-be voters about what is at stake in campaigns. In fact, commercials can be more instructive in that regard than debates.

As is true of other types of human relationships, first impressions can be very important as voters form their opinions about political candidates. A study of the 1976 US presidential race between Carter and Ford indicates that voters' initial reactions to Carter's image shaped their later voting behaviour. For Ford, initial reactions to issues played a larger role. Research on Australian elections suggests that candidates' use of the media can have a strong impact upon those who make up their minds about candidates during the campaign. Such voters are more likely to be swayed by political appeals than are people who have decided whom to choose before a campaign start. While partisan voters use the media because they are interested in politics, undecided voters refer to media sources for information about parties, candidates and issues (Gottlieb, 1992).

5.3.1 The Role of the Televised Debate in Elections

Many observers consider the 1960 debate between US presidential candidates Kennedy and Nixon to be a textbook example of television-age political campaigning. It has often been asserted that differences in the two candidates' television personae accounted in part for Kennedy's election victory. Some, however, dispute the significance of the televised 1960 debates suggesting that while visual cues undoubtedly have the potential to influence voter perceptions, the nature and extent of the influence remain a matter of speculation (Gottlieb, 1992).

Debates involving candidates for the 1988 presidential nomination carry a similar message. Results of a study of college students revealed the finding that the winner of the 1988 debate was predicted by perceptions of the candidate who projected the strongest personal image, the greatest credibility, the most logical arguments and the strongest emotional appeals. Furthermore, voter preferences expressed after a first debate were strong predictors of eventual candidate choice. In some political campaigns, even the lack of debates can have significance. George Bush's successful 1988 presidential campaign employed debate avoidance, a reliance upon emotional appeals and ridicule and a de-emphasis of issues. Both of the major US political parties have used such strategies, considered to be departures from ethical behaviour (Gottlieb, 1992).

5.3.2 Individual Voter Characteristics and the Media

Men and women tend to react differently to the media analysis that generally follows political debates. A study conducted at the University of Florida during the 1988 vice-presidential debates showed that females took less extreme views of candidates after viewing post-debate analysis. By contrast, such analysis had little effect on the extremity of views expressed by politically involved males.

During the 1988 presidential campaign, the 'gender gap', a perception that men and women viewed the leading candidates differently, was much discussed. George Bush's campaign planners were able to battle the gap through the way in which the candidate was portrayed in advertising. One advertising approach was to represent Bush as a law-and-order 'equalizer', who shared women's concerns about street crime. Another technique was to underscore Bush's belief in traditional family values. Third, the campaign used ads that underscored the candidate's ability to laugh at himself, as a way of showing his human side (Gottlieb, 1992).

Like gender, race plays a role in how people view social issues and even how people respond to questions about such issues. Various studies have indicated that a member of one race will answer questions from an interviewer of another race in such a way as to avoid alienating the interviewer. It can be argued that even when an interviewer and interviewee are of the same race, survey results should be scrutinized carefully when the interviewer's questions concern a candidate of a different race. What remains to be explored is whether race should be treated as an uncontrolled variable in political surveys involving at least one white and one black candidate (Gottlieb, 1992).

5.4 Agenda Setting

One of the powers or effects of the mass media is agenda setting. McCombs and Shaw explain that the 'mass media have ability to transfer the salience of items on their news agenda to the public agenda.... We judge as important what the media judge as important'. Media coverage of issues confers importance on them and helps the audience to treat certain issues as also being more important than others. The conferment consequently influences the attitudes or decisions of the audience towards the subjects on the agenda. The setting of agenda by the media implies that people look up to them for cues to issues of salience. People want the media to assist them to determine 'reality' and influence norms. The critic of newspapers and broadcasting see their power as lying in controlling the agenda, in their ability to select certain issues for discussion and decision and to ignore others as non-existent; and in the ability to treat certain conflicts of interests as manifestly proper material and others as too complex, or marginal, or unmanageable.

McQuail and Windahl state that 'audiences not only learn about public issues and other matters through the media, they also learn how much importance to attach to an issue or topic from the emphasis the mass media place upon it'. The basic idea is that amongst a given range of issues or topics, those which get more media attention will grow in their familiarity and perceived importance over a period of time and those which get less will decline correspondingly.

Brosius and Weimann point out that 'even though the media may not be very successful in telling us what opinions to hold, they are often quite effective in telling us what to have opinions or what not to think about'. By paying attention to such issues and neglecting others, the mass media will have an effect on public opinion. People will tend to know about these things which the mass media deal with and adopt the order of priority assigned to different issues. Agenda setting assumes that a direct, positive relationship exists between media coverage and the salience of a topic in the public mind. The relationship is stated in causal terms: By conferring status on an issue, the media structure what is important.

5.5 Campaigns and Media's Social Responsibility

The mass media are not only key avenues for providing the required information, they also determine what is available in the public domain. To achieve this, the mass media must discharge its social responsibility. McQuail highlights the main principles of social responsibility as follows:

- Media should accept and fulfil certain obligation to society.
- These obligations are mainly to be met by setting high or professional standards of information, truth, accuracy, objectivity and balance.
- In accepting and applying these obligations, media should be self-regulating within the framework of law and established institutions.
- The media should avoid whatever might lead to crime, violence or civil disorder or give offence to minority groups.

- The media as a whole should be pluralistic and reflect the diversity of their society, giving access to various points of view and right of reply.
- Society and public, following the first named principle, have a right to expect high standards of performance, and intervention can be justified to secure the, or, a public good.
- Journalists and media professionals should be accountable to society as well as to employers and the market (Charles Obot, 2013).

The mass media perform a crucial role in the democratic process. According to Gurevitch and Blumler, the mass media possess enormous powers, and their power comes from three sources—structural, psychological and normative. According to them, the structural root of the power of the mass media 'springs from their unique capacity to deliver to the politician an audience, which in size and composition, is unavailable to him by any other means'. The psychological root of the media power stems from the relationships of credibility and trust that different media organizations have succeeded in developing with members of their audiences.

Gurevitch and Blumler assert that 'it is the combined influence of these structural and psychological sources of strength that enable the media to interpose themselves between politicians and the audience and to "intervene" in other political processes as well'. This interposition, according to them, is expressed in the way in which the mass media are capable of restructuring the timing and character of political events, defining crisis situations to which politicians are obliged to react, requiring comment on issues that media personnel have emphasized as important, injecting new personalities into the political dialogue such as television interviews and stimulating the growth of new communication agencies such as public relations firms, opinion poll agencies and political advertising and campaign management specialists.

On the other hand, the normative root of media power stems from the respect that is accorded in competitive democracies to such tenets of liberal philosophy as freedom of expression and the need for specialized organs to safeguard citizens against possible abuses of political authority. From the foregoing, the mass media occupy strategic place in the polity. Besley, Burgess and Prat emphasize that a 'free or non-captured media can affect political outcomes through three routes, namely: sorting, discipline and policy salience'. Sorting refers to the process by which politicians are selected to hold office.

The kind of information media provide can be important to voters who are deciding who to put in charge. This includes information about candidate's previous track records. Their actions while in office may also be an important source of information about their underlying motivation or competence. By publishing stories or advertisements that responsibly cast light on this, the media can be a powerful force. The role of the media in achieving discipline is most relevant in situations of hidden action. This involves exposure of activities which perpetrators do not want the public to know. The media can also affect which issues are salient to voters. This would be made possible or easier through political communication or political advertisements.

Islam notes that the media industry, whether public or private, plays an important role in any economy by garnering support or opposition for those who govern, by highlighting or failing to do so the views and/or sins of industry, by providing a voice for the people or not doing so and by simply spreading economic information. The mass media do not only carry information about the economy but also message about the social, political and religious lives of the people. In the opinion of Wolfensohn, a free press is not a luxury. It is at the core of equitable development. The media can expose corruption. They can keep a check on government action. They let people voice diverse opinions on governance and reform and help build public consensus to bring about change.

It can be deduced from Wolfensohn's opinion that easy and equitable access to the mass media as well as diversity of views in media contents are not only indispensable but are crucial for the emergence of a democratic society and attainment of development. Democracy thrives on the principle of informed electorate making responsible choices and decisions. The mass media are not only key avenues for providing the required information, they also determine what is available in the public domain. Mass media enrich democracy, while democracy provides conducive environment for an efficient functioning of the mass media. It is almost impossible to have a democratic society without the full complement of a robust mass media system.

In the opinion of Curran, 'democratic function of the media system is to act as an agency of representation.' It should be organized in a way that enables diverse social groups and organizations to express alternative viewpoints. This goes beyond, however, simply disseminating diverse opinion in the public domain. Part of the media system should function in a way that invigorates civil society. It should also assist collective organizations to mobilize support; help them to operate as representative vehicles for the views of their supporters, aid them to register effective protest, develop and promulgate alternatives. In other words, the representational role of the media includes helping to create the condition in which alternative viewpoints and perspectives are brought fully into play.

According to Curran and Gurevitch, another democratic function of the media is to assist the realization of the common objectives of society through agreement or compromise between conflicting interests. The media should contribute to this process by facilitating democratic procedure for resolving conflict and defining collectively agreed aims. For example, the media should brief the electorate about the political choices involved in elections, and so help to constitute elections as defining moments for collective decision about the public direction of society. The media system should also facilitate organized representations by giving due publicity to the activities, programmes and thinking of organized groups in addition to the formal processes of government and opposition party.

But the media system is itself an important mechanism for collective self-reflection. By staging a public dialogue in which diverse interests participate, the media should also play a direct role in assisting the search for areas of common agreement and compromise. It should also provide an adequate way in which people can engage in a wider public discourse that can result in the modification of social attitudes affecting social relationships between individuals and groups. It is impossible to have a truly democratic society without an efficient mass media system. A political system that lays claim to democracy without a virile mass media would certainly be a 'malnourished' and 'still-birth' political contraption. That is why McNair (2002) has aptly pointed out that 'in democratic political systems, media function both as transmitters of political communication which originates outside the media organization itself and as senders of political messages constructed by journalists'.

He lists five functions of the mass media in a democratic society to include the following: First, they must inform citizens of what is happening around them. What we may call the 'surveillance' or 'monitoring' functions of the media. Second, they must educate as to the meaning and significance of the 'facts'. The importance of this function explains the seriousness with which journalists protect their objectivity, since their value as educators presumes a professional detachment from the issues being analysed. Third, the media must provide a platform for public political discourse, facilitating the formation of 'public opinion', and feeding that opinion back to the public from whence it came. This must include the provision of space for the expression of dissent without which the notion of democratic consensus would be meaningless.

The media's fourth function is to give publicity to governmental and political institutions—the 'watchdog' role of journalism, exemplified by the performance of the US media during the Watergate episode and, more recently, the British Guardian's coverage of the cash-for-questions scandal, in which investigative journalists exposed the practice of members of parliament accepting payment for the asking of parliamentary questions. 'Public opinion' can only matter—that is, have an influence on 'objective' political reality—to the extent that 'the acts of whoever holds supreme power are made available for public scrutiny, meaning how far they are visible, ascertainable, accessible, and hence accountable'.

There must be a degree of 'openness' surrounding the activities of the political class if the 'public opinions' of the people are to have any bearing on decision-making. Finally, the media in democratic societies serve as a channel for the advocacy of political viewpoints. Parties require an outlet for the articulation of their policies and programmes to a mass audience, and thus the media must be open to them. Furthermore, some media, mainly in the print sector, will actively endorse one or other of the parties at sensitive times such as elections. In this latter sense, the media's advocacy function may also be viewed as one of persuasion.

In short, democracy presumes an open state in which people are allowed to participate in decision-making, and are given access to the media, and other information networks through which advocacy occurs. It also presumes, as we have stated, an audience sufficiently educated and knowledgeable to make rational and effective use of the information circulating in the public sphere. Hallin and Mancini explain that 'in political markets, electors need information to judge the record of government and to select among alternative candidates and parties.' If citizens are poorly informed or if they lack practical knowledge, they may cast ballot that fail to reflect their real interests. Moreover, policymakers need accurate information about citizens to respond to public concerns, to deliver effective services meeting real human needs and, also, in democracies to maximize popular electoral support to be returned to office. Information in the political market place comes from two primary sources.

Personal interactions commonly include informal face-to-face political conversations with friends, family and colleagues, traditional campaign rallies, community forums and grass-roots meetings. These information resources remain important, especially for election campaigns in poorer democracies, and the growth of email and online discussion groups may revive the importance of personal political communications. But these channels have been supplemented in modern campaigns by the mass media including the printed press, electronic broadcasts and also more recently Internet-enabled social media.

The rise of the Internet may be a particularly important development for the process of democratization, due to its potential for interactive, horizontal linkages breaking down the traditional boundaries of space and time, and facilitating oppositional voices, new social movements and transnational advocacy networks, despite the highly uneven distribution of these technologies around the globe. Free press serves to strengthen the process of democratization and human development in their watchdog role, where the channels of mass communications function to promote government transparency and public scrutiny of those in authority, highlighting policy failures, maladministration by public officials and corruption in the judiciary and scandals in the corporate sector.

Investigative journalism can open the government's record to external scrutiny and critical evaluation, and hold authorities accountable for their actions, whether public sector institutions, non-profit organizations or private companies. Moreover, a free press can provide a public sphere, mediating between citizens and the States, facilitating informed debate about the major issues of the day. If the channels of communication reflect the social and cultural diversity within each society, in a fair and impartial balance, then multiple interests and voices are heard in public deliberation. This role is particularly important during political campaigns. Fair access to the airwaves by opposition parties, candidates and opposition groups is critical for competitive, free and fair elections.

5.6 Political Advertising

A major area where political leaders spend money to disseminate their messages to their voters is in the area of political advertising. According to McNair

> [Political advertising] refers to the purchase and use of advertising, in order to transmit political messages to a mass audience. The media used for this purpose may include cinema, billboards, the press, radio and television. Contemporary political advertising can be seen as an important means of informing citizens about who is standing, and what they are offering the citizenry in policy terms.

Since true democracy involves the participation of an informed and rational electorate, all legitimate measures and strategies should be exploited to make it possible for the citizenry to have the required information or alternatives to act on. Hallin and Mancini note that 'the mass media are assuming many of the information that political parties once controlled.' Instead of learning about an election at a campaign rally or from party canvassers, the mass media have become the primary source of campaign information. There has been a tendency for political parties to decrease their investments in neighbour canvassing, rallies and other direct contact activities, and devote more attention to campaigning through the media. The growth of electronic media, especially television, has tended to diminish the role of the party. The electronic media also make it easier to communicate events and issues through personalities.

Swanson notes that in place of or in addition to traditional campaign practices such as rallies of the party faithful, political parties and candidates relied on the sophisticated use of the mass media to persuade voters—the 'consumers' of political communication to support them at election time, and they offered campaigns that feature the appealing personalities of party leaders. Television provides an 'aesthetic' platform for the presentation of political advertising and electioneering campaign messages.

Norris asserts that 'fair access to the airwaves by opposition parties, candidates, and groups is critical for competitive, free and fair elections'. He points out that it is particularly important that State-owned or public television stations should be open to a plurality of political viewpoints and viewpoints during campaigns, without favouring the governments. Corroborating these positions, Swanson asserts that 'editorial independence, freedom from close government supervision and censorship, and the like, create credibility for newscasters everywhere'.

McNair identifies four phases of a typical US political advertising campaign: First, the basic identity of the candidate must be established as a foundation on which to build subsequent information. In this phase, positive biographical details are highlighted, such as a distinguished war record, a tactic used by John F. Kennedy and George Bush in their presidential campaigns, or an outstanding business success. Second, the candidate's policies are established in broad terms with the minimum of extraneous detail, and with emotional charge. Third, the opponent should be attacked, using negatives. And finally, the candidate must be endowed with positive meaning in the context of the values and aspirations of the electorate. In this phase, the campaign will seek to synthesis and integrate the candidate's positive features, allowing him or her to acquire resonance in the minds of the voters.

6
The Role of Television

Since its beginning, television has been interlinked with political processes of every type, ranging from coverage of major political events and institutions to effects on campaigns and elections. From its early position as a new medium for political coverage, television quickly supplanted radio and eventually newspapers to become the major source of public information about politics. Television's influence grew quickly by providing audiences with the chance to experience major political events live or with little delay.

No political event in the history of television coverage has mesmerized television audiences as the coverage of the assassination of President John F. Kennedy in 1963. Film of the actual tragedy in Dallas was played and replayed, and Jack Ruby's subsequent assassination of suspect Lee Harvey Oswald occurred on live television. By the 1970s, the live coverage of major political events had become almost commonplace, but television's ability to lend drama and intimacy to political events continues. Through television, Americans have been eyewitness to State funerals and foreign wars; a presidential resignation; hearings on scandals such as Watergate, Iran–Contra, and Whitewater; triumphs of presidential diplomacy and negotiation; and innumerable other political events.

6.1 Television and Political Campaigns

No aspect of the political process has been affected more by television than political campaigns and elections. In the USA, the first presidential election to see extensive use of television was the 1952 race between Dwight Eisenhower and Adlai Stevenson. In that particular campaign, Richard Nixon, the vice-presidential candidate, took his case to the people to defend himself on television against corruption charges in the famous 'Checker' speech. However, the most significant innovation related to the role of television in the 1952 campaign was undoubtedly Eisenhower's use of short spot commercials to enhance his television image. The Eisenhower campaign utilized the talent of successful product advertising executive Rosser Reeves to devise a series of short spots that appeared, just like product ads, during commercial breaks in standard television programming slots. Not only did this strategy break new ground for political campaigning, but many observers have credited the spots with helping Eisenhower to craft a friendly, charming persona that contributed to his eventual electoral success. Stevenson made it easier for the Eisenhower campaign by refusing to participate in this type of electronic campaigning. Although Stevenson did produce television commercials for the 1956 campaign, he was never able to overcome Eisenhower's popularity (Lee, 2015).

This early use of television for political advertising was the beginning of a trend that has grown so dramatically that televised political advertising is now the major form of communication between candidates and voters in the American electoral system. Every presidential campaign since 1952 has relied heavily on political television spots. In the 1992 election, Bill Clinton, George Bush, Ross Perot and the national parties spent over $120 million dollars for production and airing of television spots (Lee, 2015).

Several reasons account for the pre-eminence of television advertising in politics. First, television spots and their content are under the direct control of the candidate and his or her campaign. Second, the spots can reach a much wider audience than other standard forms of electoral communication. Third, the spots, because they occur in the middle of other programming fare, have been shown to overcome partisan selectivity, for example, the spots are generally seen by all voters, not just those whose political party is the same as that of the candidate. Finally, research has shown that voters actually learn more, particularly about issues, from political spots than they do from television news or television debates (Lee, 2015).

The use of television advertising in political campaigns has often been criticized for lowering the level of political discourse. Observers express disappointment over the fact that television encourages drama and visual imagery, leading to a concentration on candidate images instead of policy issues debated by him. However, scholarly research has shown that television slots for campaigns at all levels are much more likely to concentrate on issues than on images. The extensive reliance on television for campaign communication has also been blamed by many observers for the rise of negative campaigning.

Scholars and journalists alike have noted that more and more political campaigns rely on negative television spots to attack opponents. Although even Eisenhower's original spot campaign in 1952 contained a large number of critical or negative messages, and Lyndon Johnson's 1964 campaign spots attacking Barry Goldwater are considered classics, the news media labelled the 1980s as the heyday of negative spots. Over the past five decades of political spot use, about one-third of all spots for presidential campaigns have been negative spots (Lee, 2015).

6.1.1 Television News Coverage of Political Campaigns

Politics provide a great deal of natural content for television news programming. During political campaign time, the national media outlets, as well as many local stations, devote substantial amounts of time in covering the candidates and their campaigns trails. So important has television news coverage of politics become that some observers suggest its growth has been accompanied by, and perhaps caused, the demise of political parties in politics.

Because more people receive the news related to electoral campaign from television than from any other news source, there has been growing concern about how television actually covers a political campaign. Studies have shown that television's preoccupations with drama and visual imagery have resulted in television news coverage that concentrates more on candidate images and campaign strategy than on serious issues of public interest. Television news coverage of campaigns has also come to rely extensively on sound bites, snippets of candidate messages or commentary excerpts. In addition to reliance on short sound bites, television news coverage of campaigns has been characterized by reliance on 'spin doctors', individual experts who interpret events for viewers by framing, directing, and focusing remarks to favour one side or the other.

As television coverage is so important to campaigns and politicians, the question of potential bias in coverage has been raised repeatedly. Television news also plays a major role in the coverage of the candidate selection process before the party conventions. By covering and scrutinizing candidates, television coverage can help determine which candidates are perceived by the electorate as viable and which might be dismissed as unlikely to succeed. This ability to give and withhold attention has been seen by many as making television's role in the political process a very decisive one, since a candidate who does not do well in the early primaries not only faces an uphill battle in subsequent contests but may have difficulty raising funds to continue at all.

However, news media coverage of politics is not limited to simple coverage of candidates and campaign activities. Television news has also played a large role in the coverage of other aspects of the political process. In 1952, television covered its first series of national party conventions. While it was originally believed that such attention would bring the party process into the open and help voters better understand the political selection process, parties quickly learned to script their conventions for television. National television networks no longer provide gavel-to-gavel coverage of national party conventions, furnishing only convention highlights to viewers.

Televised campaign debates provide other fodder for the television news operation. The first televised debates in the 1960 Kennedy-Nixon campaign were viewed as important, perhaps decisive, in Kennedy's victory. Kennedy's success has often been attributed to his impressive appearance on television in these debates. The next set of presidential debates did not occur until the 1976 contest between Gerald Ford and Jimmy Carter, but there has been some type of single or multiple debate encounters in every subsequent presidential election. All of these cases have been noteworthy for the attention that television news has focused on the events. In some instances, such as the second 1976 Ford-Carter debate, researchers have shown that television's emphasis on Ford's famous misstatement about Soviet domination of Poland and the Eastern bloc changed the interpretation and significance of the event for many viewers.

Several innovations in television coverage of political campaigns were apparent in the late 1980s and early 1990s. One such innovation was the attention given by the television news media to coverage of political television spots. News media personnel, in conjunction with their print journalist counterparts, decided that candidate-controlled spots should be scrutinized and critiqued by the news media. Beginning with the 1988 presidential contest, the television networks, as well as local stations, began to devote increased amounts of time to analyzing candidate spots in what came to be known as 'ad watches'.

Television stations, particularly local ones, also began to take advantage of satellite technology and other remote feed capabilities to provide more on-the-spot coverage of campaigns and candidates. Traditional television news formats, however, have found themselves challenged by another innovation, the frequent appearance of political candidates on television talk shows and personality interview programmes. These shows have provided candidates with new ways to pitch their messages, often with the benefit of direct voter call-in questions. The potential influence of such shows has been enhanced by the proliferation of cable channels offering multiple distribution systems.

6.2 Television and the Rise of Political Professionals

The increased importance of television to political campaigning is also largely responsible for the growth of political or media managers. The need to perform well on television in controlled paid advertising, in debates, on talk-shows, in news interview, and on pseudo-events planned for television news coverage has created a great demand for professional campaign consultants. By the 1980s, it was possible to point to particular philosophies and schools of consulting thought and identify the specific strategies used by consultants to manipulate candidate images for television.

6.2.1 Television and the Governing Process

While television's role in political campaigns and elections is difficult to overestimate, television's significance in the political process carries over to the effects on governing the nation. Television 'keeps an eye' on government institutions and the governing process. Every branch of government is affected by this watchdog. The president of the USA probably bears the greatest weight of this scrutiny. It is indeed rare to see any national television newscast that does not contain one or more stories centred on the executive branch of government (Lee, 2015).

In addition, presidents in general have the ability to receive free network television time for national addresses and for frequent press conferences. Their inaugural addresses and state-of-the-union addresses are covered live and in full. Certainly, the White House has been a plum assignment for television journalists who have often been accused of being co-opted by the aura of power that surrounds the presidency. This unique situation has been characterized as leading, not to a traditional adversarial relationship between press and president, but to a symbiotic relationship in which journalist and politician need to use each other in order to prosper.

However, since the introduction of cameras into the Congress in 1969 and the creation of the Cable-Satellite Public Affairs Network (C-SPAN) to cover political affairs, there has been some levelling of the presidential advantage in television coverage. Although sometimes accused of 'playing to the cameras' in their legislative work, legislative leaders believe this opening-up of the governing process to the television audience has provided new understanding of and visibility for the legislative branch of government. The Supreme Court nonetheless continues to function outside the realm of day-to-day television coverage.

6.3 Television and International Political Processes

As television's role in the political system has developed over the past five decades, increasing attention has been focused on the interrelationship between television and politics in many international political environments. Although often characterized by parliamentary and multiparty systems and government-owned media, many other democracies have been influenced by American styles of television campaigning and coverage. This 'Americanization' of the media and political process can be seen in the growth of American-style political advertising and horserace journalistic coverage. Countries such as Britain, France, Germany, Italy, Israel, many Latin American countries and others have seen this trend, and newly developing democracies in East and Central Europe are also being affected. These countries have not only seen the growth of television advertising and American patterns of media coverage of politics, but a corollary lessening of emphasis on political parties in favour of candidate-centred politics.

6.3.1 Perspectives on Television and Politics

Early research into the effects of information disseminated through the mass media, particularly television, posited the so-called 'direct effects' theory that television messages had direct effects on the behaviour of audience. However, the early research did not fully support this thesis, and scholars for a time tended to discount the notion that such messages directly affected the behaviour of recipients such as voters. Recent studies have tended to show that media do affect behaviour, although not necessarily in the most obvious ways that were initially anticipated.

Television has certainly proven to have sufficiently identifiable effects to justify a belief in some direct effect of the medium in the political process. While the foregoing discussion clearly implies some direct effects of television's participation in the political process, it is important to note that there are many different theories and interpretations about the role that television and other media really play in affecting voter knowledge, opinions and behaviour. Early theorists did assume a kind of direct effect from media exposure, but were later cautioned to view the media as having a more limited role.

Agenda-setting researchers were the first to break with the limited effects model and to suggest that media coverage of particular issues in political campaigns affected the agenda of issues judged to be important by voters. Agenda-setting theory—the idea that the media do not tell us what to think but what to think about—remains an important theory of media effects, and researchers have demonstrated that the agenda of issues and candidate characteristics stressed by television and other media may become the voters' agenda as well.

Researchers interested in the political effects of television have also espoused a 'uses and gratifications' theory suggesting that voters attend to various political media messages in order to use the information in various ways. Blumler and his colleagues first proposed this theory as an explanation for why voters in Britain watched or avoided political party broadcasts.

Many other theories and perspectives on television's possible effects on political processes have been advocated. Researchers have demonstrated, for instance, that television may play an important role in political socialization, helping both children and adults to acquire knowledge about the political system and how it operates, or that exposure to television may increase voter cynicism and feelings of inefficacy.

Others have suggested that we can best understand television's role in politics by viewing it as a medium through which fantasies 'chain out' among the public, shaping views of events and political actors in a dramatic fashion. Critical and interpretive views also provide a perspective on the interrelationship between governing philosophies, societal values, and television culture. All these approaches and orientations will be essential in the future, as television continues to play a central role in the political processes that touch the lives of citizens throughout the world.

6.4 Parliament Coverage by Television

At present almost 60 sovereign States provide some television coverage of parliamentary bodies. Countries as diverse as Australia, Germany, Japan, Hungary, Bulgaria, Russia, China, India, Denmark and Egypt are among them. With varying allocations of control of the coverage between media entities and chamber officials, countries provide this form of televised information to citizens in response to three related perceptions on the part of governmental institutions: a lack of public familiarity with the Parliament and its distinctness from the executive, a lack of public knowledge of citizenship, and the desire to form channels of communication between the public and politicians that can avoid the mediation of media owners and professionals.

In 1944, the British War Cabinet argued that 'proceedings in Parliament were too technical to be understood by the ordinary listener who would be liable to get a quite false impression of the business transacted'. It favoured professional journalists as expert mediators between public and politics. Winston Churchill regarded television as 'a red conspiracy' because it had a robotic component that combined undifferentiated mass access with machine-like reproduction. But debates over televising proceedings in Britain were common from 1965, with 12 separate parliamentary proposals discussed between 1985 and 1988.

Arguments for TV rested on the medium's capacity both to involve the public in making politicians accountable and to involve politicians in making the public interested. Arguments against coverage centred on the intrusiveness of broadcasting equipment, the trivialization through editing of the circumstance and pomp integral to British politics, the undue attention to the major parties and to adversarial division that TV would encourage, and the concern that established procedures and conduct would change to suit television. Channel Four screened a programme called 'Their Lordships' House' from 1985. The Lower House rejected a proposal for coverage that year, but trial Commons telecasts commenced in late 1989, despite the then prime minister's opposition. The public had become an audience that must be converted into a citizen.

This was already a given elsewhere. In post-war Germany, televising the Bundestag was said to be critical for democratizing the public. Proceedings came to Netherlands television in 1962, via three types of coverage: live for topical issues, summaries of less important debates, and 'flashes' on magazine programmes. The first years of the system saw considerable public disaffection because MPs tended towards dormancy, absence, novel-reading and jargon on camera. Over time, members came to attend at the same time as producers, viewer familiarity with procedural norms grew, and ratings increased on occasions of moment. It is no surprise that during the extraordinary events in Czechoslovakia at the end of 1989, the opposition Civic Forum made the televising of the Parliament one of its principal demands.

Sometimes such moves have amounted to a defensive reaction, and others to a positive innovation. The European Parliament was directly elected from

1979. It has used TV coverage for the past decade in search of attention and legitimacy. Recordings and live material are available to broadcasters without cost, to encourage a stronger image for the new Europe. Second-order coverage of the Parliament had always been minimal, due to lack of media interest, but it increased markedly with live TV material. The rules on coverage are more liberal than elsewhere, even encouraging reaction shots and film of the public gallery. When Ian Paisley, a Northern Ireland member, pushed in front of Margaret Thatcher to display a poster in 1986, and interrupted the Pope's speech in 1988, his demonstration was broadcast and made available on tape. One thinks here of the chariots that go into the Indian countryside with video recordings of political rallies and speeches to be shown on screens to 5,000 at a sitting.

Direct TV politics can be a special event. Uganda adopted colour television to coincide with a meeting of the Organization of African Unity, and the first live broadcast of the Soviet Union's new Congress of People's Deputies in 1989 attracted a record 200 million viewers across a dozen time zones, a 25 per cent increase on the previous figure. A side effect was assisting in the formation of a new image overseas. For American journalists, televising parliamentary sessions helped to bring the USSR into the field of political normalcy.

In the USA, despite the introduction of a bill in 1922 providing for electronic media coverage of Congress, with a trial the following year, there were no regular radio broadcasts of proceedings until the signing of the Panama Canal Treaties of 1978. The opening of the 80th Congress in 1947 was carried on television, but this was mostly proscribed until 1971. The major drive for change stemmed from the results of public opinion polls from the early 1970s suggesting that politicians were held in low esteem. Regular closed-circuit trials were instituted in 1977. Following successful coverage of the Connecticut and Florida State Legislatures, the House of Representatives allowed routine broadcasts from 1979. After extensive tests, the Senate agreed to the same in 1986. The service is available via C-SPAN and C-SPAN II, which also broadcasts house and senate committees, prime minister's question time from the British House of Commons and an array of public policy talk fests.

The political process has also been modified by the use made of new communications technologies designed to break down mediation between politicians and publics in North America. Direct contact between leaders and their constituents has positioned them at the leading edge of applications of cable, satellite, video cassette recordings and computer-aided interaction. Alaska, for example, has a Legislative Teleconferencing Network that permits committees to receive audio and computer messages from citizens. Ross Perot linked six American cities by satellite in 1992 to convene a 'nationwide electronic rally', a metonym for the 'electronic town hall' which was to administer the country should he become president; he would debate policies with Congress and have citizens respond through modem or telephone.

The most spectacular recent examples of US parliamentary coverage are the Senate Judiciary Committee's Judge Thomas Confirmation Hearing of 1991 and the appearance of Oliver North before a congressional committee in the 1987 hearings into funding the Contras in Nicaragua. The evidence about Clarence Thomas and Anita Hill was so 'popular' that its competition, Minnesota versus Toronto, drew the lowest ratings ever for a baseball playoff. North's evidence had five times as many viewers as General Hospital, its closest daytime soap opera competitor.

Most commentators on that hearing clearly read it intertextually, referring to acting, entertainment and stars in their analysis. CBS actually juxtaposed images of North with Rambo and Dirty Harry, emphasizing the lone warrior against an establishment state that would not live up to its responsibilities. North assisted this process in his promise 'to tell the truth, the good, the bad and the ugly'. Much media attention was given to Reagan's words of admiration to North: 'This is going to make a great movie one day'. The reaction of the public was similarly remarkable. Polls which showed that years of government propaganda still found 70 per cent of Americans opposed to funding the Contras saw a 20 per cent switch in opinion after the hearings. Once the policy issue became personalized inside North, and opposition to him could be construed as the work of a repressive state, congressional television viewing became popular and influential.

Additionally, rules framed by the British Select Committee on televising the Commons prohibit cut-away reaction shots, other than of those named in the debate. Close-ups and shots of sleeping members are also proscribed. Disruptions lead to a cut-away to the Speaker. These restrictions persuaded Channel Four to abandon plans for live telecasts, although the House decided to permit wide-angle shots in 1990 in order to increase the television coverage of the occasion.

6.5 Indian Parliament Proceedings and Television

Lok Sabha TV (LSTV), a channel from Government of India, offers coverage of government proceedings and other public affairs programming. The channel broadcasts live and recorded coverage of the Lok Sabha, while Rajya

Sabha TV (RSTV) covers the sessions of the Rajya Sabha. LSTV is a Parliament channel mandated to telecast live the proceedings of the Lok Sabha—the House of the People of the Indian Parliament. The channel also produces and telecasts a whole range of programmes of general interest on issues relating to democracy; governance; social, economic and constitutional issues; and citizens' concerns. Debates, discussions and documentaries, as well as programmes on culture and award-winning films in different Indian languages are important elements in the programmes of the channel.

Select parliamentary proceedings have been telecast in India since 1989, when the President's address to the Parliament was shown on live television. After 1994, the Question Hours of both Houses were broadcast live on alternate weeks on both satellite television and All India Radio. The broadcasts were scheduled to ensure that on a given week, proceedings in both Houses were aired, one on TV and the other on radio. In 2006, DD Lok Sabha was replaced by LSTV, a 24-hour TV channel broadcasting in Hindi and English, which is owned and operated entirely by the Lok Sabha itself, broadcasting live the proceedings of the Lok Sabha and also various cultural and educational programmes and panel discussions, when the Lok Sabha is not in session.

With efforts of the Lok Sabha and Prasar Bharati, in 2004 two dedicated satellite channels were set up to telecast live the proceedings of both Houses of Parliament. In July 2006, DD Lok Sabha was replaced by LTV, which is owned and operated by the Lok Sabha itself. LSTV also airs other national ceremonies, such as the oath-taking ceremony of the President of India, conferring of awards to parliamentarians and addresses by foreign dignitaries. Private television channels are allowed to use these feeds, subject to payment and conditions laid down by the Lok Sabha Secretariat. In addition to this, video footage of proceedings is stored in the parliamentary archives. When the Parliament is not in session, these channels air general informative programmes, particularly those related to effective government.

The RSTV channel, owned and operated by Rajya Sabha, covers the proceedings of Rajya Sabha. Apart from telecasting live coverage of Rajya Sabha proceedings, RSTV also brings incisive analysis of parliamentary affairs. While focusing on current national and international affairs, it provides a platform for knowledge-based programmes for the discerning viewer. The channel offers special attention to legislative business undertaken by the Parliament.

Conscious of its role as a public broadcaster, RSTV has conceptualized programmes on the basis of the vibrant relationship between the Parliament and the people of India. It aims at providing an objective perspective on national and international affairs to the people. RSTV touches upon all the aspects of political, economic, social and cultural life of the people, while promoting scientific temper among masses. With a vision to document the story of how the Constitution of India was created, RSTV produced a 10-part TV mini-series 'Samvidhan' which was directed by Shyam Benegal.

6.6 Impact of TV on Elections

In 1952, a seasoned politician faced with a potential scandal made what must have seemed like a radical decision. He decided to address the nation— on television. That politician, Richard Nixon, wasn't running for president yet. Nixon's speech was an attempt to keep his spot on the Republican ticket with nominee Dwight Eisenhower in the wake of a major scandal. Having been accused of misusing campaign funds to fatten his salary, Nixon looked directly into the eyes of the American public and told them he had never accepted a gift. Sitting next to his wife, and telling a heart-warming story about a dog named Checkers that a supporter had given to his children, Nixon won the viewers over. Later that year, he and Eisenhower won the presidential election. Nixon would have his own problems with TV later, but the Checkers speech secured the future of his political career and marked a change in the way American politicians would campaign going forward (Sailor, 2012).

There was a time in American politics when it was seen as uncultured for presidential candidates to campaign. They might make some public addresses at campaign rallies, but for the most part they left the campaigning to the political parties and their staffs. With the rise of television, campaigns were driven more and more by the candidates themselves. But that is only the beginning of TV's transformation of the American presidential election.

In the early days of mass media, TV and newspapers and were used as tools by presidential campaigns. The candidates needed to appeal to the public, so they would use the media to do it. Today, the mass media is not just a means to an end, but one of the most important factors in determining whether a candidate for president wins or loses the election. Thanks to the 24-hour news cycle and the importance of carefully managing a candidate's image, media experts have taken a dominant role in shaping presidential campaigns.

The role of the media adviser is to control the way the public sees the candidate's image. They make sure that the candidate doesn't do anything to damage that image in interviews, at news conferences or during live speeches. Richard Nixon started the first White House Office of Communications in

1968 and pioneered the media savvy campaign strategy. Nixon was careful to limit unscripted press conferences or one-on-one interviews, and instead preferred prepared speeches that let him stay in control, without interference from reporters. In Ronald Reagan's two election campaigns, his advisers carefully managed his image by staging photo opportunities that told the story they wanted. For example, having Reagan photographed sitting on a tractor made him seem like an approachable friend to the working class. Today, most presidential campaigns take this micromanaging approach to media relations (Sailor, 2012).

When an election year rolls around, you can always count on seeing a flood of politically themed commercials. Political ads have become a huge part of campaigns. From national to state and local elections, 50 to 75 per cent of a campaign's funds are typically spent on ad production and airtime. Ads are effective because they can reach people who aren't usually interested in reading campaign coverage, attending rallies or watching the news. Campaigns buy-up time during popular programmes so they can catch these potential voters off guard. And it works. Research has shown that voters pay more attention to political spots and ads to learn about the issues of a political race, compared to other news sources. Some might see that as a sign that people are becoming more ignorant, but political ads are not necessarily misleading; they are actually more likely to engage specific issues and candidates' records than news broadcasts, which focus more on candidates' personalities (Sailor, 2012).

One of the first presidential candidates to learn the power of television ads was Dwight Eisenhower. He hired Rosser Reeves, a Madison Avenue ad executive who had produced a popular campaign for M&M's, to design ads for his 1952 campaign. Using jingles and slogans including I Like Ike, the ads painted the candidate as a friendly and personable leader. Democratic candidate Adlai Stevenson refused to use ads, and instead chose to buy up blocks of network time to deliver speeches. After being trounced in the 1952 election, Stevenson returned in the 1956 election for a rematch with Eisenhower—this time, with political ads (Sailor, 2012).

If election night coverage is the Super Bowl of the presidential election season, then televised debates are the play-offs. But political news junkies might be surprised to learn that debates have not always been a main event in national elections. In fact, before the introduction of television, presidential debates weren't very common. The most famous pre-television campaign debates in the USA were in 1858 between Abraham Lincoln and Stephen Douglas, who were running for Illinois senator, not president. In 1940, Republican challenger Wendell Wilkie challenged incumbent President

Franklin Roosevelt to debate the issues. Debates were so unheard of at the time, Roosevelt dismissed Wilkie's request, and the media accused the Republican of trying to stage a publicity stunt. It is hard to imagine a modern president refusing to debate an election challenger by calling them an attention hog.

Today, debates provide good opportunities for candidates to reach large audiences with their ideas and opinion on contentious issues. A debate may not win or lose an election, but it can change a campaign's momentum, resulting in a sudden drop or increase in the polls. Independent candidate Ross Perot was able to salvage some of his support in the 1992 election after doing well in the debates, despite having fallen drastically in the polls in the previous months. In the 1976 election, President Gerald Ford made a gaffe in a debate with Jimmy Carter, claiming that the Soviet Union did not occupy Eastern Europe. While a majority of viewers thought Ford won the debate, after newscasts focused on the mistake, support for Ford dipped (Sailor, 2012).

Before television, the presidential election cycle was relatively brief. Campaigning would take place between the conventions in the summer and the election, later in November. Primaries were held, but candidates wouldn't run full-fledged campaigns to win support. Instead, each state's party would send delegates to the national convention without consulting the public. At the convention, the delegates voted on the candidate they wanted to represent the party.

That all began to change in 1952, when the national party conventions were first televised. The thought was that covering the conventions would give the public a window into the way the parties made decisions. Few probably expected that the reverse would happen—that the coverage would move the parties to change the way they ran conventions. Playing up to the cameras, conventions became a venue for party leaders and rising stars to make speeches, not places where actual decisions were made. Today, the convention is mostly an opportunity for the candidates to stage strong starts to the general election campaign. The voting that takes place at the conventions is mostly ceremonial.

As the conventions have become less important, the primaries have become more important. The news coverage of the campaign begins 1, even 2 years before the first primary election is held, and 2 to 3 years before the general election. This has become especially pronounced as the 24-hour news networks have risen in popularity and have huge amounts of airtime to fill. For example, as early as the summer of 2009, pollsters were already testing the waters for which candidates might win the election in 2012.

Television gave elected officials and candidates for office an unprecedented way to speak directly to millions, face-to-face. Of course, it didn't take long for that direct contact to be mediated, mostly by the network executives, producers and reporters who put together nightly news programmes. Trends such as sound bites, talking heads and the dramatic nature of television news coverage have led critics to accuse TV of creating a less factual, more negative form of political coverage.

Studies have shown that since the advent of TV, the American voting public has become increasingly disenchanted with politics. Except for the 2004 and 2008 elections, voter turnout has steadily declined since 1960, the year the first televised presidential debates were held. Some argue that the increasingly negative tone of ads and political commentary has driven many to abandon interest in politics. TV has also driven a decline in party identification, replacing political parties as the entity in control of political information, as they were in the 1900s.

On the other hand, the introduction of cable news channels such as CNN and Fox News, with their 24-hour coverage, has expanded the scope of political reporting. With so much more airtime than nightly newscasts, those channels can provide political coverage with an unprecedented level of depth. Those that are politically active today could be considered more engaged than ever. Then again, there are just as many critics who would argue that the cable networks' increasing stress on images, photo ops and sound bites over the issues has driven the level of political discourse into the gutter.

6.7 Impact of Television on Voters

With large amounts of time to fill, 24-hour news stations have introduced programmes such as analysis by experts and talking heads to fill the schedule. These experts, usually paid professionals working for one party or another, try to spin the news in favour of their side. Expert speakers, independent of party control, usually lean one way or the other and offer their take on recent developments. Analysis has become so common that much of the actual political news, like speeches, has been reduced to only sound bites. News producers, anxious to keep broadcasts fast-paced, will take one important remark from a much longer series of remarks. That gives news producers a huge amount of power over how the public digests political events.

Looking at trends such as sound bites and expert talk, many media analysts have criticized television for imposing political discourse. News coverage of elections, for instance, usually focuses on developments like movements in the polls to determine who is winning. The news is less likely to focus on in-depth discussions of candidates' ideas. Given TV's visual nature, scenes of carnage after the bombing of a foreign country tend to be more powerful than a leader's carefully written speech about the necessities of war.

In recent years, media savvy political advisers have taken advantage of the power of TV and the expert speakers and commentators to get their candidates' messages across. For instance, top George W. Bush adviser Karl Rove used skilful control over the media message to help win two elections for Bush, and create momentum for controversial policies like the war in Iraq. Brilliant or diabolical, depending on which side of the political spectrum you fall, Rove used a network of conservative columnists, analysts and commentators to spread the administration's message on TV news and in print through discussions.

6.7.1 Impact of Television on Voters in India

In India, the Internet and cable television have brought about meaningful changes to public and private spheres of life more quickly than education, industrialization or any other socio-economic factor. Electronic media had no role to play for a decade after independence. Print media and radio served as the primary means of political information and mobilization. Mass media received a boost in September 1959 as a result of the introduction of television to urban India. The emergence of television in post-colonial India was characterized by competing visions. Its deeply segmented political sphere witnessed several rounds of intense debating between politicians and bureaucrats who were concerned with the efficacy of investing in television considering only a few could manage access to the medium.

The government-controlled national television network began as a 'modest enterprise' since viewers had access to one channel, while the bigger cities had access to two channels. In terms of influencing civic and political engagement, its influence was minimal since the goals of the State-regulated electronic media were restricted to educational- and entertainment-based programmes. In 1991, the Indian television network was deregulated and cable-satellite network emerged for the first time. From its modest beginning with two channels in 1990, the Indian audience got access to 515 cable-satellite channels by June 2010. Moreover, there were thirty-three 24-four hour news channels that would constantly engage in political and economic debates and conduct opinion or exit polls in election years. The number of satellite-radio stations grew from 6 during the 1990s to 312 by the middle of the last decade. These would include the community radio systems that became very successful in three states including Karnataka, Gujarat and Uttaranchal, serving as the key medium for engaging in grass-roots activism, but operating independent of state and commercial control (Satpathi & Roy, 2011).

The service providers for these stations were NGOs using radio for generating development and community education. More specifically, community radio served as a tool for empowerment that allowed local citizens the opportunity to seek accountability for state. But the success of community radio was limited to few states, due to barriers for entry created by the commerce radio lobbies and state agencies resisting citizens' accountability through enforcement of strict guidelines and high licensing fees. The deregulation of the television network in the 1990s was accompanied by the Internet revolution. From 1992 to 2010, the number of Internet users grew from none to 381,000,000 (Shaw, 2005).

In India and other post-colonial countries, television often becomes the 'compelling medium' for influencing a normative national consciousness of language, image and sound; television produces a vision of the world for its audiences. These productions link television with the political economy of nation building. If we look at the argument in the context of Indian television, we observe that the broadcast media under State monopoly helped to tentatively bridge the gap between a literate elite and the mass audience, to which print media, had formerly catered. Access to literacy in pre-colonial India was restricted, as the colonial State sought to train a select group of middle class for administrative purposes. The emergence of the cable-satellite television helped to narrow the gap between literate elite and others even further as it brought 'market forces and the power of television together by 1992' (Rajagopal, 2004).

In the post-1991 period following de-regulation of the television networks, and a growing nexus between market reforms and technological advancement, interaction between media effect on political behaviour underwent some changes. As market reforms and liberalization started influencing society, the top-down approach to economic development got replaced. Rajagopal (2004) thought that the change in the discursive narrative of State economy grew out of the complex politico-economic reality as civil society started contesting the claims of 'benign authoritarianism through which economic policy was legislated, and which had survived more than four decades of democratic elections' (Rajagopal, 2004, p. 2).

The 1990s witnessed for the first time an emerging alliance between two contradictory forces: Hindutva and neoliberalism. Gopalakrishnan (2008) compared this alliance to 'living political projects, shaped in a dialectical relationship' with their social foundations and common goals offering a space that could be in terms of the tactics used for operating the alliance. At the national level, the NDA, headed by the BJP made 'discursive adjustments' that allowed them to develop a political praxis built on the neoliberal privatization of 'education, intensified repression of social movements and the opening of the Indian economy to non-resident-Indian-driven foreign investment.' The two projects also promoted 'anti-terrorism' as the single most important agenda of the India, while attempting to dissolve its commitment to any forms of 'social justice.

Riding high on the success of what emerged as successful alliance between neoliberalism and Hindutva, in 2003, the BJP-led NDA coalition launched a nationwide television campaign with the slogan India Shining. The NDA government spent an estimated $20 million of the taxpayers' money to publish the campaign in media, in all languages (Zora & Woreck, 2004). The campaign was aired 9,472 times, making it the second-most viewed advertisement between December 2003 and January 2004 (Chandran, 2004). In the print media, similar success were achieved in terms of its popularity, as it became the fourth-most advertised insertion in the 450 national and regional newspapers.

The New York-based advertisement agency Grey Worldwide were the brainpower behind the 60-second media blitz, focusing on a 'feel-good' propaganda that was accompanied by the economic liberalization mantra along with images of India's industrial and agricultural development, the emergent middle-class and the idea of India as an emergent super power. The NDA alliance emphasized that the 'India Shining' was a government campaign that showcased India's economic progress rather than political campaign for the upcoming general elections of 2004 (*The Hindu*, 2004). The campaign plank was set up against the backdrop of the existing Indian economic development. According to Kohli (2006), the success of the Indian economy under the NDA regime was reflection of the neoliberal intervention of favouring pro-business industrial policy and de-regulation of the 'license raj'. This would also allow for greater freedom for private investors in different sectors of the economy (Kohli, 2006).

Although Internet-enabled social media are beginning to have a sizeable impact on the psyche of the voters across the globe as manifested in elections held in the USA and India in recent times, the power wielded by television hasn't waned in comparison. Television is one of the foremost preferred media of electoral campaigns because of its far better reach in countries like India. As discussed in other parts of this chapter, political debates and discussions, expert talks and analysis broadcast in television have a significant bearing on the opinions of the voters in the long run. Although, one cannot pinpoint and correlate the role played by television content pertaining to elections in influencing voters' choice, it can safely be said that over a period of time television along with other mainstream media does set agendas discussion among the public, which may tilt voters' preference over a political party or a candidate in place of others. Therefore, television medium has become an integral part of the political campaign machinery of political parties throughout the world.

7
Legal Framework for Media and Elections

There is an increased amount of law, at both a national level and an international level, governing the role of media in elections. It is very vital to understand that these legal provisions are aimed at regulating the governmental practices vis-à-vis mass media and not about regulating media organizations. Fundamental principles enshrined in international law incorporate the most important issues such as freedom of expression and information. It also includes the right to participate in governance by contesting for offices through elections.

These principles are available in Article 19 and Article 21 of the Universal Declaration of Human Rights. From then onwards, these principles have repeatedly been featured in a number of UN and regional human rights agreements. Decisions by numerous organizations, such as the UNHRC, the European Court of Human Rights and the Inter-American Commission on Human Rights, have been able to refine these principles, making them a rich and applicable source of jurisprudence.

Many other international institutions have also provided additional sources about international law on media and elections. In 1999, the UN Special Rapporteur on Freedom of Opinion and Expression introduced guiding principles with regard to the role of media during elections as well as governmental obligations to ensure media pluralism. Other international bodies such as the UN and various committees under it provide further sources on laws related to media and elections. However, it should be noted here that these laws do not have binding power over UN member states, but instead provide an important indication of prevalent international standards.

Along with a plethora of international laws and treaties, most of the countries have their own national legislations, which provide guidance and parameters for media activity and respective regulatory bodies. In many countries, especially those with a common law system, decisions of other countries' courts may be cited as an important source of guidance and precedence. Although those decisions may not have binding power just like other international guidelines, depending on the seniority of the court whose decision is being quoted, judges will take serious note of the reasoning and finding of concerned judgements.

7.1 International Law on Elections and Media

Elections and media are subjected to a number of fundamental and interdependent human rights. Fundamental rights are enjoyed by candidates contesting elections, media professionals covering elections and voters casting their ballots in elections. These rights are included in some of the important international and regional human rights conventions, including the United Nations Declaration of Human Rights (1948), Article 19, which protects freedom of expression at all times, and Article 21, which protects political participation and voting. These rights also find place in the ICCPR. These rights would also imply that discrimination against women, the disabled and vulnerable communities is strictly opposed at all times.

So far as the media relationship with the EC is concerned, two important principles come into the picture, namely, transparency and confidentiality. The concept of transparency denotes that the operations of the EC are open to public scrutiny and, hence, are accountable. And confidentiality means that the EC's operations are safeguarded against those who do not have the right to obtain such information as those people may undermine the integrity of the entire electoral process.

But practically speaking, these principles may be difficult to implement. The principles of complete transparency and confidentiality are clearly not compatible. However, specifically establishing the precedence of these principles in a given case is much easier than it appears. The activities and plans of the EC should be open to public scrutiny, except for certain valid reasons. But the process of voting by an individual voter is always confidential. It is the responsibility of the EC to take necessary steps to make voting confidential. The borderline cases that fall in between transparency and confidentiality of the voting process are likely to be very few.

After the adoption of the ICCPR in 1966, these legal guidelines therein were given binding power and, thus, it is now an enforceable law over all those States that ratified it. Article 19 of the ICCPR states that people shall have the right to freedom of expression, including the freedom to expect, get and send the information. Article 25 of the ICCPR states that every citizen shall have the right and the opportunity without any distinctions based on factors such as religion, ethnicity, and gender and so on. Additionally, citizens shall also have the right to vote and to be elected at periodic elections which shall be conducted on the basis of universal suffrage and shall be held by secret ballot, ensuring the expression of the free will of the electors.

It is clear that these two legal principles have been able to impose an obligation on governments to guarantee the diversity and pluralism of the media during election periods. There are also accepted restrictions on freedom of expression for each and every phenomenon. Although the majority of activities are completely harmless, it is clear that the notion of 'seeking, receiving and imparting information or ideas' also encompasses activities which few societies could tolerate. For instance, activities such as incitement to murder, unauthorized graffiti on public walls or the sale of pornography to children could not be justified under freedom of expression.

In order to be acceptable, limitations on freedom of expression could be put to test. First, the interference on freedom of expression must be in accordance with the law; second, the legally sanctioned prohibition must protect or promote an aim deemed legitimate in international law; and third, the limitation must be necessary for the protection or promotion of the legitimate objective. The leading regional human rights treaties—the European Convention on Human Rights, the American Convention on Human Rights, and the African Charter on Human and Peoples' Rights—have incorporated a similar combination of guarantees to the right to freedom of expression and information and right to political participation without discrimination.

In the documents adopted by the Conference on Security and Cooperation in Europe (CSCE), the participants agreed upon themselves to guarantee that no legal or administrative hindrances should disturb the access to the media on a non-discriminatory basis for all political parties and individuals willing to take part in the electoral process. However, it should be noted here that the CSCE documents are not treaties and therefore are not binding. Nevertheless, they have been accepted as part of customary international law and hence, exercise obligations on member countries. The decisions of both international and various national tribunals have provided the greater thrust to these broad principles on media and elections. In this context, the media play an important role in making governments accountable, thereby ensuring the effective functioning of a democracy. Governments are obligated to guarantee the existence of a democracy that ensures media pluralism, especially in elections. Freedom of political debate is a fundamental right (OSCE, 1990).

> Political parties and individuals have a right of access to government media during election campaigns. Government media are obliged to publish opposition views. There exists a right of reply, correction, or retraction in response to wrong statements in the government media. There may be limits

on the legal liability of the media if they reproduce unlawful statements. Political expression may be restricted only for extraordinary reasons. There is enhanced protection for criticism of politicians and government. There is enhanced protection for political opinions. There is a right to an effective remedy for those whose rights have been violated. Governments are obliged to protect the safety of media. (OSCE, 1990)

Mass media guarantee that the freedom of expression and information is implemented properly. The Inter-American Court of Human Rights categorically states a principle that is now universally acknowledged in international law and accepted by most of the countries around the world. The freedom of expression in a democratic country will have no meaning if it can only be ensured at a personal level. Freedom of expression is not just about what an individual is allowed to speak with his or her neighbour; it is also about the expression of facts and opinions and also the reception of information through the mass media.

The European Court of Human Rights goes a step further when it stated that media freedom is very important for providing citizens information in a democracy. Media freedom provides the public one of the best methods of accessing information and forming an opinion about the ideologies and principles of their political parties and leaders. It also provides politicians the opportunity to think and comment about the public issues. Thus, it enables citizens to participate in political debates freely, which is at the core of a democratic society. Media provides information on matters of public interest and act as a watchdog over the government. Not only does it have the task of disseminating information and ideas, the public also have the right to receive such information. Otherwise it would be futile to term the media as the watchdog of the democracy.

The European Court also identifies two important aspects of this democratic role of the media: to inform and to act as a watchdog. However, this role does not impose any legally binding duties on newspapers or broadcasting stations. Instead it imposes such responsibility on governments to make sure that the media are able to exercise these functions in a free and fair manner. This principle clearly leads to practical difficulties during elections. It is to be noted here that the governments have every right to regulate the technical aspects of broadcasting. The government is also under public obligation to distribute the frequencies in a fair and non-discriminatory manner. Media are also subject to the law of the land, especially in matters such as defamation or incitement. But usually as a general rule, governments do not restrict the contents of the media.

7.2 Freedom of Political Discussion

International bodies, courts and national tribunals have identified freedom of political discussion as a fundamental right. For example, the European Court of Human Rights noted in 1978 that 'freedom of political debate is at the very core of a democratic society'. Freedom of political debate means the ability to openly discuss political issues in a public sphere or in the media based on the fullest possible access to information about such political issues. It is also an expression of a range of fundamental freedoms.

In 1992, the European Court of Human Rights explained on freedom of political debate, indicating that not only is expressing opinions and receiving information important but media is also a forum for interaction between politicians and the public. Freedom of the press provides the public one of the best ways of forming an opinion about the ideas and attitudes of their political leaders. It also provides politicians an opportunity to get the pulse of the public opinion. Thus, it enables all the stakeholders to participate in the free political debate which is at the very core of a democratic society.

The importance of political debate lies in providing the voters information that enables it to exercise its political choice. The UN Technical Team on the Malawi Referendum of 1993, which chose between a single and multiparty system, stated: 'If voters are to make an informed choice at the polling station, then an active exercise of the freedom of expression is essential' (UN, 1992).

7.3 Media Pluralism

It has been stated numerous times that the media plays an important role during elections. Media role is not only about scrutinizing governmental actions but also about providing information to the voters, who should have all the necessary information at their disposal to make an informed and democratic choice. The governments also have an important obligation not to restrict the media in performing these functions. In addition, the governments also have obligations to ensure media pluralism in order to provide the public a variety of information sources. The obligation contained in Article 19 of the ICCPR, guaranteeing freedom of expression and freedom of information, applies to governments and not to individual media organizations.

The HRC stated that due to the evolution of the modern mass media, much more effective measures are required to control the media from the stranglehold of various agencies, which would interfere with the people's right to freedom of expression. The HRC elaborated on this point in 2011, stating that the government should not have monopoly over the media and should at all times promote media pluralism. Further, governments should also take suitable measures to control the undue media monopoly by privately owned media.

The UN Rapporteur for Freedom of Expression has identified both commercial pressures and government regulation as major threats to media pluralism and public interest. Some of the important challenges to independent media that the rapporteur identified in 2010 included growing concentration of media ownership, cost-cutting measures by private media organizations and existing broadcasters gaining access to new digital frequencies during the digital switchover, thereby expanding concentration and political interference in the media.

Jurisprudence from countries as varied as Ghana, Sri Lanka, India, Trinidad and Tobago and Zambia have underlined that the media monopolies are detrimental to the principles of freedom of expression, and that publicly-funded media also have an obligation to convey opinions from various spectrums other than that of the incumbent government. A number of these judgements refer to the right of opposition parties to have their viewpoints published in the public media. This right extends to different types of minorities also. The government should ensure that the members of various minority groups should enjoy the right to participate, on the basis of their own culture and language, in the cultural life of the community, to produce and enjoy arts and science, to protect their cultural heritage and traditions, to own their own media and other means of communication and to have access on the basis of equality to state-owned media.

It is important to note that the role of the media is not only about acting as a catalyst for freedom of expression in the limited sense. Media is also important as a means to enable the public to exercise their right to freedom of information, and this right is closely linked to media pluralism, because without it, the public cannot subscribe to diverse sources of information. Independent and free media should have a diversity of ownership, and it should promote and safeguard democracy, while creating opportunities and means for economic, social and cultural development.

Media should be exempted from legal liability for provocative statements and should have a right to reply. Clear demarcation should be made between news coverage of functions of government office and functions of a party candidate. Airtime for direct access programmes should be granted on a fair and non-discriminatory basis, because such programmes provide an opportunity for candidates to debate on contentious issues and for journalists to question them. Media should also engage in educating the voters. Programmes should target traditionally oppressed communities which may include women and ethnic and religious minorities.

7.4 Limits of Media Liability

Politicians and journalists are concerned with the issue of defamation, especially during election time. How far are the media legally liable if they report statements by politicians that are subsequently found to be defamatory? In his 1999 report, the UN Special Rapporteur on Freedom of Opinion and Expression came down firmly in favour of exempting the media from liability for publishing unlawful statements made by politicians in the context of an election. The type of statements envisaged might include those that were defamatory or incited to hatred. This does not mean that there would be no liability for such statements—the person who made them would still be liable—but that the media would be free to reproduce them without, for example, having to review every party election broadcast or advertisement before transmission. The special rapporteur was offering a clear guideline on a matter that has been hitherto unclear and controversial. Thus, for example, the UN Transitional Authorities in Cambodia in its guidelines took precisely the opposite view, assuming that media would be legally responsible for statements that 'incite discrimination, hostility or violence by means of national, religious, racial or ethnic hatred' (UNTAC, 1992).

The special rapporteur was reflecting a growing trend in national courts and legislatures. The Danish Parliament passed a law exempting the media from liability for publishing statements inciting racial or national hatred, providing that they themselves did not intend to promote hatred. This followed the conviction of a journalist who had been convicted and fined for broadcasting a television interview with members of a racist gang. He applied to the European Commission of Human Rights, which ruled his application admissible (UNTAC, 1992).

A newspaper cannot be held liable for publishing a statement by a terrorist organization. The right of the journalist to inform and the rights of his or her readers to receive full and accurate information constitute an objective institutional guarantee, which effectively prevents the imputation of any criminal will on the part of those who only transmit information. This reasoning is significant as it stresses that the argument against applying liability to the media in such cases has basically to do with protecting the public right to receive information.

7.5 Right to Defend Against Media Reports

Every candidate will have the right to defend himself against public criticism in the same media in which the criticism was aired. There are two basic categories of the right to reply. The first right could be called as 'right of correction' and is limited to point out erroneous information. The media organization's editors are expected to correct their mistake, but they do so in their own words. The second right is for the aggrieved individual to demand newspaper space or broadcast time from the media in order to clarify.

But the idea of creating a legally enforceable right of reply has never found favour with campaigners of freedom of expression. They fear that it might strangle free and fair expression and violate the discretion of the editors to decide what to publish and what not to. This assumes special significance in the context of elections. However, international advisory bodies and national courts have sometimes favoured such a mechanism, especially in instances where the criticism in question originates from government-owned media, to which the opposition parties have limited access. The UN Special Rapporteur on Freedom of Opinion and Expression has cautioned against a government-mandated right of reply and stated that the right should in any case be limited to allegedly false facts. It is of the view that if a right of reply system is to exist, it should ideally be part of the industry's self-regulated system and can feasibly apply to facts and not to opinions.

7.6 Restrictions on Political Speech during Elections

It should be noted here that freedom of expression is not an absolute right and it may be subjected to certain restrictions based on circumstances. However, such restrictions should conform to properly defined standards. It is not legitimate to restrict political speech before it is spoken. So the implied meaning is that while a person who is defamed may have a legal remedy, it is not acceptable to apply prior censorship to politicians' words to guarantee that they do not contain defamatory content. Article 19 of the

ICCPR provides a number of instances in which the right may be restricted. The exercise of the rights provided also carries with it special duties and responsibilities. It may therefore be subject to certain limitations such as respect of the rights and reputations of others and the protection of national security or of public order.

Article 20 of the ICCPR also puts restrictions on propaganda for war and advocacy of national, racial or religious hatred that constitutes incitement to discrimination, hostility or violence. The UN Technical Team on the Malawi Referendum applied these principles to national law governing an election campaign. It stated that restriction on freedom of expression should not be broadly defined as to leave it to the discretion of the law enforcing authorities, since uncertainty over legal boundaries has a negative effect on the exercise of this right to freedom of expression.

7.7 Criticism of Politicians and Incumbent Governments

International tribunals are clear that politicians and governments may be subject to greater criticism and insult in comparison to ordinary individuals and, subsequently, the law also offers them less protection. This is due to the fact that politicians have great responsibility for leadership and representation of their constituents and their country, and because they have greater access to solutions than most common people. But more often than not, officials invoke charges such as criminal defamation against critics.

The civil law of defamation can be a legitimate tool to protect reputations against reckless and malicious allegations. In recent times, many national courts have ruled that the scope of defamation law must not prevent the media from exercising their proper function. Public figures have far easier access to channels of communication to counteract false statements. Hence, media should be given a free hand to perform its functions. In recent years, this approach has been adopted in countries such as the UK, Australia and India.

7.8 Right to Effective Remedy

International law states that any individual who believes that their rights are challenged shall be entitled to an effective solution in a national court. In relation to media and elections, this implies that there is an expectation that the courts are ready to modify any unjustified restrictions on media coverage; denial of access to the media' denial of the right of reply' defamatory or inflammatory material; or any other issue where media, parties and candidates, or the electorate feel that their rights have been violated.

The notion of a remedy should actually offer the complainant a timely and practical solution in the context of an election. For example, if defamatory or inaccurate information is aired, it should be corrected while it is still fresh in the voters' collective mind. Although the normal courts will still be the ultimate arbiters of whether rights have been infringed, many countries also have administrative procedures that deal with complaints more rapidly. It may be a regular complaints mechanism operated by a broadcasting regulator or a media council backed by the government.

7.9 Restrictions on Media during Elections

Most of the countries across the world do not have appropriate provisions in their laws to control the media during elections. Even in matured democratic countries, there are differences of opinion about what extent the media may be subjected to regulation during elections. While the USA has got the tradition of minimal media regulation, Europe favours establishment of enforceable rules vis-à-vis media during elections. Unlike the USA, Europe has a history of state participation in internal broadcasting. This may be one of the major reasons for the evolution of such practices. What it implies is that the all-important public resources of broadcasting and frequency spectrum is to be allocated and used in a fair and non-discriminatory manner so as to reflect the views of the different candidates and not just favour the ruling party.

Notwithstanding the existing differences in terms of political culture with regard to media regulations, it is universally recognized that the media does have a very important role to perform in providing information to the voters. Hence, it is rather surprising to note that there are very few number of legislations that deal with media content during elections across the world. This may indicate towards the presence of matured media environment where there is a free and fair exchange of political ideas and where every political party and candidate has an equal and fair chance to have media access to get across his or her ideas.

In countries where major media organizations are publicly owned or under the control of a power political group, it is imperative for the lawmakers to set out some basic guidelines for the coverage of elections. There has to be a marked difference in terms of provisions relating to public and private media. The provisions may be focused on aspects such as time and space given to political parties and its respective candidates, whether paid advertising is allowed, duty pertaining to educating the voters, debates of the candidates and space and time be given to the candidates to defend themselves in case of factual misrepresentation in the media.

Regulations could also directly address the more specific issues such as news blackouts, restrictions with regard to coverage of opinion polls and policies pertaining to defamation. The law or regulations will probably come out with a statutory body with the responsibility of media watching during election. The responsibility could also be assigned to some other existing body such as, for example, an EC or broadcasting regulator to carry out this work. In order to address the complaints about the media coverage, the provision to set up a speedy mechanism could also be included in the law.

7.10 Safety of Media Professionals

Journalism is a dangerous occupation. Statistics collected by media freedom organizations show that each year dozens of media professionals are killed or injured in the course of their work. Elections can be dangerous for journalists, and tense and sometimes violent campaigns or announcement of results can expose those trying to report honestly and accurately. The responsibility for protecting the physical security of everyone within its territory rests with the government, which has a particular obligation in relation to the media.

There are certain fundamental measures that governments can take to guarantee protection to journalists. Governments can make it a specific offence to carry out violence or threats against the media. Violence or threats against the media are investigated promptly and those responsible are brought to justice. International humanitarian law makes specific reference to the protection of journalists, stating that 'journalists engaged in dangerous professional missions in areas of armed conflict shall be considered as civilians' and provided with the same protection as civilians.

Additional protection should be extended to war correspondents who are accompanying armed forces. In such cases, correspondents should be accorded prisoner of war status if captured and other rights equivalent to civilian members of armed forces should also be extended. The International Committee for the Red Cross has a dedicated hotline for journalists in trouble in conflict zones. Thus, journalists covering elections in conflict-affected areas are protected under international law, although implementation of these protections by national governments often remains as having a lot to be desired. In addition, electoral commissions can promote a code of conduct that stresses the importance of both political parties and security forces allowing journalists to go carry out their work without restrictions.

7.11 Responsibilities of Public and Private Media

Public-owned media is an important resource of information for the electorate as it is funded by the public money. The generally accepted norm in any media is that it should not be politically biased in its electoral coverage. In his 1999 report, even the UN Special Rapporteur on Freedom of Expression has also spoken on similar lines. He has urged that the public-funded media organizations have the responsibility to provide the voice to a variety of opinions and warned against using it as a propaganda machine by a political party. Media also have the responsibility of providing education to the voters and to provide a platform for various political parties and their respective candidates.

Whether the public fund goes towards a building, a vehicle or a television station, the use of public resource for a particular political party's campaigning carries the same legal and ethical implications. It is exactly for this reason that in many countries, there are clear-cut regulations to protect public media against the interference of the government. However, the obligations of the private media are not similar to that of public media. The broadcasters and journalists should not be told what to write and what not to write. In addition, various political viewpoints should also be provided with enough space and time. Importantly, it should be noted here that the private media also have obligations towards the public. The professional journalistic standards expect professionals working in private media to be accurate and to carry out balanced reporting.

Usually, the government allocates licenses to broadcasting stations with necessary terms and conditions. It may relate to whether they are allowed to support any political party or to broadcast news or views pertaining to them. Conditions such as obligations with regard to public service announcements to educate voters should also be incorporated. Any general law or regulations related to media coverage should apply to both public and private media. Provisions related to blackout periods before the voting or the coverage of opinion polls is a case in point. Similarly, general legal provisions such as the law of defamation will still apply equally to both public and private media.

Though governments make a distinction between public and private media, a number of aspects of the law or regulations governing the media during elections would definitely affect both sectors. Regulations related to expenditure procedure for hearing complaints against the media by the public or political parties, reporting of opinion polls, provisions related to hate speech, policies related to news block outs before or during the elections, right of the journalists to have access to electoral events, accreditation of journalists and provisions to guarantee the safety of journalists would definitely affect media professionals, whether they belong to public or private media.

7.12 Implementation Mechanism

The responsibility of implementation is one of the most important practical aspects of the law or regulations on media during elections. Media editors and regulatory bodies will often have a day-to-day communication during elections in comparison to normal times. Hence, the relationship would in all probability be collaborative in nature. Issues arising during elections could be addressed by existing regulatory authority. Even the media can establish its own controlling mechanism, taking political parties on board. The EC invariably takes up this responsibility in many countries. However, a special body could be set up especially during elections to control media organizations. Even the judiciary can step in to contribute during such times. Ultimately, media will definitely have the right to appeal in case of infringements of its rights.

The media coverage of elections is often looked after by the existing regulatory authorities in collaboration with the EC. Media organizations should disseminate news and other information pertaining to elections in an objective and impartial manner and must treat all political parties fairly. The role of media, however, does not drastically change during elections as in the normal times. But the broadcasters will have more responsibility during elections to provide equitable news coverage to all political parties without compromising on the news values.

7.12.1 Self-regulation by Media

Many independent commentators view self-regulation by the media as an ideal solution during elections. If the independent media is in place along with the established tradition of democratic elections, this method will definitely work out because even the coverage is in tune with the long-established ethical practice. The best know example of this approach is in place in Britain, where the Broadcasters Liaison Group (BLG) allocates direct access party election broadcasts. BLG was formed in 1997 and comprises of representatives of broadcasters. The BLG works in collaboration with the EC to ensure consistency.

The state-owned Polish Radio and Television has adopted a mixed approach. Here the State Electoral Commission allocates direct access broadcasting, but in their news coverage related to electoral campaigns, radio and television are answerable to the general regulatory body, called the National Broadcasting Council. The Polish Radio and Television management has issued detailed guidelines to their staff, which are as follows: Polish Radio and Television should disseminate exhaustive coverage of the campaign and information about the candidates. While providing information about the parties and candidates, they should avoid any bias in favour of any political party or views. The principle of equality of access is to be maintained while providing airtime to parties and candidates.

7.12.2 Election Commission

In many cases, the EC will take the responsibility for implementing regulations on the media during election campaigns. If the EC has sufficient guarantees of independence and expertise to conduct the specialized role of media regulation, it is often seen as appropriate. In 1994, Malawi held its first democratic elections. Interestingly, it offered a good example of an EC's role in a new democracy. The independent commission was able to guarantee fair share of coverage from the government-funded broadcaster for different political parties and candidates. The commission was able to accomplish this with the help of a media subcommittee which had the experience and expertise to deal with broadcasters.

In a small country with plenty of institutions, an EC may be a preferable option. For example, in Barbados, the Electoral and Boundaries Commission looks after the overall electoral process, including media regulations. In 1987,

Nicaragua's Constitution established the electoral council as an independent body of the government. One of the major responsibilities of this council is to implement the mass media law during elections and manage a complaints procedure. It has also set up a special mass media department to deal with broadcasters, especially in attempting to deal with changes in practices.

7.12.3 Elections Media Commission

Many countries have preferred to establish a special body to regulate media during elections. This option has worked out best in transitional elections where media role is not properly spelt out. In 1994, South Africa had set up an Independent Media Commission (IMC) in addition to a widely respected Independent Electoral Commission (IEC). Similarly, Bosnia-Herzegovina has also set up a specialized body called the Media Experts Commission (MEC) for regulating the media in elections. However, it worked only during a short transitional period.

7.12.4 Judiciary

The responsibility of electoral administration would lie with a special branch of the judiciary in some of the countries. For example, in Uruguay, the Electoral Court administers voting; it can also rule on any disputes between the political parties and investigate challenges posed to the election results. This specialized body can also consider the complaints raised against election campaigning in the media. Latin American countries have this common model across the continent. For example, in Costa Rica, elections are administered by a body called as the supreme electoral tribunal. It also regulates media coverage. It is an independent constitutional body comprised of judges, funded by the legislature and, more importantly, independent from the executive of the government.

7.13 Complaints Procedure

An important element of most media regulatory authorities, in the course of elections and at other instances, is a complaints procedure technique. This is a method by which the public, political parties and the media themselves can try to find adjudication on alleged breaches of the law or regulations on election coverage. Since the election duration is normally quick, the complaints mechanisms will need to be fostered closer to the fast resolution of complaints. If, as an example, the complaint is about inaccuracy that can have an impact on citizens' intentions, there's little use in correcting the error once the election is over.

Complainants will continually have the right to take legal proceedings that are laid down inside the country. And there should always be an inherent appeal process that provides scope for dejected complainants or the media themselves to go for a higher judgement from an independent court of law. But in general, the thrust is on a swift, cost-free and non-confrontational resolution of disputes. This is very important, especially in a situation where there is hostility between political parties and communities. There are various types of complaints procedures, just the like different types of regulatory authorities. Where there is no single uniform procedure in place, a hybrid system may be used.

7.14 Regulating Opinion Polls

Opinion polls are an important aspect of election coverage in most of the countries as it is tried and tested method to gauge the voters' intentions and attitude towards political parties and candidates. Hence, the publication of opinion poll results often arouses strong reactions and responses from various quarters.

> Sixteen of the twenty-seven European Union countries, for example, ban reporting of polls, although timeframes range from a full month to just 24 hours before Election Day. Only three countries—Italy, Slovakia and Luxembourg—have bans of more than seven days. In many of the EU countries, legal challenges in recent years have reduced the time period over which the ban applies. (2009)

However, in the USA, the media coverage of opinion polls is considered as an important part of the freedom of expression during elections. The problem with opinion polls is that the results are not just the mere reflection of public opinion but would definitely have the ability to influence the opinions of others. It may not be an exaggeration to say that the voting behaviour of a sizable number of people would depend on the results of the opinion polls.

It is precisely for this very reason that regulations would try to control how opinion polls are presented in the media.

However, a total ban on reporting opinion poll findings is not desirable and would be impractical for the larger interest of democracy.

France had long had a ban on the reporting of opinion polls in the week before elections. In the 1997 legislative elections some newspapers broke this regulation. They included Le Parisien and La Republique des Pyrennees. *Liberation* got round the ban by putting the findings of an opinion poll on its Internet site, which is linked to the Tribune de Geneve in Switzerland. France Soir followed this by publishing a poll before the second round of voting took place. This seems a fairly clear case of a law becoming ineffective once it has fallen into disrepute—despite the fact that it had been respected for many years—and the French ban has since been reduced to 24 hours. (Darbishire 1998)

7.15 News Blackouts

In some countries across the world, there is a practice called as news blackout, a silence period on election campaign news before or during voting. It implies that the media should stop covering campaigns for a designated time preceding the voting day. The intention of such measure is to provide the voters with the opportunity for reflecting on their choice, independent of opinions and views reflected in the media. More often than not, this is a voluntary arrangement.

In France, news blackout is legislated and, hence, the government has to spend its resources to implement the same. In Israel, the Independent Broadcasting Authority has been given the responsibility of observing campaign news, especially of news blackout. News blackouts are usually for 24 hours or less. For example, Armenia, Bosnia and Herzegovina, Croatia, France, Hungary, Philippines, Russia, Singapore, Spain, Slovenia and Macedonia, have this system in place. In some countries like Indonesia, a 3-day blackout is carried out.

7.16 On Hate Speech

For those concerned with media freedom, hate speech is a very problematic issue. The concept is generally used to refer to attacks in support of national, racial, religious, sexual or other issues. The problem here is to determine as to what extent it is acceptable to limit the right to freedom of expression, when the views that are expressed are infringing the rights of others. One of the problems is that hate speech might just be a matter of opinion. One person's hate speech could be other person's considered opinion. Hence, it is rather difficult to impose restrictions on matters of expression.

When the elections are going on, this dilemma becomes even more acute for various reasons. One should remember that in a democratic set-up, it is during the elections that a variety of political opinions are expressed. If restrictions are imposed on such points of views, it potentially impedes the right to freedom of speech and also the right to participate in a democratic process. And also, the highly charged election campaigns would also sometimes lead to inflammatory statements by the candidates or political leaders which are likely to instigate people into violence.

Such issues are nearly impossible to address, especially in a country with a history of communal clashes or ethnic violence. In many instances, even the media are known to have played a role in fanning hostilities between communities. The issue of defamation also has a similar problem like that of hate speech. Defamation is an area where freedom of expression is legitimately restricted for the protection of the rights of others. However, during election campaigns, it does not have the similar impact. Debates are always part of democratic campaign. Even international jurisprudence has clearly stated that political leaders must have thick skins. In comparison to ordinary citizens, they should have less protection. So far as the media's point of view is concerned, during election campaigns, the similarity between defamation and hate speech lies in the issue of who will be held responsible for any unlawful statements. Is it the media which reports it, or is it the person who makes the hate speech?

7.16.1 International and Comparative Law

International law and various national courts do not offer any clear-cut answer to the contentious issue of balancing freedom of expression and protection of other rights. More often than not, the issue of balance is determined by national and local conditions and contexts. Although international treaties do provide a definitive basis for criminalizing hate speech, the general consensus is that in interpreting this balancing act, focus should be on promoting many voices to counter the impact of hate speech instead of banning those voices that express uncomfortable and outrageous views.

7.16.2 Media Liability

There are two important dimensions to discussion of hate speech and the media liability during elections: one is about the media reporting hate mongering by politicians and the other is about the media directly indulging in hatred. So far as the former factor is concerned, the international consensus is towards absolving the media from liability for reporting the speeches and remarks of politicians, within the limited time span of an election campaign. This implies that a journalist or media organization would not be open to either a civil or criminal case for reporting remarks by a political leader advocating hatred. But it would not absolve the journalist from a professional responsibility of balancing such statements with counter points of view.

7.16.3 Attempts to Regulate

When the media itself openly advocates or incites hatred, it cannot expect to be free from liability. In such instances, the regulatory authority is expected to monitor the media coverage very carefully. But this can create practical as well as ethical problems. For example, it would be difficult to differentiate between irresponsible reporting of violent statements and active endorsement of such viewpoints. So the distinction between editorial and non-editorial content becomes crucial. Non-editorial content, especially the direct access material, is beyond the control of the media as they are generated by the political parties. The regulatory authorities will have to determine to what extent it chooses to allow the content of direct access items.

7.16.4 International Law on Hate Speech

International consensus on the question of hate speech is determined by a balance of Articles 19 and 20 of the ICCPR. Article 19 'guarantees the right to freedom of expression; this right shall include freedom to seek, receive and impart information and ideas of all kinds, regardless of frontiers'. Article 19 then outlines possible restrictions to this right, including 'for respect of the rights or reputations of others'. Article 20 states that 'any propaganda for war shall be prohibited by law; any advocacy of national, racial or religious hatred that constitutes incitement to discrimination, hostility or violence shall be prohibited by law' (UN ICCPR, 1976).

The American Convention on Human Rights suggested the states to declare advocacy of hatred on national, racial or religious grounds as a criminal offence. The European Convention on Human Rights and the African Charter on Human and Peoples' Rights do not prohibit hate speech. The Convention on the Elimination of All Forms of Racial Discrimination (CERD) has an even broader definition prohibiting hate speech. Article 4 of CERD mandates all the states who are party to the treaty to declare 'all dissemination of ideas based on racial superiority or hatred, incitement to racial discrimination, the provision of any assistance to racial activities' as a criminal offence.

7.16.5 Decisions of International Courts

The principle of incitement to crimes against humanity itself being a crime against humanity dates back to the decisions of the Nuremberg trials of Nazi leaders in the 1940s. In recent times, the International Criminal Tribunal for Rwanda has found four journalists and the former Minister of Information guilty of incitement to genocide through media reports. The Israeli Supreme Court has stated that freedom of expression would be infringed only when there is an imminent probability that the statement will result in damage to public order. It ruled that the Broadcasting Authority had violated the rights of the leader of an extreme anti-Arab political party by reviewing his statements before broadcasting them. In Sweden, the Freedom of the Press Act prohibits the expression of threats or contempt against racial, ethnic or religious groups. In 1991, a newspaper editor was prosecuted for publishing a letter from a reader expressing racist opinions. The editor's argument was that such opinion should be allowed to given space to allow for a debate. The Hungarian constitutional court ruled a provision of the law on incitement to hatred as unconstitutional. The provision had made it an offence to insult or humiliate the Hungarian nation, or a group of the population based on religion, race or similar features.

The UN Special Rapporteur on Freedom of Expression has firmly stated that the media should not be held legally liable for unlawful statements that they cover in the course of election campaigns. This was always a controversial issue in the past, with some international authorities taking the contrary view. The assumption that the media should not be prosecuted in a civil or criminal suit for reporting the hate speeches of politicians reinforces a trend that was laid down by the Spanish constitutional court. It emphasizes the right of the public to be informed about what politicians say, even if it is unlawful and incites violence. It has to be noted here that this is different from a situation in which the media itself deliberately incites violence.

The removal of liability impacts news coverage as well as direct access programmes. Newspapers or media organizations may no longer refuse to run direct access or advertising material from a party saying that it would expose the media organizations to prosecution. For example, the German constitutional court ruled that decision on unlawful statements should be taken by the courts and not the media. But one can expect the media to perform this review process if they are definitely not legally liable. If a media organization runs the risk of being prosecuted for publishing or broadcasting the contents of a direct access broadcast, then obviously they should have the right to refuse to run it. Since it is virtually impossible to do so, the views advocated by the UN Special Rapporteur stands vindicated.

7.16.6 Right to Reply to Criticism

Right to reply, although not so popular in the media, has found favour among international tribunals of late. Journalists should accept the fact that this is a better option rather than exposing themselves to be held responsible for endorsing the opinions of one candidate or another. But if journalists have to avoid right of reply of political candidates and leaders, they should ensure that the coverage is a balanced one. During election reporting, all important political parties should get a fair say in news and current affairs programmes. Television channels are expected to offer a reasonable chance for conflicting opinions.

Sometimes, only the general approach of fairness may not be sufficient.

> The personal attack rule under the US Communication Act requires that if an attack is made on the personal qualities or character of an individual, then that person should be notified and given an opportunity to respond. In the South African election of 1994 there was a provision, slightly broader than the US personal attack rule, but based on the same principle. This is a common rule in election laws and regulations and provides a sensible opportunity to achieve balanced debate. It stated that if a criticism were levelled against a political party without that party being given the opportunity to respond at the time, or without its view being reflected, then the broadcasting licensee was obliged to give the party a reasonable opportunity to respond to the criticism. (Entman, 1995)

If a broadcaster intends to broadcast a programme in which a particular political party was criticized within 48 hours of the beginning of the vote, then it also should give the party the opportunity to respond within the programme or as soon as possible afterwards. These provisions only apply to coverage under the editorial control of the broadcaster and not to political advertisements. Brazil has a right of reply provision that applies specifically to knowingly making false statements in the course of direct access broadcasts. Here, the offended party can appeal to a judge. If the application is successful, the complainant wins an amount of free time for rebutting the false statements. The amount of free time is taken from the time granted to the offender.

7.17 Right to Access Election

The question of who is a practicing journalist is best left to journalists' organizations, although governments, through an information ministry or similar authority, have a system for accrediting journalists. Whatever the merits and demerits of these systems, an accreditation is required for journalists, specifically during elections. This is very important because the media is entitled to attend electoral events such as material transportation or the counting, which might not be open to ordinary people. The preferable system for accreditation of journalists during elections is one that is jointly carried out by the EC and the media regulatory body. Accreditation should be available to journalists belonging to local, national and international news organizations on the production of credible identification. The accrediting authority does not have the discretion to refuse credentials to any journalist.

The requirement to provide access to accredited media staff should be conveyed to the police department responsible for providing security during the elections. Accreditation identity cards consist of a laminated photo, clearly identifying the bearer as a media representative. Guidelines are also being made known to the political parties, who in turn are expected to ensure their members and supporters facilitated access to those bearing media credentials. When the approximate date of an election is announced in advance, accreditation of most local journalists can be organized in time, and there should not be a limit on the number of media personnel to be issued with accreditation. News organizations also do not have any obligation to limit the number of journalists who are accredited. But it would be reasonable for organizers of an event to limit the numbers from a particular news organization that are allowed into any particular event or location in order to provide access for the widest range of media.

A photo identity card is a very useful mechanism which works perfectly at many public events connected with elections when the security of electoral process is at stake, especially during voting or counting. At such times, logistics determine that only a limited number of journalists can have access. Journalists can operate a pool system wherein they chose their representatives to attend a particular event and later they share the information that is gathered. Even electoral officials can set up a rotation system to ensure that some journalists are present at all times, thereby allowing journalists to decide among themselves to determine that the best possible time slots are available for all of them. Hence, it can be safely said that accreditation is just an administrative tool that occasionally has a security dimension. The meaning is that, in principle, anyone can have access to the public electoral process and write or broadcast about it.

Whatever is applicable to local and national journalists with regard to accreditation and the journalists' right to access election events applies equally to any foreign media professionals who are present to cover the same. It is important to emphasize here that this is a matter of principle. The fundamental sources of the right to freedom of expression—the Universal Declaration of Human Rights and the ICCPR—explicitly define this right as entailing the communication and receipt of information 'regardless of frontier'. In most cases, there will be foreign correspondents residing in the country on a long-term basis. Since these journalists will invariably have some kind of accreditation as a condition of their residence in the country, getting accreditation to cover the election presents little problem in principle or practice. A problem is more likely to arise if the election is a matter of some international interest, with the possibility of large numbers of foreign media staff arriving at the last minute to cover it.

Exact arrangements have to be made between the agency usually responsible for accrediting foreign media and the organizers of the election. For immigration reasons, all foreign journalists will have to be accredited. But, as with domestic media personnel, neither the government nor the electoral administrators will have any discretion to decide who may or may not get the accreditation to report the election. Accreditation is an administrative measure to facilitate election coverage and not a means of keeping people out. Common sense implies that a measure of prior planning is required to determine the number of foreign journalists likely to cover the elections. If that is done, accreditation can be planned in advance and other facilities such as telephone and computer links from the media centre could also be arranged in time.

Elections are organized for the benefit of the voters and not the international media. Hence, it is prudent for the foreign media professionals to be patient and understanding of the situations. International accountability is also part of the process of organizing free and fair elections. Foreign media indirectly play the role of external election observers. It is therefore in the best interests of democracy that they are allowed in the entire election process and enabled to do their job. The media cannot cover elections properly if they are not allowed to gain access to important events and places. But unfortunately, many countries that are embarking on democratic elections for the first time do not have the experience of the media freedom culture.

The purpose of any law or regulation on media during elections is to create a situation in which the media can carry its work in a free and fair manner. Elections are not state secrets to keep the dedicated investigative journalists out. On the contrary, elections should be conducted in the public eye. Hence, the journalists should be given the fullest access to election events. The EC should understand that if the media are present at events such as briefings and news conferences, then it will be much easier for to convey its messages and concerns to the public. Transparency will also result in more credible elections, which mean more credibility for the EC also.

In order to ensure access to certain activities of the election, it is necessary for an EC to establish some form of media accreditation. In principle, this should not be necessary for all events, as the ultimate responsibility for determining a journalist should lie with the relevant media professional bodies and not the state. It is also important to ensure that access should be based on a non-discrimination principle. For example, it would be unacceptable if journalists from certain media organizations were excluded from rallies by certain political parties. The EC should explicitly state in its code of conduct that the parties should allow free access of all media to all their public events. It would be catastrophic if electoral authorities themselves start exercising any discrimination in providing media briefing materials inviting media professionals for press conference.

The media's right to access is directly linked with the principles of freedom of information. Freedom of information also means that the media are entitled to investigate and report critically on the efficiency and probity of the EC also. This scrutiny should not be determined as interference with the commission, but rather as a means to promote its credibility and efficiency. The EC should understand that efficiency is the result of a broad principle of accountability. If the media have good access to the EC, then they can report and educate the voters about its activities to the public in a quick manner.

7.18 Provisions for Public and Private Media

Most of the laws and regulations apply to both publicly and privately funded media. In addition to ethical obligations related to all journalists and broadcasters, public media are also accountable to the voters, who are ultimately their owners. Hence, it is usually presumed that public media should be politically impartial. There are also certain obligations that could be related to public media only. Direct access broadcasting is the term used to refer the access given to parties and candidates to broadcast their campaign material. It is distinguished from election campaign news coverage. Another important aspect of the responsibility of the public media stems from the government's obligation to inform and educate the voters as to how to exercise their democratic rights in an election.

7.18.1 Time Allocation to Candidates

According to the EU, particularly 'in a media system characterized by a private audio-visual media sector shaped along political lines, state broadcasters have a particular responsibility to be a genuine public service and create a forum for all campaign messages during the election period' (EU, 2009). An electoral framework should be stipulated to determine how the media will allocate direct access broadcasts. Legislation to this extent must be comprehensive and carefully worded.

Regulatory frameworks should spell out whether direct access to media by political parties will be free or paid or, as is often the case, a mixture of the two. Sometimes all parties are given free direct access but can top this up with paid advertising. Different rules are also often adopted for print and broadcast media (OSCE, 2001). In a paid advertising system, time is simply allocated to those who can pay. However, if direct access broadcasts are to be allocated by a regulatory authority, how will it be done? What criteria are required to allocate available broadcast time or print space? Is should be done on the basis of equality so that every party gets equal time. Different countries have adopted widely varying systems.

7.18.2 Equitable Direct Access Coverage

One of the basic decisions to be made in managing direct access broadcasts by the parties is to come to terms with whether time slots are to be given on the basis of equality or equity. Equality clearly means that every party or candidate gets the same access. Equity means that everyone gets fair access, meaning that a party with a large popular support should have more airtime compared to a less popular party. Equal direct access coverage stipulates that everyone is provided an opportunity to present their points of view to the electorate. The voters in turn choose whichever party is popular. The broadcaster will not have a role of determining the popularity of a political party. It is very simple system to administer, and everyone can understand it.

However, if direct access is allocated on a fair or equitable basis, it means that parties are given an opportunity to convey their opinions to the voters based on the proportion of their popular support. This means that the electorate gets to hear the arguments between the major contenders for elections along with other parties with lesser support base. The important determining factors for equitable access are a party's strength in previous elections and the number of candidates it is fielding. Usually, there will be a minimum allocation of time to all parties. In Netherlands, the regulatory authority has some discretion to allocate additional time to the major parties. Even some equality-based systems such as Denmark, Norway and Japan require political parties to fulfil the criteria such as number of seats contested or a minimum number of public signatures.

In many new democracies, the equity system qualification threshold is set low, because of the difficulty of understanding the level of popular support each party enjoys. For example, in South Africa, all parties receive a minimum allocation. But in established democracies, the threshold is usually higher. It is advisable that the threshold is determined by the number of seats contested rather than the number previously held, because it would act as a great obstacle to the emergence of new parties. Hence, in the 2010 General Elections in England, the threshold was 89 contested seats or about a sixth of the total. In parliamentary elections, the nature of the voting system clearly determines how significant smaller parties are likely to be to the larger outcome, and that will in turn determine what time allocation they receive.

7.18.3 Length of Direct Access Slots

Another important factor with regard to direct access slots is timing. Any broadcast aired at a time when everyone is asleep or at work will be of little use to political parties and candidates. So, just like commercial advertising, all parties will go after a 'prime time' slot. A method that was very much in vogue in the past was the simultaneous broadcast of party election broadcasts on all channels. But it has been generally abandoned in favour of a practice where viewer's choice is supreme. The second important issue is the length of broadcasts. Traditionally, the purpose of law and regulations has always been to ensure that slots are long enough for parties to get their messages across to the public.

But in the age of slick advertising and sound bites, it is increasingly felt that the 10-minute election broadcast is not required any more. Earlier in the UK, the main parties were allocated five 10-minute slots. But the parties preferred to forego half their time allocation in order not to bore the voters by going on at too great length. Recently, the timeslots have been shortened to less than five minutes.

7.18.4 Political Advertising

The type of ownership of media organizations and the type of regulatory mechanism influences the policymakers to take decisions on paid political advertising in mass media. When it comes to print media, generally, the issue of paid advertising for political parties and candidates is not problematic. Usually paid political advertising is allowed with limitations on campaign spending and sometimes restrictions on the kind of content used in promotional material. But paid political advertising is a tricky business when it comes to electronic media, especially in television and radio. The cost of television advertising is also quite expensive and the broadcasting stations either are owned by the government or receive their share of frequency spectrum from the public authority.

Hence, the approach with regard to paid political advertising in electronic media is quite different from that of print media. In spite of this, these factors do not automatically lead to a ban on political advertising all-together in electronic media. Countries with a long history of public-funded broadcasting stations such as France, the UK and Denmark have been strict towards paid political advertising. But countries with a stronger commercial broadcasting history such as the USA treats political advertising more liberally.

However, a country like Canada, although having a public broadcasting tradition similar to that of Britain, closely follows the USA on the issue of political advertising. The BBC has always followed a strict prohibition on commercial advertising, but French public broadcasting has allowed it since the 1960s. But both the countries maintain equally strict regulations on political advertising. When it comes to public broadcasters, they provide free direct access slot as per predetermined criteria, whereas the private broadcasters sell advertising slots to parties and candidates based on commercial interests of their organizations.

Those in favour of paid political advertising cite freedom of speech as a supporting factor. They are also of the opinion that political advertising promotes greater diversity of views, fosters public debate and is also not putting a tax burden on the ordinary citizens. Some research reports have also indicated that political advertising could be an educational tool to promote long-term change in the attitude of the public towards governance and politics. During the time of elections, news could be sensational or subjective, but sometimes political advertising could be more substantive and sophisticated. A high level of policy-related content advertised by different political parties could contribute in the increased level of political awareness among the public. The news coverage which focuses more on the candidate's character, scandals surrounding elections and the horse race is limited in this aspect.

Those who are against paid political advertising bring in the equality factor. They say that all political candidates should have an equal and fair chance to access direct broadcasting without the money factor. Many countries that favour direct access broadcast system almost have a ban on paid political advertising. Some argue that paid political adverting increases the risk of propaganda in political debates, because most of the paid political advertising are shorter in duration in comparison to direct access slots, focus mainly on selling the candidates and do not worry about developing a political discourse or a debate.

Paid political advertising would also force the candidates to depend on other funds to carry out the campaign, thereby affecting the very sanctity of democracy. In order to attract donations from different quarters, political leaders tend to utter lies and make promises which are impossible to fulfil instead of acting in the best interests of their constituencies. Despite these drawbacks, many countries across the world have a mixture of paid and free direct access broadcasting during elections. A country which follows paid political advertising should grapple with the unlimited political advertising by political parties and candidates, unlike free direct access broadcasts which provide only limited share to all the political parties. But this problem can be fixed as in the case of Canada, which has a ceiling on the amount of advertising time each political party can buy, just like allocation of time on free direct access broadcasting.

It is rather surprising to have a system which is characterized by paid political advertising without free direct access. For many years, Finland had this system in Europe. Venezuela, for example, does not allow any political advertising on its two government television channels but allows unlimited political advertising in private commercial broadcasting channels, although political parties are prepared to pay the same tariff like any other advertisers because they do get subsidy for advertising spends. In Venezuela, the incumbent government can also buy advertising. But the ruling party is not allowed to promote itself. In 1978, the then incumbent government had spent an equal amount on television advertising as the rival political parties. According to an estimate, Venezuela spends an extremely high level of amount on political advertising. Although the USA has a well-established paid political advertising system, it is well regulated in terms of curbs on campaign donations for instance.

7.18.5 Regulation of Direct Access Content

When it comes to direct access political content on broadcasting stations, the important question for the regulatory authority is to determine whether they should control the content or format of programmes and whether they are free election broadcasts or paid advertising. Given the hostility of international law on prior censorship of any kind, strict regulations are virtually ruled out. But there has to be some sort of order that needs to be in place; hence, regulation of format to ensure a serious political message is advisable and also regulation of content to prevent broadcasting of illegal material could be followed. Another important aspect to this whole issue of regulation is to determine the extent to which the media is legally liable for the political content that it broadcasts. If the media feels that they would be subject to legal proceedings for broadcasting such content, they would be the first one to favour the implementation of strict regulations on political content. Perhaps Israel provides the solution in this regard, where party broadcasts have to be approved by the EC before being aired online.

Attempts to regulate on the basis of good taste are highly difficult because it is subject to a culture. Countries can follow the Finnish approach with regard to direct access broadcast where negative campaign is strictly banned. Strictly speaking, the difference between regulation of content and form is a rather artificial one. Some countries advocate a minimum duration for political broadcasts to guarantee that there is a serious argument being made and not just an advertising message.

Among the advanced democracies, France has a far greater degree of regulation in these matters, aimed at maintain the quality of the messages being disseminated. For example, in the 1988 presidential election, only one of the broadcasts allocated to each candidate was allowed to be filmed outside the television studio and only 40 per cent of each broadcast was allowed to contain archived film materials. The aim of these restrictions was to ensure that the candidates present their policies to the camera, and in order to avoid personal attacks on opponents, archival footage was not allowed to be used without the consent of those who appeared in them.

Some countries have a blanket ban on personal attacks. But in political advertising, it is accepted that certain kinds of false statements and promises could be communicated. International jurisprudence has indicated that such statements cannot be a basis for refusing political advertising.

> It is not within the power of a broadcasting station to deny an election slot with the argument that its contents appear unconstitutional, since the competence to decide upon the constitutionality of a party and its announcements lies only with the Federal Constitutional Court. The station has however the right to expect that the party uses its airtime only for legal campaigning, and in particular that no relevant and evident breach of criminal law will take place. The station is therefore entitled to control the content of the slot and - in the case of such a breach of law - to refuse transmission. (Druck, 1995)

Another way of indirectly regulating paid political advertising is to limit the campaign spending. Although such limitations are widely applied, usually, most of the campaign budget is allocated for television advertising. Hence, the impact will definitely be felt. Canada has put breaks on spending, which means that parties can never use up their allocated share of advertising on television. South Africa has a policy which states that all political advertising is subject to legal limitation of campaign spending. Venezuela, which supposed to be the highest per capita spending on political advertising in the world, does not have any limit on spending. In the USA, all political advertisements should carry a disclaimer indicating who paid for them. In Japan, candidates are not allowed to buy broadcasting time, but the political parties can do that provided their advertisements are for support of the party and not for specific candidates.

7.18.6 Balanced Media Coverage

There is a general obligation on the public-owned media to have a balanced coverage of the election process. In some countries, these obligations would be spelt out in specific regulations, especially laws related to broadcasting. Even the public-funded media would have in its founding legislation an objective and balanced coverage of news and current affairs. More often than not, self-regulation is the only advisable approach to keep track of this. For example, the BBC keeps a record of the time given in news bulletins to the various political parties in order to keep the balance in conformity with the proportional allocation of time for party election broadcasts. There should not be any distinction between private and publicly owned media when it comes to regulations, especially with regard to the obligations that are placed upon them during elections. A common approach is to impose certain public service obligations on the private broadcast media in license agreement. This system is in place in the UK. Thus, a direct access programme regulation applies equally to public service broadcasters as well as private broadcasters.

Whatever might be the approach, the regulatory authority will have a role to play with regard to non-editorial material such as advertisement, direct access slots and voter education content aired by private broadcast media. The regulator will be responsible for supervising adherence to guidelines and rules governing media. Although the regulator will not intervene with the private media to ensure balanced news coverage, the private media should adhere to the same policies on hate speech and defamation and also be subject to a complaints procedure.

In principle, a pluralism of ideas and political points of view is best maintained by having independent media that are relatively free and without interference to carry out their business. And the regulatory authorities have to strive towards facilitating this. If the media behave in unfair manner and obstruct the information to the voters, then the regulator can always step in. This should always apply in relation to non-editorial content.

It should be noted here that most of the provisions that are laid down by the law are often violated, ignored or contradicted in practice in all sectors; media is no exception to this rule. Sometimes, governments also fail to implement laws and regulations to create a necessary level playing field to all political parties and candidates. Even the strong political outfits and leaders would have the audacity to flout all the norms and ignore the legislations in place. It is rather sad to note that, in spite of having strong constitutions with robust emphasis of freedom of expression, countries fall short of expectations when it comes to stricter implementation of existing mechanism to deal with violations.

8
International Case Studies on Media and Elections

Mass media in its various forms have influenced human life. They have basically disseminated information and entertainment to the audiences. Earlier print media was the leader for a long period of time. But in recent times, print media is facing severe competition from television and Internet-enabled social media, which is influencing the myriad responses from the society. Even the radio has also pitched in by providing news and views along with the dosage of entertainment. Of late, the Internet and Internet-enabled new media or social media have become a decisive player in the society. It has created a situation where information could be disseminated in real time across the world.

According to normative perspective, the media has to consider public interest as the single most important criterion in its functioning. Public interest criteria could be comprised of freedom to publish, pluralism in media ownership, diversity of information and diversity in terms of culture and opinion. And very importantly, media should consciously lend its support for the democratic political system, thereby acting in favour of public order and security. The security of the State is another important aspect that media should focus on. The quality of information transmitted to the general public and respecting the human rights of individual in specific and the society in general should be the guiding principles of media coverage. Media is often called as the fourth estate in the public sphere because of the kind of social responsibility that is expected from it.

Media's responsibility becomes much more important during elections, without which democracy has no meaning. Media practices during elections have come under the scanner in recent times, especially in growing economies. For example, in India, many issues such as paid news, paid advertising and preferential media coverage have been in the news recently. Corrupt and unethical journalistic practices are not only unprofessional but also detrimental to the very foundations of democracy. It is in this context, understanding the various instances from different parts of the world with regard to media and elections become important. In the following paragraphs, some of the international cases are being discussed.

8.1 Italy: Access to Media

In 1993, the Italian Parliament passed a law about access to the media by candidates with regard to the election of the House of Deputies and Senate of the Republic. The law also created a different procedure for the public and private media. The law stipulated that the public broadcaster Radiotelevisione Italiana (RAI) is accountable to the Parliamentary Address and Surveillance Commission, which consisted of 20 members of each house of the Parliament. In order to provide equal opportunities of appearances for all the political parties participating in the election campaign, the commission issued guidelines to RAI in 1994. To monitor the RAI coverage during election campaigns, it established a viewing centre. The commission also framed guidelines for direct access election broadcasts by the parties on RAI.

So far as the private media was concerned, a regulatory authority called as the Guarantor for Radio, Television and the Press was created by the law of the press, extending its mandate to radio and television in 1990. On the basis of parliamentary recommendation, the president of the Italian republic appointed the guarantor. The guarantor had additional powers with regard to elections under the law. The guarantor was mandated to guarantee equal access to political parties and the press as well as to private broadcasters. He was also responsible for determining the maximum and minimum fees for political advertising and was entrusted with the responsibility of issuing a regulation governing the coverage of elections. The guarantor was assisted by existing regulatory authorities called regional committees for radio and television which helping in a monitoring and informing role.

8.2 United States: On Bloggers

In recent times, successive US presidential elections have been termed as the emergence of the Internet elections. The 2004 elections indeed saw the emergence of a phenomenon called as blogging that very few had even heard of so far. But since then, blogs were considered as highly influential by many commentators. Some of the most celebrated bloggers were conservative who were believed to be the biggest contributors to the re-election of the then incumbent President George W. Bush.

As early as 2004, a US district court judge had ruled that the Federal Election Commission should apply the law on campaign finance on the

Internet as well. But the Bipartisan Campaign Reform Act which was passed in 2002 exempted the Internet from its provisions. This law was trying to address the issues of soft money and sham ads unconnected with the campaign. The judge was extremely critical of the commission's regulation excluding the Internet from its provision. He stated that to allow such expenditures to be made unregulated would lead to rampant corruption. To allow an entire class of political communications to be unregulated is clearly permission for a candidate to evade campaign finance laws, thereby creating a potential for gross abuse. Opposing the court's verdict, the blogging community has put forth the argument that, as journalists, they are free to express their opinions and views. They said they may be subject to regulation on the issue of whether they have received money from the candidate. Paid political advertisements on the Internet could declare as to who funded the advertisement just like the practice with broadcasters.

8.3 Canada: Prohibition on Bloggers from Reporting Results

In January 2006, the Supreme Court of Canada gave a verdict that the media could not report results of the elections until all the polling stations are closed. The prohibition extended to the Internet websites, social media and blogs as well. This verdict regulating the Internet during elections gave rise to the debates on whether the Internet could be termed as a media in the conventional sense. A lot of people would vehemently argue that the interactive and personal character of the Internet sets it apart from the traditional media such as print and electronic media. Their argument was that the Internet facilitates only debate, unlike a television channel reaching out to huge masses at a single point in time influencing their decision-making. Notwithstanding the sentiments expressed by many independent commentators and political bloggers, the Supreme Court of Canada included the Internet in the gambit of media in its all-important verdict.

In countries like Canada, the issue of reporting of election results is a serious one because it straddles several time zones. For example, even after the counting is completed on the eastern side, the polling stations would still be open on the western seaboard of the country. In 2000, a blogger from British Columbia on the West Coast named Paul Bryan deliberately broke the law and published election results on his website electionresultscanada. com. According to Section 329 of the Canada Elections Act, this was an offence. As per the section, no person was allowed to transmit the election results of a particular electoral district to the public in another electoral district before the closure of all polling stations in that electoral district.

And therefore Mr Bryan was charged with the offence and was faced with a maximum fine of $25,000. Arguing that the verdict violated the Canadian Charter of Rights and Freedom, he challenged the constitutionality of the provision. In February 2003, hearing the case, the Provincial Court of British Columbia ruled that Section 329 is justified in a freed democratic society even though it did limit the right to freedom of expression. Subsequently Mr Bryan was convicted of violating Section 329 and was fined $1,000. But in October 2003, Mr Bryan was acquitted on appeal by the Supreme Court of British Columbia, as the court found that Section 329 did infringe the Charter of Rights and Freedoms. The Canadian EC and the attorney general were granted leave to appeal the decision. But even before the case was heard, the 2004 elections were held. And the EC did not enforce Section 329 to maintain the uniform application of the Act throughout the country. As a result, the media reported the results from the eastern provinces as soon as they were announced by the authorities.

But in May 2005, the British Columbia Court of Appeal reversed the decision of the Supreme Court and termed that Section 329 was constitutional. The court gave Mr Bryan leave appeal, but the case was not heard by the time of the next general elections held in January 2006. Subsequently, the elections commission of Canada announced that it would enforce the provisions of Section 329 across the country following the court's verdict. Thereafter, a group of media organizations appeal to the Supreme Court to vacate the ban, pending Bryan's appeal, saying that the impact of reporting the results would not be huge and would infringe the expression of several millions of Canadians. But the Supreme Court ruled that the existing law would continue unaffected.

8.4 Canada: Paid Political Advertising

Canada's experiments with the regulations pertaining to media during elections are very interesting. Unlike countries with a strong presence of public broadcasters going for strict prohibitions on paid political advertising, Canada adopts a more liberal approach. The Canadian Radio-television and Telecommunications (CRCT) Commission has laid down certain guidelines for the allocation of time for paid political advertising in publicly funded broadcast stations. In 1990, the government set a ceiling for the total amount of time allowed at six-and-a half hours. The duly registered political parties were eligible to buy this airtime. Once eligible parties apply for the airtime, the CRTC arranges for a meeting of the party representatives to allocate airtime among them. CRTC retains the right to allocate airtime if the party representatives do not come to a consensus in this regard.

The criteria which was agreed upon by the representatives of the party for the allocation of time for paid advertising in the 1979 and 1980 general elections were comprised of factors such as the percentage of vote each party received in the last general election, the number of seats held by the respective parties in the national House of Commons prior to the dissolution of the same and the number of candidate nominated in the past elections. However, this was not a rigid method as it was flexible in the sense that, for example, if a party fielded a new candidate in a particular election, it was open for a different formula. But once the time was allotted for political parties, they were free to buy as much of the time that is given to them and could use that time as per their requirements. Due to the overall ceiling fixed on elections spending, no political party was able to buy its full allocation of time.

8.5 United Kingdom: On Hate Speech

In 1997, the British National Party (BNP) lodged a complaint on election broadcasts with the Broadcasting Standards Commission which looks after complaints against broadcasters including on election matters. BNP described the broadcasts as racist and stated that it may encourage racial hatred because the nature of the illustrations used in television broadcasts and sensational headlines used in newspapers would foster racial violence.

When the commission started to look into this complaint, the responses that it received from the broadcasters were interesting as it illustrated the kind of difficulties faced by the media while disseminating such extreme statements. Most of the broadcasters had sought prior legal advice to determine whether the broadcasts constituted incitement of violence, and they were told on the contrary. Their contention was that even the voluntary guidelines for broadcasters on party election broadcasts states that the party broadcast could be impartial. The BBC accepted that the broadcasts did promote a party whose opinions could be termed as offensive, but also defended itself saying that it was not the function of the broadcaster to impose its discretion of judgement on voters.

The independent London Weekend Television stated that it was unreasonable and inappropriate to expect the broadcasters to decide upon public policy, whether it is racist or not. The commission appreciated the broadcasters for behaving with responsibility and, hence, did not uphold the complaints. The commission said that it fully understands the concerns of the affected party, but it was of the view that the balance of rights are always tipped in favour of freedom of speech during election and expected the electorate to make a judgement on a party's policy at the time of voting.

8.6 Russia: Complaints Procedure

In 1993, during the parliamentary elections in Russia, an ad hoc body called as the Arbitration Court on Information Matters was set up to look into electoral disputes. During that tumultuous period, the temporary body was successful as an impartial adjudicator of ensuing disputes. Therefore, the government decided to set up a permanent complaints body in place of this ad hoc body. That is how the Russian Judicial Chamber for Information Disputes came into existence. It is an independent state body which comes under the president of Russia. The body is entrusted with the independent responsibility of performing a number of functions related to the role of the media in elections.

This disputes authority had the mandate to guarantee truthful and non-partisan media coverage in the matters of public interest besides assuring the principle of parity in the mass media. It also had the mandate to implement the principle of political pluralism in television and radio news from time to time in larger public interest. The regulations setting up the disputes body mandates that it shall adjudicate the disputes and other cases involving the mass media. The Russian law would be of great help to the chamber in resolving the disputes besides the guidance of universally accepted international law and journalistic ethics. Although it is referred to as the judicial chamber, it is not similar to normal courts. It implies that a complainant can file a separate court case even after the chamber has heard the matter.

8.7 Gambia: Communications Plan from Election Commission

In 2004, the IEC of the Gambia decided to come out with a communications plan as it felt that the commission had very limited resources with regard to communication. The commission was of the view that a communication plan would allow it to focus on human as well as material resources wherever it was needed very badly. Such a plan would also help in marshalling its resources in preparation of materials as well as distribution of the same to the media. The IEC wanted to be proactive in media relations rather than being reactive to its requests as it used to be. Besides, the commission wanted to prepare the material at its own convenient time instead of rushing through at the eleventh hour of the elections.

The IEC thought the communication plan would bring in discipline and would also help to have clarity in its objective and the kind of messages it wanted to disseminate to the different audiences at different points in time. This would enable IEC to determine the most effective media for transmitting messages. Communication planning would also allow the IEC to integrate all its communication work such as media relations, voter education programme, contacts with political parties and so on. It would also guarantee that the commission and its staff would be speaking in one voice.

In order to have better media relations, the communication plan would help the IEC to develop a toolkit of techniques and measures. Because the IEC had already completed the process of strategic planning, it was placed in a very strong position to focus on its communication needs. IEC adapted the process developed by the Canada-based Institute for Media, Policy and Civil Society. The method incorporated important factors such as situational analysis of the organization as well as external environment, the general objectives and communication objectives of IEC, the target audiences, important messages, strategies and tactics, and timeliness of delivering messages.

8.8 Zimbabwe: Biased Coverage

In recent years, Zimbabwe provides a very interesting case study of media coverage during elections because it was extensively monitored. In 1999, a non-governmental organization called the Media Monitoring Project of Zimbabwe (MMPZ) was set up to monitor the role of media during elections. It monitored a series of controversial elections right from the referendum on constitutional reform in 2000. Although elections held thereafter were characterized by biased coverage in government-controlled media, the 2000 referendum provides a clear-cut example because international norms on allocation of time were in place at that time. So each political idea should have gotten the equal direct access airtime. The government-owned media should also have covered the positions of each campaign equally.

At that time, broadcasting in Zimbabwe was still under the State's monopolistic control. The Zimbabwe Broadcasting Corporation (ZBC), formally an independent body, was running both radio and television. Even the leading daily newspaper *The Herald* was also controlled by a public trust. It was also well known in Zimbabwe that the editors were appointed and fired by the Ministry of Media, Information, & Broadcasting Services.. The launch of the privately owned *Daily News* put an end to the monopoly enjoyed by *The Herald* and its sister paper the *Chronicle* as it very quickly acquired a mass readership. Subsequently, a number of other newspaper with predominant urban presence also found acceptance among the readers.

The quantitative analysis of ZBC coverage of the 2000 referendum revealed that there was an overwhelming bias in favour of acceptance of the draft constitution. For instance, a current affairs programme in television gave 16 hours of coverage in favour of the acceptance of draft constitution whereas it gave only 1.33 hours against it. Similarly, there were 17 editorial articles in *The Herald* favouring the draft constitution and not even a single editorial against it. Out of the 38 opinion pieces published in state-controlled newspapers, all of them favoured draft constitution. The sources of information employed by new media were an important criterion in the methodology of the MMPZ.

The government-owned media also fell short of expected standards in voter education. It grossly failed to explain what the outcome of the referendum would be—an elementary drawback. It was assumed that if the campaign succeeded, the Constitution would automatically become a law. But this wasn't the case. The positive vote only implied that the constitution bill would have been placed before the Parliament for vote. There was an even catastrophic failure with regard to voter education material prepared by the constitutional commission. In an animated advertisement meant to educate the voters as to how to complete the ballot, the box next to the word 'yes' was shown as being filled with a tick. This was a clear breach of principle of impartiality.

When the elections were held in February 2000, the Zimbabwean voters rejected the draft constitution by a very large margin. MMPZ in its report mentioned about this ironical situation and, analyzing on the impact of media coverage, it stated that voters would have ignored the biased coverage or would have been repelled by it and, hence, voted against the draft constitution. Or it may have been the case of media coverage becoming irrelevant for the voters. MMPZ accepted that its methodology did not provide any basis for reaching to any conclusions. So it discounted other factors and only concentrated on the question of media coverage and concluded that the information was lamentably inaccurate and biased.

8.9 Nigeria: Impact of Media Ownership

In Nigeria, media ownership is highly concentrated in the hands of political leadership. Broadcast media is especially owned by the Central or state governments. So clearly, this would have had impact on the journalists working in these media organizations. The Institute of War and Peace Reporting (IWPR) had surveyed around 100 working journalists to find out the impact of media ownership on their journalistic practices. Around 45 per cent of the journalists who participated in the survey stated that the owners would often influence the editorial content in the media to a great deal. Even the analysis of media coverage of previous Nigerian elections has been far more damning. In 2007, the Commonwealth Observer Group stated in its report that the government's significant ownership of the broadcast media had negatively impacted the media coverage and heavily influenced the coverage in favour of incumbent political parties.

Significantly, the group also noted that a number of officials and candidates had complained to them that they have been denied airtime and media coverage because of the political bias of media owners. The Nigerian Election News Report (NENR) was set up by IWPR in March 2011 in the run-up to the national elections later in the year to enhance the abilities and skills of local journalists in covering Nigerian elections. A politically neutral NENR provided a much-needed platform for news reports in the larger public interest in the run-up the elections as well as post-election period. The observer group noted that journalists who were associated with NENR were of the opinion that it was an authentic source of fair and balanced news.

For example, a journalist named Bulama Yerima, a NERN contributor who hails from the conflict-prone state of Borno, works for state-owned Borno Radio Television Corporation. He says that the stories that he has sent to NERN would never have been aired on his station because of censorship. But unfortunately, some of the independent journalists whose wages are very poor do take bribes from the politicians in order to meet their ends. Whatever might be the reasons, when journalists accept money from the politicians, it will definitely have a diminishing effect on the democratic system.

In order to undermine the negative impact of poor wages on the Nigerian democracy, NENR offers an alternative income for the journalists by providing monetary rewards for good and balanced news reports, thereby providing the public with reliable news at a politically sensitive time. The service has also won praise from the Guild of Editors. NENR is a programme funded by USAID under IWPR that has trained over 100 working reporters and 40 trainees. The training sessions provided the journalists the confidence to carry out difficult interviews with political leaders, get views from street, write in-depth stories and cover conflict situations in a sensitive manner.

One of the trainers of the course, Ivor Gaber, a journalism professor, has said that one of the major challenges was to make the journalists think beyond the political horse trading that dominates election coverage across the media. But the people want to know who will solve their practical problems such as power shortages, pathetic roads, poor transportation and lack of employment and so on. So journalists were told to focus on issues rather than political leaders. They were also given inputs as to how to stay safe in a country where elections are violent. When violence erupted in northern Nigeria during elections, these skills proved crucial as NENR was able to report from the worst affected areas also.

8.10 Egypt: New Media and Transparency

New media played an important role in the wave of Arab Spring that began in 2011, a fact that was given considerable worldwide attention. But commentators have failed to notice that new media has also played an important role in providing transparency in post-revolution elections. This case study throws light on one such election transparency effort highlighting how 'netizens' organized to broadcast information about voting day activities in the 2011 parliamentary elections in Egypt.

In the Arab Spring revolution countries, new media is not a new phenomenon. Over the years, Facebook, blogs, Twitter, YouTube and other social networking sites gained momentum there, just as they did elsewhere. But the revolution did provide the fillip to an environment that further fostered dramatic proliferation and diversification in the usage of new media. However, it is not advisable to claim that the revolutions were results of new media alone.

The revolutions were actually born from a host of circumstances which gave rise to social unrest. An unprecedented hike in wheat prices, decades of political repression, poverty and other country-specific circumstances lead to the revolution. Precisely at this historical time, new media tapped and facilitated hitherto unprecedented means for social unrest to mobilize support and organize. New media was able to put information in the hands of ordinary citizens through its Internet-based social media. New media was also able to evade strict environments censorship in each of the Arab Spring countries.

Due to the recent development of these events, the academic discourse is still evolving, and there is still a very limited data and analysis of the role of social media in the Arab Spring. This is not to say that there is a lack of information. But the sources of information are something which is hitherto unheard of. For the first time in the tumultuous history of Arab world ordinary people were able to effectively cover the ongoing movements through Twitter, Facebook, online blogs, and videos on YouTube.

According to the 2011 Arab Social Media Report, 94% of Tunisians get their news from social media tools, as do 88% of Egyptians. "Both countries also relied at least on state-sponsored media for their information." Equally noteworthy, in Egypt there are now more users of Facebook than there are subscribers to newspapers. In addition to Twitter, Facebook and YouTube, personal blogs have been used as an insider perspective to the ongoing revolutions. The fact that these tools of social networking that have previously had a reputation strictly for socializing is now being used as sources for information and data, speaks volumes of their relevance in contemporary political mobilization. (Storck, 2011)

It is also important to note the impact of new media in providing transparency to elections which were held subsequently along with analyses of its role in facilitating the revolutions and political mobilization in general. Since the overthrow of the monarchy in 1952, the parliamentary elections held in Egypt in November 2011 was the first genuine attempt at electoral democracy that the country has witnessed. And this time around, new media was around to observe, analyze and scrutinize the elections along with the so-called mainstream media.

However, it should be noted here that the responses from the new media were not as spontaneous as one would have thought. Because less than a year before the revolutions started, the ground work was done by an activist organization called as U-Shahid (You are a witness). The organization was working on mobilizing social media savvy citizens to observe the 2010 parliamentary elections which were to be later characterized by issues such as oppression of the opposition parties, infringement of media freedom and rigged results.

So it was a near impossible task which the organization was trying to achieve through monitoring of the ensuing elections. Nevertheless, that election provided the organization the much-needed experience to put their methodologies and techniques to test and allow them to garner more support from the public. But once the revolution took place resulting in the ouster of Mubarak rule, U-Shahid found itself working in a whole new public sphere where new media was one of the major players. This was also the time in which traditional media and election observers were struggling to cope up with evolving environment of freedom in the country.

8.11 Georgia: Media Monitoring

When Georgia went for parliamentary elections in 2008, the attention was on how the country's television reporters were influencing voters' behaviour. The overarching opinion among the civil society intellectuals was that the journalists cover only press conferences and publish statements of politicians but do not worry about follow-up stories, thereby affecting the voters negatively. The Organization for Security and Cooperation in Europe (OSCE) in its April 2008 interim report focused on the coverage of the election campaign. It said that coverage given by national broadcasters Rustavi 2 and Mze and the other local broadcasters was biased. All these stations were providing positive and neutral coverage for the United National Movement, the incumbent party and opposition parties were not neutral to say the least and not positive at all.

The nine-party United Opposition Movement held almost a month-long boycott of Rustavi 2 and Mze for biased coverage. May be this could have tilted the coverage in its favour because Rustavi 2 announced later that it was cancelling coverage of the opposition parties citing that the channel was being insulted by them. OSCE reports had also stated that there was a visibility of political influence on the main television networks leading to biased coverage. Subsequently, the Georgian Public Broadcasting station, an important target of opposition's criticism during the presidential elections was praised by OSCE for improving the balance of its coverage of the campaign.

Once the new president and board of trustees came on board, the very outlook began to change with new programmes such as election debates twice in a week and a political platform presentation show once in a week. It also started offering free airtime for party presentations three times in a week. It had also signed an agreement with political parties to provide objective and balanced coverage. In spite of these positive measures taken by the public broadcaster, when it comes to paid advertising, it was still dominated by the United National Movement. Only two political parties had taken paid advertising slots. So far as the free airtime was concerned, time slots ranging from 30 seconds per hour on private stations and 60 seconds per hour in public broadcasting stations were available only for parties with more than four per cent of votes in the 2004 parliamentary elections. And hence, the dominance of leading political parties continued, notwithstanding the positive developments that took place post the presidential elections in 2008.

8.12 South Africa: Gender and Elections

In 2009 Jacob Zuma emerged as the president of South Africa when the elections were held. The African National Congress (ANC) narrowly missed a two-thirds majority in the elections. When it comes to gender parity in politics after the elections, South Africa rose to third place from seventeenth in the global ranking of women in parliament with 11 per cent increase in women's representation, rising from 34 to 43 per cent. Now Rwanda is at the top with 56 per cent, followed by Sweden with 47 per cent ahead of South Africa.

Although elections and media coverage of the same were deemed free and fair, some observers lamented that the media coverage lacked depth. Institutes like the Freedom of Expression Institute expressed apprehensions about lack of serious coverage of issues involved in the elections. With regard to the media coverage of gender issues, it constituted only 2.4 per cent of the overall election coverage. Even the coverage given was stereotypical. For example, most of the reports in media focused on president elect Jacob Zuma's polygamous lifestyle and was centred on speculating who would be the first lady and what would be the cost that tax payers have to be burdened with and so on. Stories focusing on his opinion on the Constitution and women's rights rarely found place in the media coverage.

Freedom of expression means that views from different quarters are heard. Formal censorship is a way of silencing such voices. But sometimes, a far more worrying censorship takes place when the views and voices of certain groups of society are systematically excluded from the mainstream media. That is how gender issues get sidelined in the public sphere. In South Africa, women constituted 24 per cent of all sources in 2009 elections, which is higher than the global average of 21 per cent given by the GMMP in 2005). In spite of the presence of 43 per cent of women members in the Parliament, the responses from editors was that they only report what is newsworthy.

According to Kubi Rama, deputy director of Gender Links, media coverage of elections were largely dominated by events rather than issues. Had issues such as poverty, education, crime, gender violence, HIV and

AIDS been covered with seriousness, had journalists bothered to consult them on critical matters of life and death, the voices of women would have been loud and clear, he stated. Many examples of blatant gender stereotypes were found when the qualitative analysis of election coverage was conducted by Gender Links. The male dominance of politics was characterized by many news reports bearing the headline 'All the President's Men'. And news stories with headlines like 'All the President's Women' focused on rumours and allegations concerning women.

Despite this. many positive developments were also witnessed. For example, sexist comments by ANC youth league leader Julius Malema on women had prompted a well-positioned opinion piece in the *Mail* and *The Guardian*. Likewise, SABC International, South Africa's public service broadcaster hosted a debate on polygamy in Africa with panellists and questions from the viewers over the phone. A lot of South African newspapers had also published lengthy profiles of leading women in politics, including new and emerging leaders in opposition parties.

Although white male commentators and analysts dominated the media, the *Mail* and *The Guardian* frequently used black female experts and opinion leaders, such as Nikiwe Bikitsha and Phumla Gobodo-Madikizela, who expressed refreshing views on the gender issues. The *Mail* and *The Guardian*'s election coverage was balanced as it consistently consulted ordinary men and women in equal number in presenting their views on the elections. *The Guardian*, in fact, brought out a supplement on women's economic empowerment. Although coverage often ignored gender dimension, there is a growing recognition within the South African media that focusing on both sexes definitely makes a good business sense for media organizations.

8.13 India: Ashok Chavan's 'Paid News' Case

In May 2014, the Supreme Court bench comprising Justice Surinder Singh Nijjar and Justice Fakkir Mohammed Ibrahim Kalifulla dismissed a plea by former Maharashtra Chief Minister Ashok Chavan, who had challenged the Delhi high court order, holding that the commission can inquire into the allegations of paid news if the same was not disclosed by the candidate while filing his or her election expenses returns. The apex court had stipulated that the EC hold a day-to-day hearing and decide the complaint in 45 days.

In the 2009 assembly election, Mr Chavan had won from Bhokar constituency in Nanded. His opponent, Madhav Kinhalkar, had filed a complaint with election commission, accusing him of hiding expenses on a 'paid supplement' titled *Ashok Parva* (the era of Ashok) in a leading Marathi daily. However, Mr Chavan and the daily's management had denied the allegation and maintained that the supplement was not a paid one. Thereafter, the election commission started its inquiry into the allegations. The Delhi high court in 2010 declined Mr Chavan's plea seeking the stay of the proceedings. He had then moved the apex court in November 2011 seeking the halt to the entire exercise, which the bench dismissed.

8.14 India: *State of Uttar Pradesh V/S Raj Narain*

On 12 June 1975, Justice Jagmohanlal Sinha of the Allahabad High Court convicted the then Prime Minister Indira Gandhi of electoral malpractices and not only disqualified her from the Parliament but also debarred her from holding any elected post for 6 years. Indira Gandhi had won the 1971 Lok Sabha election from Rae Bareli constituency in UP, defeating socialist leader Raj Narain, who later challenged her election alleging electoral malpractices and violation of the Representation of the People Act, 1951. He had alleged that her election agent Yashpal Kapoor was a government servant, and that she used government officials for personal work.

'The respondent no. I (Indira Gandhi) was thus guilty of a corrupt practice under section 123(7) of the Act ... accordingly stands disqualified for a period of 6 years from the date of this order ...', Justice Sinha pronounced to a stunned Indira Gandhi who was present in person in the court. But on an appeal filed by Indira Gandhi, Justice VR KrishnaIyer—a vacation judge of the Supreme Court—on 24 June 1975m granted a conditional stay on Justice Sinha's verdict allowing her to continue as prime minister. However, she was debarred from taking part in parliamentary proceedings and draw salary as an MP.

Interestingly, the very next day she imposed the Emergency, suspending all fundamental rights, putting opposition leaders in jails and imposing censorship on the media. While the Emergency was in force, the Supreme Court later overturned her conviction on 7 November 1975. It could be argued that Justice Sinha's judgement changed the course of Indian politics as Mrs Gandhi was forced to impose the Emergency and had to change the law retrospectively to get over his judgement. That judgement was hailed all over the world as a great triumph of an independent judiciary in India.

8.15 India: T. N. Seshan and Electoral Reforms

T. N. Seshan was the chief election commissioner of India who served in his office from 12 December 1990 to 11 December 1996. He was revered for his extraordinary stint as the chief election commissioner of India. Seshan, who believed in democratic principles, wasn't afraid of taking on the mighty and powerful in the political circle. He was credited with ushering in electoral reforms in India which were continued by his successors.

Seshan was different from his predecessors. He acted swiftly in resolving electoral cases. He would hear the case once and settle it. During his tenure, he reviewed more than 40,000 cases of alleged false election returns and disqualified 14,000 potential candidates for public office. Seshan also insisted that state employees who are deputized should fall under the jurisdiction of the commission. Hence, it was essential that they obey the directives of the commission and perform their duties honestly and efficiently. The Supreme Court also ruled in favour of commission's authority over deputized personnel. One of the positives results of the verdict was that the illegal 'commands' of local officials and political leaders were drastically curbed.

The Parliament, wary of Seshan's tussles with bureaucracy and the political system, amended the Constitution and added two additional commissioners to share power with the chief election commissioner. Although he fought back for a brief period of time, Supreme Court ruled that the position of the chief commissioner vis-à-vis the other two commissioners was 'no more than that of the first among equals'.

Seshan also made great efforts in creating public awareness about voters' right. The commission circulated publications on voters' rights and duties. Voters were constantly reminded that it was their responsibility to safeguard the freedom and fairness of elections and also to choose their leaders wisely. In 1992, in order to negate the rampant practice of voter impersonation, Seshan called for the government to issue photo identification cards to all legal voters. However, politicians bitterly opposed this move. After waiting for 18 months for the government to act, Seshan announced that if identification cards were not issued to the voters, elections would not be held after 1 January 1995. In fact, a number of elections were postponed because voters were not issued cards. Finally the Supreme Court had to intervene and ruled that voting was an inherent right of citizens, thus voting could not be postponed indefinitely due to any reason.

In an effort to curb overspending by candidates during elections, Seshan implemented Section 77 of the Representation of the People Act of 1951, which made it obligatory for the candidates to keep accurate accounts of expenditures. He added the following requirements: (a) all election expensed must be explicitly accounted for, (b) the accounts must be filed accompanied by an affidavit of oath and (c) the accounts must be certified by the district election officer. He also brought in campaign spending limits: 20,000 to 40,000 rupees for assembly candidates and 150,000 to 170,000 rupees for Parliament candidates. One of Seshan's more controversial policies concerned with election displays. He prohibited election graffiti, noisy campaign convoys, loudspeakers, wall writing and posters on public and private property. Notwithstanding some of his controversial policies, T. N. Seshan is best remembered as the man who brought in electoral reforms in India.

9
Media and Elections in India

Media plays an influential role in the political process, right from creating and moulding public opinion to agenda setting. Media would also keep a tab on the people who are in power by expecting transparency in their activities. Imagine a situation where the government is controlling the entire information process. Obviously there will be no scope for accountability in such a dispensation. That is exactly why an independent media is needed to act as an effective observer and critically monitor the government's power and influence over its citizens. With the emergence of TV and radio networks, many governments in Europe and America came out with new legislations to enable the broadcast media to remain neutral. Before we move further in examining this issue, it would be apt to understand the role of media in defining the political future of a country during elections.

Media has an undisputable role in a democracy. A free media is considered the watchdog of the government. A stock of the media behaviour, therefore, is crucial, largely because of the process of agenda setting and gatekeeping attached with media. Every media student knows that media acts as a gatekeeper in setting the limits for political discussion and sometimes even for candidacies for public office. A disconcerting fact is media being an oligopoly. This is a concern in many liberal democracies as this means only a few individuals have enormous powers to influence the political opinion and destabilize the existing political establishment.

Hence, it is important that media doesn't set the agenda of the selected big business houses that control it and that only journalistic considerations form the basis of gatekeeping. Else the polity of a nation would be threatened by crony capitalism—an unholy nexus of politicians and big business houses. Any such prospect would spell doom for our democratic political structure. Internationally, the power of the media to define politics has been forensically examined. In Western liberal democracies, the governments have been pressured to institute major inquiries into where the buck stops in media governance. It has been a constant endeavour of the torchbearers of free opinion to ensure that media does not just remain a propaganda tool of vested powers but plays a larger role of creating informed citizens with constructive public opinion.

The media is a vital cog in a democracy. In fact, the survival and success of Indian democracy owes a lot to the vigour and vibrancy of the media institutions. In the past few years, both electronic and print media have grown enormously in India. And this explosion has led to a situation wherein voters are flooded with a surge of information, thereby narrowing to some extent the gap between politicians and voters. More significantly, the nature of media has tilted from government control to overwhelming private control. The new private media is hard-hitting and questions everything. It has been a driving force behind the exposure of many scams. Indian media was responsible for making corruption a significant issue in the 2014 general election. Media is at the heart of modern political life, especially during the time of elections. But media performance during elections sometimes leaves a lot to be desired.

With thousands of newspapers and hundreds of news channels in several languages, Indians are spoilt for choice and diversity. But in many ways, such growth and diversification has come at the cost of accuracy, journalistic ethics and probity. Even as the number of news sources has grown exponentially, the information given by these countless sources is quite similar. This raises serious concerns about the trivialization of content and the impact of the increasing concentration of media ownership in the hands of large corporate groups. Since much of the media is privately owned and driven by profit motives, commercial compulsions distort the free and fair dissemination of information. Television news, which reaches out to those who cannot read and write, has clearly become an integral part of our democracy and must be central to an analysis of media and elections. Besides, it sets the agenda which the print media is prone to follow.

The role played by the media during the 2014 Indian general election is very significant, and it needs an introspective and critical analysis and debate. Never has the mass media been misused to set the political agenda like it happened during the election. A lot of evidence can be cited to prove that opinions had been manufactured, structured, slanted and bent to suit a particular political party in the run-up to the impending Lok Sabha election. The media coverage for the 2014 election began as early as December 2012 when Narendra Modi was re-elected as the chief minister of Gujarat for the third consecutive time. It was an ideal situation for him to step in as a prime ministerial candidate for the BJP given the anti-incumbency factor working against the ruling UPA. Media played up the 'Modi wave' until the BJP was defeated by the AAP in the Delhi assembly election in December 2013 in a stunning manner. Television news channels and social media had little time for any leader other than Prime Minister Modi.

As indicated by the media, Mr Modi could guide the nation out of the emergency by giving solid initiative, and the administration vacuum was driving the baffled electorate into the BJP's lap. This vigorously developed construct—unequivocal administration is the solution for India's burdens—has been spread by the corporate segment and the urban working class, which saw the Congress as degenerate, dynastic and wasteful, and a neglectful supporter to poor people. This involved a high-voltage crusade to increase hostility to incumbency against the UPA, which unfurled with a supported assault on the UPA government. Given that the white collar classes are furious about the financial stoppage and consider the UPA in charge of it, it is not shocking that the political 'talk' has been amazingly homogeneous in its accentuation and pushing of the accompanying focuses: reprimand of the UPA, particularly defilement, feedback of the impediments of Congress initiative and the line and the Gujarat model of advancement. Seemingly, the media has moved from 'assembling assent' to 'assembling dispute' against the current government before it returns again to making assent.

Taking a clue from Mr Modi, a few media houses and editors have named the 10 years of UPA standard as a 'squandered decade', totally overlooking its positive commitments. Going further, we were informed that nothing has happened in the last 60 years and voters must give Mr Modi a shot of 60 months to change India. In one stroke, the entire past has been pulverized. However, the media did not challenge this, in actuality, and it lent confidence to this by basically rehashing the corruption of India's contemporary history. The media has been close-lipped regarding the critical destitution-easing activities of the UPA government. However the rights-based welfare plans were under assault and berated as 'dolenomics', despite the fact that it has gradually offered assent to the rule of social obligation satisfying individuals' fundamental needs. There was an extraordinary assault on the National Food Security Act (NFSA) as an occasion of flippant populism that will crush the development.

Reporting for the 2014 elections will be remembered for its almost complete spotlight on individuals, scarcely ever on the issues at the ground level. As such, this is the manner in which the political talk in the run-up to the 2014 general elections shaped up. Modi had assumed an overwhelming persona, overshadowing every single other element of the political talks and issues. Short of adequate staff during the elections, TV news channels depended vigorously on the live feeds from the two major parties, most obviously from the Modi camp. This new pattern permitted channels to connect to the BJP's live feeds and transfer it to clueless viewers, resulting in media hype. It is just when a few editors brought up uncomfortable issues in their respective internal meetings that a few channels began distinguishing it as 'BJP feed' on-screen in an undersized font.

One irreplaceable impact of this build-up was over and again recommending a Modi wave. The implied Modi wave was witnessed only on lopsided media surveys, and not in ground level reports. The emphasis was completely on identities, disregarding the bigger issues including the election itself. All in all, different components matter more: the choice of candidates, local level alliances and the performance of state governments. What frequently gets neglected is that opinion surveys reduce the media coverage of elections into a horse race and a media spectacle. There were convincing reasons why some social researchers contend that opinion polls not only measure opinion but also boost false awareness and end up as self-satisfying predictions.

The media's fixation on a one-sided narrative was overwhelming political diversity and pluralism of elections, especially the clout of regional parties and marginalized sections and their worries. There is a propensity to acknowledge obviously the terms of discussion as set by specific groups, paying little heed to whether this clashed with the current standards of the majority rule system. Subsequently, the media was not vexed about Mr Modi's part in the 2002 Gujarat riots; it did not scrutinize the procedure of examination, especially the role of the special investigation team (SIT) that prompted his acquittal by a lower court. Rather, the media obliged his exoneration as the vindication of his purity in the 2002 riots in spite of the availability of contrary evidence.

There have been various instances of the routes via which the mass media constructed images that could have been appropriated for political purposes. The media's way to deal with the Ayodhya issue is a valid example. Once again, secularism and pluralism have been reduced to 'minority appeasement', pretty much as it was done in the 1990s when L. K. Advani set 'positive secularism' against 'pseudo-secularism'. Rather than venturing back and analysing the conspicuously political motivation behind the recharged critique of secularism, the media as a rule assimilated the political agenda and argument as set out by the Hindu nationalist groups. What represents the readiness of the media to get tied up with the promulgation, paying little respect to whether it was a precise representation of his genuine political aims and individual states of mind? Edward S. Herman and Noam Chomsky, in their 1988 book *Manufacturing Consent: The Political Economy of the Mass Media*, discussed the impact of 'propaganda' and 'systemic biases' in the mass media and explained how consent for monetary, social, and political policies is manufactured in the minds of the people, a consequence of the way advertising and media ownership is structured.

The significant changes in the media scene that were apparent in the new structure of media ownership can better explain the phenomenon. The pattern was clear: media houses have transformed into huge business; huge business groups are purchasing tremendous stakes in the media; political leaders, political parties, and people with political affiliations own and control expanding segments of the media; and media proprietors are also entering into politics in a big way. The media is huge business and enormous business is in the media. There should be no worries about the expanding centralization of media possession and cross-media ownership in the hands of huge corporate houses which firmly sponsored Mr Modi as the next prime minister since he had pushed the political discourse more toward markets, reforms, and investments. The media's treatment of the AAP changed inversely once the political party began hitting at corporate corruption, through their position on power tariffs, and all the more perceptibly after AAP party leader, Arvind Kejriwal, went to Gujarat to 'review' and 'assess' the Gujarat model of development and started bringing up issues of crony capitalism in Gujarat.

Make no mistake, there's a media bias out there. The media in India does not merely report and provide coverage, it is very much a part and parcel of Indian politics and electoral system. Although there may not be a collective attempt on the part of the media to block independent voices, it does take sides and, more often than not, tends to editorialize news reporting. However, it should be noted here that media bias is not a unique feature of the Indian media. It is true of media practices everywhere. For instance, the bias was very clear in major sections of the US media coverage of the 2012 presidential election. But it is commendable how the US press has handled accusations of media bias. Not denying the tilt, the US mainstream media identified those charges of partisan coverage and put them on record, while some of them have not only taken note but have also attempted to analyse the charges in the public domain. Hence, there was a serious debate in the USA on the role of media and its biases. Numerous leading US newspapers are quite open about their political affiliations, but strangely in India media bias is not a topic of discussion during or after the elections!

Interestingly, the Indian media's perception and practice of fairness and objectivity is to systematically pose questions to all political leaders and criticize all parties. The media is allergic to any discussion on bias. The freedom of the media is supposed to be sacrosanct despite mounting evidence of distorted practices such as 'paid news', 'coverage packages', 'private treaties' with big corporations, and 'doctored opinion polls', not to mention a slant towards the Right wing in all media platforms, including satire, spoof, and parody. Yet, the media is still averse to criticism, which is legitimate and long overdue.

9.1 National Emergency and Press Censorship

During the summer of 1975, as then Prime Minister Indira Gandhi became more threatened by the increasing criticisms of her government, she declared a state of emergency in the country. Thereafter, she took control of the press, prohibiting reporting of all domestic and international news. The government expelled many foreign correspondents and withdrew accreditation from more than 40 Indian reporters who usually covered New Delhi. In recent years, this has probably been the one of the most significant events in the history of the Indian press. Post-Independence, the Congress party had remained in power in one form or another until March 1977.

The 1975 Emergency was a major turning point in the history of the country. The government suspended the fundamental rights of the citizens and imposed press censorship. Dissent was smothered mercilessly by the high handedness of the authorities at the helm. Arbitrary actions were initiated without the fear of punishment. Initially, the country was in a state of shock and stupor, failing to comprehend the ramifications and impact of the governmental actions. Overnight, tyrants who were close to the seat of power sprouted at all levels.

The reason why the Emergency was a ground-breaking event was the abject manner in which the pressmen caved in. The media ownership began to realize that journalists only boast of big things and courage, but hardly ever displayed the courage when it came to confrontation. The Emergency also exposed the bureaucrats and others government functionaries who were found to be timid. It also exposed journalists who, in the words of BJP leader L. K. Advani, 'were asked to bend but began to crawl'. After Mrs Gandhi came back to power in 1980, the press was generally run by the proprietors. They developed the clout due to the failure of journalists to live up to the expectations during the Emergency. This was also the time when the newspaper started to transform as a product. Media owners were more interested in sales of the newspaper and were not interested in lofty ideas which most of the journalists did not practice. This was the time when the Working Journalists Act was pushed to the background. Proprietors introduced the contract system. As the journalists were given contract for 2 or 3 years, they 'behaved' as per the likings of the owners. They began to lose their sheen because the job was more important than ideals.

Right after Independence, India adopted democratic principles and declared itself as a democratic socialist country. However, numerous incidents that occurred during the reign of Indira Gandhi clearly brought out the fact that the country was threatening to drift away from parliamentary democracy. The state of national emergency, which is legally valid under the Indian Constitution, lasted for about 19 months. Unable to tackle the mounting pressure on the government by the opposition parties on issues of corruption, inflation and economic instability, the government opted the wrong way out by imposing the Emergency. Indira Gandhi's government, instead of taking this up as a political challenge, clamped national emergency and imprisoned the opposition party leaders, including all critical voices from the media.

The Indian Constitution considers freedom of the press as an integral part of 'freedom of expression'. Indian courts, in the past, have treated press freedom as a fundamental right. Article 19 of the Indian Constitution implies limitations on the various types of freedom. It says that the 'states shall be authorized to make any law restricting the exercise of the freedom of speech in the interest of the security of the state, friendly relations with foreign countries, public order, and decency and good conduct'. The states are also authorized to apply restrictions on press freedom 'in order to check slanderous articles and promotion of disaffection towards or contempt of court'.

With the radio already under government ownership, Indira Gandhi successfully controlled the media in India for over a year and a half. Unfortunately, during censorship, most of the dailies 'filled with fawning accounts of national events, flattering pictures of Gandhi and her ambitious son, and not coincidentally, lucrative government advertising'. But two prominent English language dailies, *The Indian Express* and *The Statesman* were an exception to this. They fought courageously against Indira Gandhi's arbitrary decisions of press censorship. Despite some bold stands taken up by these two newspapers, it was quite evident that Indira Gandhi had a strong hold on the Indian press.

9.1.1 1978 Chikmagalur Bye-election

In 1978, a small, rural parliamentary constituency in South India named Chikmagalur made political history for the whole South Asian subcontinent. During the March 1977 general elections, Indian voters mortified the Congress party government and turned it out of office. However, in 1978, a record 76 per cent of the eligible voters cast its ballots to give back the dubious former prime minister of India, Mrs Indira Gandhi, to the national Parliament. As Western daily papers have solemnly recognized, Gandhi's presence as the informal leader of the parliamentary opposition put her one step from the office of prime minister.

It was the ruling Janata Party's goal to make any electoral challenge against Mrs Gandhi, enormous or little, a noteworthy trial of its political strength. So Chikmagalur turned into the scene of boisterous standoff battling, with the Janata Party sending all its gathering powerhouses, including even the prime minister, Mr Desai himself, to battle against Gandhi. The Janata put before the electorate its vision for a rural India, with Desai charging that a vote in favour of Mrs Gandhi was 'a vote in favour of dictatorship'. And the Janata Party lost. 4 November 1978 was Mrs Gandhi's day. The triumph was the most vital stride in her offer for a political comeback.

As far back as her disfavoured exit from office in March 1977, the restriction has endeavoured through false arrests, anti-corruption commissions, criminal accusations and even dangers to change the Constitution, to close Gandhi from the eye of the general public. It is to the credit of a little gathering of political consultants and Mrs Gandhi's own bold battling that the Chikmagalur decision was a success. Her advisors, specifically the Karnataka State Chief Minister Devraj Urs, who also worked as her campaign director since Chikmagalur falls inside his state, rejected Janata Party's provocations to battle on false issues. In mid-July, when disillusionment with the Janata Party's mismanagement was at a high point, Urs and Gandhi picked the constituency, the planning and all the battle issues. In all cases, the Janata Party was outflanked. Gandhi began with a strong pro-science, pro-industry campaign style, and the largely rural population, much to the World Bank's dismay, chose industrial development, despite the Janata's ruralist slogans.

9.1.2 Mrs Gandhi's Campaign

Gandhi's campaign strategy was to attack against the Janata government's policies. The ground for her battle was laid when Gandhi, at the invitation of Urs, laid the foundation stone for the Mangalore steel plant. The plant is a few miles away from Chikmagalur. Gandhi's plan of action was critical of the Janata government and the World Bank backed back-to-the-village movement. When Congress-I made the announcement of her candidacy in mid-July, it was ridiculed, but within short span of time, the small constituency transformed into a mini India. Gandhi addressed seven to eight election meetings in a single day, and made visits to the villages to discuss the impact of national policy and the need for industry and science with her audiences. She did not speak like the representative of the state. Gandhi spoke as a national leader in English or Hindi and Urs translated her speeches to the people. Gandhi deliberately chose a constituency from South India because she thought, given the Janata government's policies against her, that she could not have received a fair election in the north. A political analyst summed up the electoral atmosphere of the Gandhi campaign: 'A large section of the rural population thinks that in Chikmagalur they are voting for the next Prime Minister'.

9.2 Political Slogans

Although Indian political campaigns may not be compared with US elections, the slogans used in campaigns do provide the humour, interest and enthusiasm to the voters and experts alike. The history of Indian politics is adorned with so many unforgettable slogans such as *Garibi Hatao* (eradicate poverty) and *Jai Jawan, Jai Kisan* (hail the soldier, hail the farmer). Any good slogan can bring people together towards a cause, irrespective of religion, caste, language and regional considerations. This becomes especially important for a country like India which has such diversity. An analysis of the history of India's election slogans provides insights about the country's political history. For instance, former Prime Minister Indira Gandhi secured a landslide victory for Congress Party in 1971 with the powerful *Garibi Hatao* slogan which reverberated across the country.

9.2.1 Desh Bachao

During 1977, the Indian economy was in a dire straits and as a result the poor people of the country saw a ray of hope in the opposition party's slogans such as *Indira Hatao, Desh Bachao* (remove Indira, save the nation) and *Sampoorna Kranti* (total revolution). These slogans seemed to transcend divisions across the country. When Indira Gandhi's elections ended in a catastrophe, as the court declared her win as invalid, she clamped a state of emergency in the country, jailing opposition leaders and putting severe restrictions to freedom of the press. As a response to it, opposition parties united to form the Janata Parivar and fought the elections with the above-mentioned slogans. The bloc swept the 1977 election.

India's first Prime Minister Jawaharlal Nehru was better known for his speeches than slogans. However, he did coin the famous slogan *Hindi-Chini*

Bhai-Bhai (Indians and Chinese are brothers) in the early 1950s. But this graciousness backfired due to the deteriorating relationship between the countries regarding border disputes. This resulted in a full blown war in 1962. His successor, Lal Bahadur Shastri, came up with country's most popular slogan after independence when India was fighting the war with Pakistan in 1965. There was a severe food shortage at that time. It was at this critical juncture Shastri gave the slogan *Jai Jawan, Jai Kisan*, which boosted the country's sagging confidence at the time of a crisis and also helped the Congress party's success at the elections.

The slogan was tweaked by former Prime Minister Atal Bihari Vajpayee after the nuclear tests in 1998 as *Jai Jawan, Jai Kisan, Jai Vigyan*. The slogan emphasized the increasing investment done by the government in science and technology at the time. In 1996, the BJP came to power on the back of many famous slogans centred around Mr Vajpayee, whose clean image made him an ideal face for the party during elections. *Sabko Dekha Bari Bari, Abki Bari Atal Bihari* (we have seen several others, but now it is Atal Bihari's turn) was the catchphrase among the supporters of BJP in the run-up to the elections. But the most famous slogan which related directly to a political leader was coined for Indira Gandhi. During the Emergency, Congress party member Dev Kant Baruah created the slogan Indira is India and India is Indira indicating the power that Mrs Gandhi wielded at the time.

9.2.2 Modern Slogans

In the 2004 national general elections, political parties hired professional public relations firms to create slogans and run campaigns. By outsourcing this work, parties also ran the risk of falling out of favour with the people. The BJP had a taste of this after its much-publicized India Shining campaign tanked in a big way in 2004. At the time, voters recognized the fact that India's economy had been performing fairly well, but was far from shining. As a result, they chose the Congress party over the BJP. The Sonia Gandhi-led Congress fought the elections with a more realistic slogan *Aam Aadmi Ko Kya Mila?* (what did the common man get?), offering a strong counterpoint to the India Shining campaign.

When it comes to slogans, regional parties appear to be performing better than their national counterparts. For instance, in 2011, Trinammol Congress chief Mamata Banerjee ran a successful election campaign with a popular slogan *Maa, Maati, Manush* (mother, motherland and people) and came to power in West Bengal. After decades of rule by communists, people saw freshness in Mamata's campaign and gave her a chance to rule West Bengal as per her vision.

9.3 Revival of *Garibi Hatao*

In 2006, the Congress Party-led UPA government had chosen to restore the populist slogan *Garibi Hatao* initially promoted by Indira Gandhi amid the 1971 parliamentary elections, with the expectation that it could give political boost to another wave of neoliberal reforms. In particular, the UPA government was intent on opening up the public infrastructure projects to private capital, introducing 'market-pricing' for electricity, privatizing public sector companies and establishing special economic zones (SEZs), emulating the Chinese model in which companies enjoy tax benefits and relatively less stringent labour regulations.

As soon as the UPA cabinet decided to place the *Garibi Hatao* slogan at the centre of the government's propaganda, the then Prime Minister Manmohan Singh and other important ministers left for a series of big business programmes at which they promised to intensify the pace of economic reforms. The Congress wanted to clear the confusion within the business circles that the resurrection of Indira Gandhi's slogan of *Garibi Hatao* would not affect the business class. Even with revised 20-point programme *Garibi Hatao* would be updated with special reference to economic reforms of the Indian economy. Congress's revival of *Garibi Hatao* was not just a matter of electoral calculations. The Congress and the UPA were involved in a precarious and increasingly untenable balancing act, posing as a party concerned with the *aam aadmi* (common man), simultaneously implementing neoliberal, socio-economic reforms; increasing massive military spending; and seeking to have a strategic partnership with US imperialism.

To its great surprise, the Congress-led UPA shot to power in the 2004 elections after the campaign made a consorted appeal to popular discontent over the increasing unemployment, economic insecurity and poverty that have resulted from the neoliberal programme. But predictably, the Congress' promise of 'reforms with human face' has proven to be a cruel hoax. The UPA government has pursued an economic and geopolitical agenda that is all but a carbon copy of the policies implemented by its predecessor, the NDA.

9.4 Advertising and Politics

Why is there a need to go to town and take control of the airwaves and flock the Internet? What is exactly at stake here? Have political parties finally understood the power of branding and consumer marketing? And more significantly, does this kind of advertising even work? Let's focus on few instances. The first election 'slogan' was *Garibi Hatao* coined by Indira Gandhi in the early 1970s. It might seem a very simple idea today, but it reflected a vision that was attractive to the larger people it targeted. Doordarshan was still in its nascent stage, and even if we were to presume that some of the newspapers were particularly favourable to the Congress apparatus, one has to concede that it was a powerful slogan that fired the imagination of the people. And non-paid media was there to take the message across.

The true era of political advertising started in 1984 when Rajiv Gandhi employed an advertising agency to manage the advertising campaign for the general elections after the demise of Indira Gandhi. When the Congress won the elections, the advertising agency was lauded for its 'brilliant' campaign. But strangely, 5 years later, it was blamed for its horribly negative campaign, Mr Clean, over the Bofors scam. This seems to be a simplified analysis. No sane person would have bet against Rajiv Gandhi and the Congress in the aftermath of Indira Gandhi's assassination. And it would have been pretty clear that the Bofors scandal, which was the first publicly discussed corruption scandal in the country, would claim its pound of flesh. Advertising might not have had a serious role to play in the fortunes of the Congress, but it still ended up getting acclaimed initially only to have bad reputation later.

In 1996, the Congress campaign centred on the 'Gandhi' brand name and the sacrifice made by the family for the country, and BJP's campaign was totally about patriotism. Interestingly, the 1996 election results did not favour any one political dispensation. In the late 1990s, BJP marketed brand 'Atal' to counter the Congress' 'Gandhi' brand. But it is the 2004 elections that most publicity pundits have a say about. A track record of good economic growth prompted the BJP to come out with the India Shining campaign.

The target group was huge and the State-run Doordarshan was chosen because of its wide reach. On-ground campaigns were undertaken in the form of *yatras* by top BJP leaders across the country. It was during the same election campaign that the Congress Party also came out with a simple yet powerful slogan *Congress ka Haath, Aam Aadmi ke Saath* (Congress' loyalty rests with the common man). Congress believed and executed in its campaign that the much talked about prosperity had continued to elude the common man. Before the ballots were cast, most experts believed that the BJP's India Shining campaign was a winning strategy as they counted on the impressive growth rates in the years preceding the elections. Even the social indices were seeing an upward trend at the time. Many experts thought that the campaign 'reflected the mood of the nation'. But the whole country knows how well the campaign went for BJP. After the results were out, one of the major reasons cited by political pundits was the failure of the India Shining campaign and the successful campaign strategy of the Congress centred on 'aam aadmi'.

9.4.1 Failure of 'India Shining'

In independent India, every election was fought on some slogan or the other. Hence, it came as a great surprise that the 2004 general elections were not fought on any political slogan. The ruling NDA instead chose to rely on what it termed as a 'feel-good factor.' To strengthen this, the government spent close to ₹5 billion on the India Shining advertising campaign. NDA leaders were claiming from rooftops that they have done more for the country in just 5 years compared to previous governments that ruled for 50 years. According to them, India was on the way of becoming a superpower. To support their claims, they presented statistics.

The common man on the street looks at the statistics with a bemused look. He understands no statistics. He believes that all data generated by the government is fudged either intentionally or inadvertently. The credibility of government institutions was eroded on one hand by immoral corrupt politicians who head them, and on the other hand by employees and officers who are too lethargic to do any serious data collection. Initially, when the election campaigning was just beginning, the so-called experts flanked every other TV channel espousing feel-good factor with statistics flying all around. However, among the common public, feel-good had become a big joke.

Another important aspect for the failure of the campaign was its language, which must be the one that touches the heartstrings of target audience. Feel Good and India Shining did not translate well into Hindi and other Indian languages. At no point during the course of Indian modern politics has there been a political campaign which was conceived in English. It was ironical that a party whose base is basically in the Hindi-heartland of the country had chosen to express its key electoral plank in a language alien to its own cadre. This illustrates the distance that had come between the party cadre and its leadership.

The flavour of the campaign was indicated by one poster, which featured smiling women in yellow sari playing cricket and the slogan 'You've never had a better time to shine brighter'. A number of commentators have pointed to the glaring and obvious gulf between those well-off Indians and the vast majority of the population who are condemned in poverty and lack access to the most basic services. Even as the Indian economy was booming, the country had slid further down the ranking in the UN Human Development Index from 124 to 127. Cutbacks to government social spending had impacted essential services, including health care and education, as well as basic infrastructure such as clean water, roads and electricity. The oppressive poverty and chronic unemployment had driven millions to the cities to look for work. As a result, these people lived in the oppressive slums that surround the major Indian cities.

9.5 General Elections 2014: Obsession on Narendra Modi

History will remember the 2014 general elections of India as the country's first intensively televised elections. Never before in the history of the country close to 400 news channels in a wide array of languages had communicated political messages to the masses from an equally diverse spectrum of political classes from across the country before 2014 2014. But, ruefully, most of these news networks were obsessed with one man: Narendra Modi. Most of the television channels were dishing out stories related to his persona for more than 6 months, bordering on a saturation point. This is indeed an unprecedented coverage, even by global standards. Only Barack Obama's campaign, which officially began in April 2011, for a second term in 2012, eclipses it (Bushan, 2014).

But it was difficult to fathom the cost of this media blitzkrieg. One could speculate that there could be a trade-off between Modi and television networks. Or was it the obsession with television rating points? Or was it a matter of political ideology? Clear answers are difficult to obtain for these questions. Various factors may have played a role in varying proportions during the electoral coverage. India TV editor Rajat Sharma has said at a seminar that the TRP of his new channel increases by more than 60 per cent when Narendra Modi is on their television. That perhaps explains why India TV chose to focus so heavily on Mr Modi. A similar TRP-chasing coverage was on during the Anna-Hazare-led anti-corruption movement in Delhi in 2011. Even that event was covered to the saturation point.

So far as CNBC-TV18 is concerned, it is still not clear as to what has happened to the network after Mukesh Ambani took control of it. But beyond the obvious and implied pressures that have influenced television news, the real twist in the narrative has been a fundamental change in the very grammar of television content. The television coverage trends that have emerged during the elections have clearly tilted the balance towards the studio and the anchor. The reporter's perspective is no longer as important as it used to be. It is clear from the experience of this election that, hereafter, elections in India—be it parliamentary or assembly—will be fought more on television screens and less on streets.

9.6 TRP and Salability of Politicians

One of the important factors that is in play in television coverage in India is the salability of politicians. If the candidate or the leader does not garner impressive TRPs, news channels will not make programmes on them. Another factor which determines a leader's coverage is his or her 'telegenic' personality. Thus, for example, even a prominent leader like Mayawati, with a large base of Dalit support, find it difficult to feature in prime time television coverage. News networks also consider whether the persona is amiable to the manufacturers as well as the so-called general viewers or prospective consumers in order to promote products and services. The market as a determining factor of a politician's 'salability and worth is the elephant in the room.

The Delhi-based national media hit a final nail in the coffin of reportage during the 2014 general elections. There was a glaring reporting deficit on display as reporters were pushed to the background by the domineering studio anchors. Most of shows on television were characterized by sameness with similar discussions on Narendra Modi and with the same set of 'experts' appearing in different new channels. For example, in NDTV, during the coverage of Varanasi constituency where Narendra Modi was contesting, Barkha Dutt hogged the limelight, overshadowing a fine story by the reporter Rahul Srivastava on Dalits just outside Varanasi. That story was only shown on a few times, but not during the prime time.

Most of the election rhetoric that was grabbing space in prime time television was largely about entertaining and dumbing down debates and not about serious and meaningful discussions on issues. Political leaders were also wilfully competing to create controversies in their campaigns in order to find themselves or their topics in the studio discussions during the six-hour

(6 pm to 12 midnight) band of prime time. Politicians such as Azam Khan, Amit Shah and Giriraj Singh did this with certain degree of success. Even the studio discussions were less on tolerance and meaningful debate and more on creating studio rage. It was like television and politicians were feeding off each other for mutual gain.

9.6.1 Impact of TV on Print

Another vital issue needs to be explored is the impact of the television news channels on print media. The format used by '*The Guardian* online' providing minute to minute coverage of events like the 'Arab Spring' was replicated by newspapers like *The Indian Express*, in an attempt to match the speed of television news. Newspapers like *The Times of India*, by having an understanding with the group-owned television network, offer short video clips of important news events in its online platform. Although all the news channels talk about strengthening democracy in their studios, they hardly have shown commitment in creating news content that reflects the country's real issues, at least during elections.

9.7 Uttar Pradesh Assembly Elections 2017

In 2017, BJP won a landslide victory in the election held for the 17th UP Legislative Assembly, exceeding the expectations of the most optimistic party supporters! The overwhelming three-quarter majority of winning 325 seats is astounding and comparable only to the 2014 Lok Sabha Elections in the magnitude of the victory. The party contested the elections without projecting a chief ministerial candidate, a deviation from the poll strategy executed in other state elections in the recent past. BJP is said to have capitalized on the collective party leadership and political clout and charisma of its leader, Prime Minister Narendra Modi. In fact, he was their lead campaigner in the elections.

Samajwadi Party (SP), which had its own internal feuds to cope up with, and the Congress party, without a charismatic mass leader, had a pre-poll alliance. But the coalition failed to make an impact on the electorate, as both the parties sank to a heavy defeat. Bahujan Samaj Party (BSP), which was in power not so long ago, led by Mayawati sank to almost obscurity with only 19 seats to boast. The UP election results are interpreted as Prime Minister

Narendra Modi's political clout and BJP President Amit Shah's political acumen and caste engineering.

Journalist Rana Ayyub (2017), analyzing the electoral results, has credited Amit Shah for the thumping victory. She says Amit Shah used the formula which was once used by Kalyan Singh in 1991, by successfully managing to cobble an alliance of the upper class, non-Muslim, non-Yadav and non-Jatav vote along with the unified Hindu vote including Dalits, seen as the Mayawati support base. 'Amit Shah combined astutely the weaknesses of the three other partied and stitched them with the unifying "Jai Shree Ram" slogan that he raised in Gorakhpur' (Ayyub, 2017). She says that the likes of Yogi Adityanath and Sakshi Maharaj did their allotted work efficiently despite many internal differences with the party. Amit Shah has hit the bull's eye with the list of handpicked candidates and many rebels from other parties, This is a familiar strategy which has worked wonders for the party, although it did not yield results in some of the other states. Clearly, BJP's victory can be analysed as a mandate against the weaknesses and internal squabbles of other parties rather than for the BJP. This becomes all the more clear if one can just glance through the voting percentage of other major parties. SP has polled 28 per cent of voting with a negative swing of 7.35, whereas BSP has managed to cling on to 22.2 per cent with a downward swing of 3.71 per cent. The combined voting percentage of these parties stands at 50.2 per cent which is way higher than BJP, which was polled at 41.4 per cent.

9.8 Karnataka Assembly Elections 2013

In 2008, BJP came to power under the leadership of powerful Lingayat leader B. S. Yedyurappa. However, it had to take the support of few independent MLAs to form the first ever government in South India. Mr Yedyurappa became the chief minister of Karnataka. However, the 5-year BJP rule was not smooth, to say the least. It was mired in many controversies.

Just a few months into power, the BJP launched 'Operation Kamala', which encouraged Congress and Janata Dal (Secular) or JD (S) MLAs to defect to the BJP to bolster its strength in the assembly. Mr Yedyurappa also had to face opposition from his own party members over his style of functioning. The Reddy brothers—Karunakara Reddy, Somashekara Reddy and Janardhana Reddy—and B. Sriramulu, a faction led by Mr Balachandra Jarkiholi and BJP loyalists led by Ananth Kumar troubled the chief minister. To add to his woes, many party legislators, including the chief minister himself were accused of corruption and nepotism.

Mr Janardhana Reddy was arrested in the Bellary illegal mining scam in 2011. Leaders such as Katta Subramanya Naidu, S. N. Krishnaiah Setty and even Yedyurappa were imprisoned for some time for their role in individual land scams. Yedyurappa was also accused of encouraging illegal mining. BJP ministers and MLAs such as M. P. Renukacharya, H. Halappa, K. Raghupathi Bhat, Krishna Palemar, Laxman Savadi and C. C. Patil were involved in sex scandals. In 5 years, BJP had three chief ministers.

Cashing in on these scandals, revolts and constant change of the chief minister, the Congress party, under the leadership of Mr Siddaramaiah and state Congress president Mr G. Parameshwara, launched campaigns. At the height of the illegal mining scam, the Congress leaders undertook *padayatra* to Bellary with the slogan *Namma Nadige Bellary Kadege* (our journey toward Bellary). During the elections, the Congress fought with a catchy slogan *Sakappa Saku* (Enough is enough), indicating the numerous scandals and scams the leaders of the BJP were involved in. It was also suggesting at the incumbent party's misrule in the state.

During the initial days of BJP rule, erstwhile Janata Pariwar leader and former Deputy Chief Minister Mr Siddaramaiah led the campaign against the BJP and JD (S) with the clever *AHINDA* (Minorities, Backward classes and Dalits) caste combination, which became a kind a movement in the state. When he joined the Congress party, this *AHINDA* tag worked in favour of the party. When the elections were held in May 2013, the Congress party won it with an absolute majority of 122 seats, comfortably crossing the majority mark of 113 seats. Thus, the party came back to power after the gap of nearly 9 years, with Siddaramaiah becoming the chief minister.

9.9 Social Media Role in Indian Politics

The US presidential election of 2012 confirmed the significant role of social media in politics. At the time of the Republican primaries, most of the Republican candidates were fighting it out on social media to create awareness and support for their respective political candidature. The battle did not end with the primaries. It continued during general election campaigns as well. During the general election campaigns, Barack Obama and Mitt Romney used social media to create a following, engagement and reach. The initial debate between the two principal candidates generated more than 10 million tweets.

In India, recent developments in the field of communication technologies have compelled the erstwhile traditional political leaders to embrace new age digital media. Initially viewed with apprehension, social media has become an integral part of the promotion strategy of almost all political parties. The ruling BJP, Congress and AAP have been at the forefront of this social-media-driven political activism. Almost all prominent national leaders belonging to different political parties have their own Twitter and other social media handles. Some of them, such as Prime Minister Narendra Modi, Aravind Kejriwal and Shashi Tharoor, are very active in social media. Parties are beginning to set aside a budget for social media along with hiring professionals to carry out political activities through social media.

In June 2012, India had 137 million Internet users and it is expected to have 330 million Internet users by 2016. This rise in the number of Internet users will lead to an increase in digital influence on people's opinion towards the political entities. According to ComScore Metrix, March 2011, social networking sites reach 84 per cent of the web audience in India, and take up 21 per cent of all time spent online. From March 2010 to 2011, there was a 16 per cent growth in the number of people using social networking sites in India, which is higher than the regional as well as global growth. 75 per cent of Internet users in India are below 35. As the Internet is becoming more and more approachable for the Indian public, social media sites are becoming more popular among the users. Moreover, Indian Internet users are more likely to discuss politics than those in many other countries (Rajput, 2014).

A Pew research study in December 2012 revealed that nearly 45 per cent of Indian web users use social media to discuss politics. Only Arab countries scored higher than India in this aspect. Social media played a very significant role during Anna Hazare's anti-corruption movement in 2011 and 2012. Social media has become a vital medium for civic and political debates. In fact, it emerged more strongly in late 2012 and early 2013 public protests against the Nirbhaya gang rape in New Delhi. It could be said that the social media has become an effective alternative to mainstream media. Even the mainstream media is also using social media as an important source of news, views and latest developments. Twitter- or Facebook-based news stories are commonplace in news channels.

Twitter along with other social media will play a vital role in Indian politics in the days to come. These media offer politicians a platform to directly communicate with the public. However, it should be noted here that social media can never replace traditional media such as TV, newspaper, radio etc. It can only be used to complement the existing media network. With the Internet users are increasing by the day, politicians can no longer afford to undermine the power of social media. The use of Twitter in Indian politics is still in its nascent stage and there is obviously a long way to go. Left parties even now do not have a presence in social media. Only BJP, Congress and AAP are trying to attract the tech-savvy Indian youth. With its well-established social media cell, clearly, BJP has an edge over other parties in this regard.

As stated previously, the last decade has witnessed a rapid Internet penetration in India. Hence, the Internet's socio-economic impact is also becoming more and more visible now. The Internet is playing a role in different aspects of life such as education, socialization, healthcare, communication, entertainment and development. And now, the Internet is emerging as a vital platform for political strategists. People are now entitled with the Internet's ability to facilitate them to connect and learn about politics, political parties and their leaders. Almost all major political parties in India have their presence in the Internet through websites, Facebook pages, Twitter accounts and blogs.

The Internet is definitely emerging as a new force to be reckoned with in Indian politics. In the coming days, Internet use will bring a paradigm shift to Indian politics. Right now, the Internet is offering new possibilities for political mobilization and participation. These are still early days for the Internet in Indian politics, and it is difficult to predict with certainty what would be the impact of Internet on Indian elections which usually revolve around public rallies, sentiments, television, print or radio ads and popular welfare schemes. But now Indians are now more comfortable with social media, especially when it comes to discussing critical or sensitive issues such as politics, corruption, poverty and economy.

9.9.1 Impact of Social Media on the 2014 Lok Sabha Elections

The 2014 Lok Sabha Elections had a high social media impact, considering the fact that it has entered deep into mainstream politics. Here is how social media played a vital role in the most influential elections in India. Narendra Modi, popularly known as NaMo, acquired the tag of the first social media prime minister of India. He was also the second most liked politician on Facebook. BJP carefully entered social media platforms engaging the users in important conversations. The tagline *Ab ki Baar Modi Sarkaar* became viral on social media. The party's social media cell carefully orchestrated the conversations with common people, with its ever-obliging volunteers chipping in to create a buzz around Modi.

Direct connection with users: Politicians were trying to form a direct contact with the potential voters through Facebook and Twitter by posting and tweeting regularly. The active users were also started to engage with each other on the political front. Hence, social media became a tool both for party leaders as well as the voters to understand each other's perspectives. Indian politicians also used hashtag strategy discretely on Twitter to drive home the point. Hashtags such as #Election2014, #NaMo and #ArvindKejriwal were trending during elections.

Impact on young voters: Youngsters were in the forefront when it came to using social networks as a tool of discussing political content. Social media savvy politicians such as Modi and Kejriwal made the most of the opportunity and had a mind-boggling impact on young voters, especially the first-timers. Politicians and youth had a mutual impact on each other with their active participation in social media platforms such as Facebook and Twitter.

Image boosting: Politicians have used social media to boost their images just like big brands. For example, every time Modi was scheduled to address a political rally, there was an update on Facebook and Twitter. His campaigns were turned into online campaigns, thereby connecting with the people who were not part of his offline campaigns. Social media was also flooded with images of Modi and his campaign and what he spoke on those rallies, registering his image in the minds of the users, many among them were impressionable first-time voters. This strategy did help him to create an aura around his persona during the elections.

Overtook the mainstream media: Social media was able to bypass the mainstream media such as newspapers and television during the elections. Dedicated accounts and pages of the parties doled out images, videos and activities continuously over the social media platforms to digital savvy party followers. They got the minute-to-minute updates on their smart phones when on the move. Through Twitter and Facebook, parties tried to reach out to vast number of voters and pulled them into the political conversation. In a new changed mainstream, media is no longer the first-hand source of news for the active social media users.

Powerful media for freedom of speech: Social media is an incredible platform to express, share thoughts and create awareness. As it offers space for the people to express their views, it becomes easier for politicians to understand them. Manufacturing consent, the famous treatise by Noam Chomsky, has had a major application during the 2014 general elections. Social media has emerged not only as a medium of freedom of expression but also as a source of content for mainstream media to develop and build stories around them. BJP and AAP are initiating the changes in tone and tenor, images and messages in this regard. With changing times, elections no longer are won by giving subsidies, doles and gifts before and after; entitlements, rightful gains of growth and economic development and the like are becoming important for the increasingly conscious and demanding voters, especially the younger voters.

The Indian Left parties which were traditionally banking on the labour and lower classes along with a section of the educated middle class are increasingly being left out of the new emerging political discourse in the country partly due to social media. It is the neo-left like AAP, which mixes *Inquilab Zindabad* with *Bharat Mataa ki Jai*, capturing public imagination now. AAP has managed to carve a niche for itself within a very short span of time thanks to social media.

9.10 Conclusion

Mass interest in politics is slowly changing. A very large number of youths influenced by BJP and AAP have become politically active in recent times. Thanks to this new-found interest, women are also voting in large numbers. With the backup of social media, ordinary and less powerful candidates, especially belonging to AAP, were able to put a strong fight in many seats. In fact, AAP gave the media-driven, corporate-funded election juggernaut BJP a run for its money. Some parties have begun to present constituency specific manifestoes to make their respective candidates accountable post elections. Thanks to social media, this time around Indian democracy went into participatory mode with millions of young voters participating in the electoral process. One can only hope that this unprecedented participation now leads to empowerment in a holistic sense.

10
Ethical Considerations in Election Coverage

Democracy thrives in an atmosphere where people are free to express their opinions and are well informed to cast their ballots at the elections. It is the media organizations and journalists who should play a critical role in the electoral process by disseminating the news and the diverse views of the public to the larger masses. Media provide detailed information pertaining to candidates, parties and their programmes. And journalists who work for media organizations contribute their bit towards citizens' participation in democratic debates. They ensure that issues of public interest remain intact at the centre of election campaigns. Journalists are also vital in ensuring legitimacy of the electoral results, and their responsibilities are more in countries emerging out of a political crisis. But, in order to carry out their all-important activities, journalists should have the right to provide information without being pressured or threatened. At the same time, they also have the duty to provide the information in an objective and constructive manner.

A journalist has to face numerous pressures during elections. The pressures may come from the government or from political parties, from a professional superior or from a stakeholder, or from the editor or owner of the news organization. Governments may create problems for the journalists and their respective news organizations by cutting down advertisements. Political parties may play various tricks to get a favourable coverage, and the editor may impose an editorial policy to help a political party or candidate and snub the journalists. But the general public expects journalists to be apolitical and objective, and devoid of sympathies when it comes to the coverage of politicians.

Journalists must rest on the ethical principles and moral values in order to resist pressures and perform to the best of their abilities during elections. Although a universal charter pertaining to these aspects of the journalism profession does not exist, ethical codes framed by respective countries around the world are similar. Most of these codes liken journalism to truth and objectivity. Professional journalists must be accurate, balanced, neutral and human-oriented in their approach. A sense of moral responsibility is paramount to a journalist as he or she is required to provide space for opinions which are sometimes contradictory to his or her own liking. Irrespective of political or any other considerations, a journalist's fundamental responsibility and loyalty should always be with the citizens. Media should never become part of a government, a political party, and powerful groups or individuals. Journalists who work for media organizations are expected to exercise their right to free expression through their profession.

10.1 Rights and Responsibilities of Journalists

Article 19 of the Universal Declaration of Human Rights of 1948 and Article 19 of the ICCPR of 1966, which is signed and ratified by 154 countries, provides protection to journalists. Major regional human rights conventions like that of Africa, the USA and Europe also guarantee these rights of the journalists. These covenants and agreements recognize the rights of the journalists to seek, receive and disseminate information in a free manner without systemic interference. Journalists should not be intimidated or harassed by government officials while exercising their responsibilities.

10.1.1 Rights and Responsibilities

A journalist has every right to speak with candidates belonging to different parties during electoral campaigns, including leaders who strongly oppose the policies of the government. Journalists should be able to get the information which they consider as important for the larger public and the country. The 1966 covenant also recognizes that freedom of expression should be enjoyed by every individual. Hence, during political campaigns, freedom of expression is to be guaranteed to the candidates as well as the citizens. Political parties and candidates should have the right to express their opinions through media platforms. At the same time, journalists should have the right to present programmes pertaining to political parties and leaders. Incumbent governments should not deny candidates the opportunity of organizing election rallies nor should a political party pressurize citizens to favour them during the elections.

10.1.2 The Legality of Press Restrictions

However, the 1966 covenant does allow a limited number of legitimate restrictions on freedom of expression. In order to protect the rights and reputations of individuals, to safeguard the country from security threats and to maintain the public order, morality and decency, restrictions may be imposed. But the covenant also strictly stipulates that these restrictions must be regulated by the laws of the countries where the elections are held. But, there is always a possibility of a government using these justifications to censor journalists who are not favourable to them.

So, what is the recourse a journalist has when restrictions are imposed on his or her coverage? If a journalist is hampered by any legal restriction, he or she should first determine whether the restrictions are legitimate under international law. Censorship to prevent the incitement of racial hatred is a legitimate restriction under international law. No candidate can use the pretext of national security to duck the objective and critical coverage. In general, a journalist should not be restricted to present a range of ideas and opinions during elections under the premise of laws pertaining to information and communication.

10.1.3 Protection of Sources

If a source has requested for anonymity, a journalist has every right not to reveal the name publicly or to the government. But journalists should be very careful not to fall prey to sources that provide inaccurate information. So, it is the responsibility of a journalist to test the reliability of a confidential source by verifying his or her information. And to safeguard himself or herself, he or she may reveal the identity of the source to his or her superior.

10.1.4 Safety of Journalists

In case a journalist feels unsafe in any place, he or she should report it to their respective organization and regulatory authorities immediately. They can provide a detailed report including threats and attacks aimed at him or her, or his or her colleagues, to human rights commissions or related government agencies. It is advisable that a journalist should not work alone in a volatile country to safeguard himself or herself. Members of international or national media bodies may accompany journalists covering conflict zones. It would be easier to handle the problems which may arise during coverage.

10.1.5 Co-operative Media Regulation

Ministries of information and broadcasting or law, government regulatory agencies or self-regulatory bodies, administered by professional journalists, may come out with a media regulatory system. A synergy can be established between the government and self-regulatory authorities during normal or crisis periods. For instance, the government may support the action taken by the media organizations against unethical professional conduct by their staff members. During the run up to the elections, journalistic bodies may come out with their own professional guidelines and codes of conduct and submit the same to all political parties in order to protect themselves from harassment by their supporters. Government or self-regulatory bodies may think of setting up election media-monitoring committees comprising well-known personalities and thrust upon them the responsibility of investigating threats or aggression against media personalities and act on it.

10.2 Objectivity Challenge

Every day journalists face the challenge of objectivity, impartiality and balance. Their professional ethics would pass through a litmus test during elections. During those times, political parties and candidates running for office would be more than willing to manipulate the media and control information. But the media must understand that it's first and foremost responsibility is to provide the citizens with authentic opinions and ideas and factual information canvassed during the campaigns.

Media should basically act as a facilitator between the political leadership and the voting community. Media should not act as a voice of politics alone; its loyalty should always be with the public. Hence, media should provide information to ordinary people by upholding the ethical practice while electoral reporting. Journalists should be wary of politicians who can behave in a worse manner. Violence rhetoric and offensive opinion about minorities and vulnerable groups are common place during elections. Journalists should never indulge in inciting violence or hatred. They should help the police personnel to maintain the law and order in the society.

Just like other citizens, even journalists are entitled to have their own political opinion. But when it comes to their profession, they should remain non-partisan, especially while covering elections. Opinions of the media with regard to politics should be confined to editorial columns or programmes. But so far as the reporting of news and current affairs is concerned, media must be fair to all political parties and candidates. It is unethical for a journalist to take part in any election activity such as contesting, campaigning or making financial donations to political parties. Accepting gifts or cash is a strict no for journalists because the entire society may have to pay a price for it. Media professionals have a responsibility towards the society as a whole.

Journalism was always intended for the larger public interest and not to act as mouthpieces of individuals or other interest groups. Hence, it is very important that journalism is devoid of political interference. To serve the larger public interest, sometimes journalists can defy advertisers as well as their proprietors. In order to reinforce professionalism and independence and ease the pressure on working journalists, media should set up internal mechanisms.

Journalists must understand that the most important people during elections are the voters and not the political party leaders or candidates. Hence, the media focus should always be on the people who vote. They will have to examine the promises made by the candidates during campaigns and pose relevant questions from the voters' or community's perspective. Election time news media bias is not unusual. For instance, a political party or a group may consider the omission of certain news items or issues from media as deliberate bias. But one should discount the fact that journalists make these choices on the basis of sound professional judgement.

It is difficult for the journalists to weigh these factors because of the tight deadlines and pressures. Nevertheless, they do strive for fairness and make their publication decisions solely on the basis of news value. In fact, strictly adhering to news values would go a long way in establishing the credibility of a journalist. Yes, there will be political pressure and pressure from the owners, advertisers and other interest groups. But, it is the responsibility of a journalist to rise above these and work in the interest of larger public.

But media can sometimes express biased opinion. There is nothing wrong in openly offering support or promoting a political party in editorial columns, but news stories should be devoid of these orientations. Liberal newspapers tend to be left of centre in their editorial columns and conservative newspapers will favour right of centre politics. Usually, the editorial column which acts as the voice of a newspaper on wide range of issues will be biased as it expresses an opinion. But such opinions should always be based on authentic facts. Even column writers and television anchors have the right to express their opinions, but never at the cost of balance and fairness. Deliberate distortion of facts through improper presentation and suppression of vital facts are strictly forbidden. Preferential news coverage to one party or using deceptive camera angles to either snub or enhance the impact of campaign rallies is also totally uncalled for.

News reporters must act as a bridge between the voters and the candidates. The desire of the people to involve themselves more in political process is a phenomenon that is here to stay in the era of social media and open journalism. And hence, journalism should not focus only on the glamour and glitz of celebrities or political leaders. They should also denounce the 'horse race' model of coverage of elections. It is the duty of journalists to dig deep into the serious issues that are of concern to the voters.

It is important for media organizations to provide training to their staff members regarding the coverage of elections. In order to inculcate political pluralism among the reporters and editors, they need to be explained about the electoral aspects from the point of view of voters and political candidates. An understanding of the constitutional and legal framework of the electoral process is fundamental. Authentic information pertaining to political parties, candidates and manifestoes are equally important. Reporters make sense of it based on credible sources who provide insights on issues cropping up during elections. An understanding of safety and security issues is significant as journalists and media staff cannot afford to take unnecessary risks. Campaign events can be robust and dangerous for journalists. Hence, the media organizations should ensure that their staff members employed at various levels are paid properly and are with permanent contracts.

10.3 Ethical Standards during Elections

Coverage of news stories as per the highest legal and ethical standards and credibility could be termed as media professionalism. While exercising freedom of expression and information, journalists must strictly adhere to media professionalism at all times. Journalists belonging to new democracies which have emerged from highly restrictive political system would definitely lack the professional skills of their counterparts from the USA or the UK that have a long history of media freedom. The experience of an authoritarian system could also positively influence journalists. For instance, in some cases, fearless journalism has played a vital role in putting pressure on dictatorial regimes to open up the political space for others. Those journalists who have worked in such hostile environments and successfully produced stories would have acquired unmatched professional skills. This holds them in good stead while covering elections as well.

The ethical and professional issues that journalists encounter are not so different from what they face in their day-to day-working lives. But these dilemmas would have acquired an all-together different dimension during elections. News value and uniqueness of the event should typically drive the news coverage. But the voters also need fair and balanced reportage pertaining to electoral manifestoes and agendas of different political parties. One of the reasons why media is considered as a significant part of a democracy is that they are in a position to investigate, verify and expose the corrupt practices during elections. The administration of an election depends on the lawmakers, and the scrutiny of this process depends on the professionalism of journalists.

It is a common practice for politicians to make inflammatory statements during election campaigns to influence the masses. Election time is a tricky situation for journalists to be in, because it is during the election campaigns that different political points of views are expressed while at the same time inflammatory speeches are also made. Journalists will confront the challenge of reporting these inflammatory political speeches in an accurate but subdued manner so as to keep the tempers down. Media organizations operate with bare minimum resources in developing countries and even journalists are underpaid. Editors will face ethical problems as not many are taking up the journalistic profession due to this. In some cases, journalists are allowed to receive honorariums or other rewards from the candidate for covering the story. Notwithstanding the pay-related drawbacks, journalists accepting favours from the candidates clearly amounts to bribery and, hence, is not good for independent coverage.

10.4 Code of Conduct during Elections

Every country has its of codes of conduct containing principles to guide the performance of media and journalists. Governmental agencies, ECs or journalistic associations, or any other regulatory authorities may come out with their own code of conduct during elections. An in-house code prepared by media associations would be effective if journalists and editors themselves participate in bringing it out. The international federation of journalists has its own code of conduct which enunciates many principles that are relevant in covering elections. Accuracy, impartiality and honesty are the canons of this code.

A journalist has to report accurately without any bias and in accordance with facts. Suppression of essential information is strictly uncalled for.

Observing professional secrecy with regard to sources is important. During the times of allegations, journalists should seek comments from both sides. If a published information is found to be inaccurate, a journalist should do the utmost to correct them. When it comes to opinions of political parties, it is advisable that journalists try and report in their own words. But journalists should avoid using language or expressions which may offend individuals or communities or which may heighten the violence on the grounds widen the discrimination based on race, sex and sexual orientation, language, religion, political or other factors. Journalists should never accept any gifts or rewards from any politicians or candidates, and he or she should not make any promise to them regarding news coverage. Plagiarism, malicious writing, libel or slander and unfounded accusations are grave professional offences of journalists.

10.5 Legal Provisions during Election Coverage

A journalist should have a thorough understanding of the laws governing elections for reporting elections. Senior editors who are involved in planning the coverage of elections should understand their legal obligations. Laws and guidelines pertaining to programming and news content to be understood as well. Media organizations can put their own system in place to fulfil these obligations. They also need to understand the restrictions pertaining to access during the electoral process such as counting and the official announcement of results. Precautionary measures pertaining to ballot boxes, plans for ballot box transportation and security of storage facilities are some of the important electoral activities a journalist needs to know.

10.6 Accuracy and Impartiality in Reporting

Accuracy stands for details such as proper spellings of candidate names, precise numbers, exact quotes of the candidates and correct attribution, and things like that. It is the responsibility of journalists to put texts and events in a proper and accurate context. If a context of a statement is not accurately placed, a news story can easily become biased. One possibility is to include the candidates' statements in verbatim. Timeliness is a virtue for journalists; so is accuracy of facts and figures. A casual approach with regard to gathering of factual information and presenting the same would be detrimental to a journalist's career as well as to media professionalism.

10.6.1 Impartiality

Impartiality is one of the major canons of news reporting. It is also closely related to accuracy. Although accuracy is a precondition to impartiality, it will not guarantee impartiality. For instance, sometimes accurate reporting which conveys the position of one political party or candidate will be one-sided if it does not provide alternative opinions. A balanced news story will always contain different points of view. And a journalist should always strive towards establishing balance in a particular news story. If, for example, a journalist is assigned to a particular political party beat, he or she can only get the comments from that party. In such instances, it is the responsibility of the editors to arrange for alternative opinions from other parties by compiling composite stories or by presenting other point of views.

If a journalist wants to express his or her own opinion, it should be presented as such. A clear separation should be there between facts and comments, especially during election coverage. This is applicable even to campaign journalism. Media organization may not be forbidden to endorse a political party or a candidate, but their overall election coverage should be impartial and accurate. Media organizations and management are also bound by ethical obligations just like individual journalists. But journalists can express their own opinions in favour of a political party or a candidate in clearly earmarked opinion sections.

Expectations from public media differ from that of private media when it comes to bias in electoral coverage. Public media is expected to present a wide range of views in its news columns and less of editorial content. Public media owned by the public invariably have a large national reach and can be very influential because these audiences would have limited access to media infrastructure. Therefore, impartiality should be the hallmark of public media. It is also important for journalists not to hold any important positions in political parties to be impartial. Of course, they are free to have political opinions and loyalties personally, but news columns should free of such expressions. Any political affiliation would definitely undermine the credibility of a journalist. As mentioned before, a journalist should always avoid bribes from the candidates or political parties. But election-time bribery is a common phenomenon in countries where journalists are underpaid.

Although conventional type of 'cash for coverage' exists in most parts of the world, there are other subtle manifestations of bribery such as gifts and vouchers that are used by parties and candidates to induce journalists.

10.7 Conclusion

It is unethical for journalists to accept any sort of gifts or inducement to write favourable or negative reports on politicians or any other candidates. Media organizations can try to overcome the problems of inducement by initiating strict actions against a journalist involved in bad practices. They can also provide ethical training to their staff members and provide incentives to underpaid journalists. In addition to this, press councils and media ombudsmen can also uphold the code of ethics for journalists. Transparency with regard to salary in the media sector is an important factor in enforcing ethics.

Journalists have ethical obligations to their audiences, to the society as well as to the media organizations. Election reporting is not different from general reporting when it comes to exercising ethical principles. A journalist should never indulge in dishonest or illegal methods of information gathering nor should he or she breach the confidentiality of sources when they may be in danger. As mentioned earlier, freedom of expression, critical to human rights, is essential for the smooth functioning of democracy. Media organizations are entrusted with this serious responsibility to exercise freedom of expression for the larger public good. Journalism is not just a job, but a profession which seriously influences the society. Hence, it is important for the journalists to be accurate, impartial and objective at all times to remain as a credible source of information to the society.

Bibliography

ACM. (2005). 'Association of Caribbean Media workers calls on Guyana government to ensure safety of media workers'. Retrieved 30 August 2015, from http://acmpress.org/files/2014/11/20050829-GuyanaMediaSafety.pdf

Anetwesonga. (2015). Covering elections. Retrieved 1 September 2015, from https://anetwesonga.wordpress.com/category/uncategorized/page/4/

Arterton, F. C. (1987). *Teledemocracy: Can technology protect democracy?* Beverly Hills, CA: SAGE Publications.

Article 19. (2015). Free expression, media freedom and 2015 elections in Myanmar: Global campaign for free expression. Retrieved 30 August 2015, from http://www.article19.org/data/files/medialibrary/37712/14-09-10-elections.pdf

———. (2007). Freedom of expression and the Angolan elections. Global campaign for free expression. Retrieved 30 August 2015, from https://www.article19.org/data/files/pdfs/publications/angola-foe-elections.pdf

Ayyub, R. (2017). How Amit Shah won Uttar Pradesh for Modi. NDTV. Retrieved 12 March 2015, from http://www.ndtv.com/opinion/how-amit-shah-won-uttar-pradesh-for-modi-1668378

Badawi, A. M. (2011). *Peace for a better world: Inspired from Egyptian revolution*. US: Xlibris (p. 115).

BBG. (2012). Nigeria media use 2012, Broadcasting board of governors. Retrieved 23 August 2015, from www.bbg.gov/wp-content/media/2012/ gallup-nigeria-brief.pdf

Behnke, P. (2010). *Social media and politics*. Singapore: Konrad-Adenauer-Stiftung.

Besley, T., Robin, B., & Andrea, P. (2002). Mass, media and political accountability. In J. D. Wolfensohn (Ed.), *The right to tell: The role of mass media in economic development* (pp. 45–60). Washington, D.C.: World Bank Institute.

Bhushan, S. (2014). 'How the television news industry scripted the Indian elections', Caravan. Retrieved 5 September 2015, from http://www.caravanmagazine.in/vantage/television-scripted.

Blanchard, R., (Ed.). (1974). *Congress and the news media*. New York, NY: Hastings House.

Blood, R. W. (1991, 23–27 May). *Time of voting decision: Knowledge and uncertainty*. Paper presented at the Annual Meeting of the International Communication Association, 41st, Chicago, IL.

Blumler, J. G., & McQuail, D. (1979). *Television in politics*. Chicago, IL: University of Chicago Press.

Bormann, E. G. (1972). Fantasy and rhetorical vision: The rhetorical criticism of social reality. *Quarterly Journal of Speech* (58), 396–407. Baton Rouge, LA.

Castells v. Spain, Judgment of April 23, 1992, Series A no. 236, para 43.

Carver, R. (2001). Media and elections. Retrieved 30 July 2015, from http://aceproject.org/ace-en/topics/me/onePage

Chandran, B. (2004). India shining glows on TV ads list. *Business Standard*. Retrieved 30 July 2015, from http://www.business-standard.com/india/news/india-shining-glowstv- ads -list /144965/

Chomsky, N., & Herman, E. S. (1988). *Manufacturing consent: The political economy of the mass media.* New York, NY: Pantheon Books.
Cisilin, A. (2013). Deconstructing social media in India. *Journal of South Asia Woman Studies, 14*(1).
Clancey, M., & Robinson, M. (1985). General election coverage: Part I. *Public Opinion, 8* (6, (December–January), 49–54. Washington, D.C.
Crain, W. M., & Goff, B. (1988). Televised legislatures: Political information technology and public choice. Boston, MA: Kluwer Academic Publishers.
Coronel, S. S. (2002). The role of media in deepening democracy. Retrieved 27 July 2015, from http://unpan1.un.org/intradoc/groups/public/documents/un/unpan010194.pd
Coronel, S. S. (2011). 'Role of media in deepening democracy' (p. 1). Retrieved 12 August 2015, from https://www.academia.edu/7113362/THE_ROLE_OF_THE_MEDIA_IN_DEEPENING_DEMOCRA?auto=download
CSCE (1975). Conference on human dimension of the CSCE. Retrieved 2 September 2015, from http://www.osce.org/odihr/elections/14304?download=true
Curran, J. (1991). Mass media and democracy. In J. Curran, & M. Gurevitch (Eds), *Mass media and society* (p. 81). London: Edward Arnold.
Darbishire, H. (1998). Media and the electoral process. *Media and democracy* (p. 96). Strasbourg: Council of Europe.
Devlin, L. P. (1993). Contrasts in presidential campaign commercials of 1992. *American Behavioral Scientist, 37,* 279–90. Princeton, NJ.
Devra, C. M., & Singh, N. (2009). Whose news do you trust? Explaining trust in private versus public media in Africa. *Political Research Quarterly, 64*(2), 276–92.
Diamond, L., & Plattner, M. (2012). *Liberation technology: Social media and the struggle for democracy,* Maryland: The Johns Hopkins University Press.
Document of the Copenhagen Meeting of the Conference on the Human Dimension of the CSCE (1990). Retrieved 3 September 2015, from http://www.osce.org/odihr/elections/14304
Dostie-Goulet, E. (2009). Social networks and development of political interest. *Journal of Youth Studies, 12*(4).
Druck, H. (1995). Germany: Equality within the constitution. In Y. Lange & A. Palmer (Eds), *Media and elections: A handbook.* Dusseldorf: European Institute for the Media.
Dwivedi, R. (2011). The penetration of social media in governance, political reforms and building public perception. *Manthan: International Journal of Mass Communication, 6*(1), 163–67.
Engstrom, E., Gentry, J., & Melwani, G. (1989, 10–13 August). *Evidence for differential effects on males and females in the wake of post-debate analyses.* Paper presented at the Annual Meeting of the Association for Education in Journalism and Mass Communication, 72nd, Washington, DC.
Entman, R. M. (1995). 'The media and US elections: Public policy and journalistic practice. In Y. Lange & A. Palmer (Eds), *Media and elections: A handbook.* Dusseldorf: European Institute for the Media.
EU. (2009, 7 June). Final report, Lebanon parliamentary elections. Retrieved 10 September 2015, from http://www.europarl.europa.eu/meetdocs/2009_2014/documents/dmas/dv/raport_final_/rapport_final_en.pdf
FNJ. (2008). An agenda for change: The right to freedom of expression in Nepal. Retrieved 30 August 2015, from https://www.article19.org/data/files/pdfs/publications/nepal-agenda-for-change.pdf
Frank, R. S. (1973). *Message dimensions of television news.* Lexington, MA: Lexington Books, D.C. Heath.

Franklin, B. (Ed.). (1992). *Televising democracies.* London: Routledge.
Gallup. (1988). The Gallup report. Retrieved 31 August 2015, from https://www.udel.edu/htr/American/Texts/campcov.html#note17
Garay, R. (1984). *Congressional television: A legislative history.* Westport, CT: Greenwood Press.
Garber, M. (1993). Character assassination: Shakespeare, Anita Hill, and JFK. In, M. Garber, J. Matlock, & R. L. Walkowitz (Eds), *Media spectacles* (pp. 23–39). New York: Routledge.
Garner, J, Gobetz, R. H, Garner, J., Leland, C. M., Scott, & David, K. (1990). *Television news and presidential campaigns: The legitimization of televised political advertising.* Paper presented at the Annual Convention of the International Communication Association, "Television news and presidential campaigns: The legitimization of televised political advertising." *Social Science Quarterly,* 74(2), 274–85. University of Texas Press.
GMMP. (2015). *Who makes the news?* London: WACC.
Golding, P., Murdock, G., & Schlesinger, S. eds. (1986). *Communicating politics.* Leicester: Leicester Universith Press.
Gopalkrishnan, S. (2008). Neoliberalism and Hindutva. Concurrent.org. Retrieved 12 August 2015, from http://www.countercurrents.org shankar301008.Htm
Gotllieb, S. S. (1992). The media role in political campaigns. Retrieved 1 September 2015, from http://www.ericdigests.org/1992-3/role.htm.
Graber, D. (1976). Press and television as opinion resources in presidential campaigns. *Public Opinion Quarterly, 40* (3), 285–303. New York, NY.
Granovetter, M. (2005). Impact of social structure on economic outcomes. *Journal of Economic Perspective, 19*(1, Winter), 33–50.
Griffin, E. (1991). *A first look at communication theory.* New York, NY: McGraw-Hill.
Gurevitch, M., & Jay, B. (1977). Linkages between the mass media and politics: A model for the analysis of political communications system. In J. Curran, M. Gurevitch, & J. Wollacatt (Eds), *Mass communication and society* (p. 270). London: Edward Arnold.
Gurevitch, M., & Blumler, G. (1990). Comparative research: The extending frontier. In D. Swanson & D. Nimmo (Eds), *New directions in political communication* (pp. 305–19). Newbury Park, CA: SAGE Publications.
Halberstam, D. (1981). 'How television failed the American voter'. *Parade, 11,* 7. Retrieved 31 August 2015, from https://www.udel.edu/htr/American/Texts/campcov.html
Hallin, D. C., & Paolo, M. (2004). Americanization, globalization and secularization: Understanding the convergence of media systems and political communication. In F. Esser & B. Pfetsch (Eds), *Comparing political communication: Theories, cases and challenges* (pp. 25–44). Cambridge. Cambridge University Press.
Hess, S. (1991). *Live from Capitol Hill! Studies of Congress and the media.* Washington, D.C.: Brookings Institution.
Hetherington, A., Weaver, K., & Ryle, N. (1990). *Cameras in the commons.* London: Hansard Society for Parliamentary Government.
Hofstetter, C. R. (1976). *Bias in the news.* Columbus, OH: Ohio State University Press.
Horwitz, R. B. (2001). *Communication and democratic reform in South Africa.* Cambridge: Cambridge University Press.
Hussain, A. (1999. 29 January). *Report of special rapporteur on the protection and promotion of the right to freedom of opinion and expression* (UN Doc. E/CN.4/1999/64). E/CN.4/1999/64. Retrieved 12 September 2015, from https://documents-dds-ny.un.org/doc/UNDOC/GEN/G99/107/66/PDF/G9910766.pdf?OpenElement

Hutchinson, J. (1989). *The big picture on the small screen.* Canberra: Department of the Senate.
Islam, R. (2002). Into the looking glass: What the media tell and why—An overview. In J. D. Wolfensohn (Ed.), *The right to tell: The role of the mass media in economic development* (pp. 1–26). Washington, D.C.: World Bank Institute.
ITU. (2010). Monitoring WSIS Targets; A Midterm Review. *World Telecommunication/ ICT Report 2010.* Geneva: ITU, p. 10.
Jordan C. (2013). Social media, American interests, and the Arab spring. *Dalhousie Journal of Interdisciplinary Management,* 9(Spring), 1–13.
Joslyn, R. A. (1980). The content of political spot Ads. *Journalism Quarterly.* Urbana, IL.
Just, M., Crigler, A., & Wallach, L. (1990). Thirty seconds or thirty minutes: What viewers learn from spot advertisements and candidate debates. *Journal of Communication, 40*(3), 120–33.
Kaid, L. L. (1981). Political advertising. In D. Nimmo & K. R. Sanders (Eds), *Handbook of political communication* (pp. 249–271). Beverly Hills, CA: SAGE Publications.
———. (2015). 'Political processes and television'. Retrieved 5 August 2015, from http://www.museum.tv/eotv/politicalpro.htm
Kaid, L. L., & Johnston, A. (1991). Negative versus positive television advertising in U.S. presidential campaigns, 1960–1988. *Journal of Communication, 41*(3), 53–64. New York, NY.
Kaid, L. L., & Holtz-Bacha, C. (Eds). (1995). *Political advertising in western democracies.* Newbury Park, CA: SAGE Publications.
Kaid, L. L., Gerstl, J., & Sanders, K. R. (Eds). (1991). *Mediated politics in two cultures.* New York, NY: Praeger.
Kaid, L. L., Gobetz, R., Garner, J., Leland, C. M., & Scott, D. (1993). Television news and presidential campaigns: The legitimization of televised political advertising. *Social Science Quarterly, 74*(2), 274–85. Austin, TX.
Kern, M. (1989). *30-second politics.* New York, NY: Praeger.
Keyton, J., Wall, V. D., Golder, & James L. (1989, 6–8 April). *Political values and political judgments: Analysis of responses to the 1988 presidential debates.* Paper presented at the Annual Meeting of the Southern Speech Communication Association, Louisville.
Klapper, J. T. (1960). *The effects of mass communication.* Glencoe, IL: Free Press.
Kline, S. L., & Kuper, G. (1994). Self-presentation practices in government discourse: The case of US Lt. Col. Oliver North. *TEXT, 14*(1), 23–43. The Hague, Netherlands.
Kohli. A. (2006). Politics of economic growth in India, 1980–2005, part I: The 1980s. *Economic and Political Weekly,* 40(13): 1251–59.
Kolbert, E. (1992). As political campaigns turn negative, the press is given a negative rating. *The New York Times,* 1 May 1992.
Kraus, S. (Eds). (1962). *The great debates.* Bloomington, IN: Indiana University Press.
Lamb, B. (1988). *C-SPAN: America's town hall.* Washington, D.C.: Acropolis.
"Law on the Establishment of Radio and Television Enterprises and their Media Services", law number 6112 Turkey, as found on *WIPO Resources*webpage. Retrieved 26 August 2015, from http://www.wipo.int/wipolex/en/text.jsp?file_id=24185
Lichter, S. R., Amundson, D., & Noyes, R. (1988). *The video campaign: Network coverage of the 1988 primaries.* Washington, D.C.: American Enterprise Institute for Public Policy Research.
Lingens v. Austria, Judgment of July 08, 1986, Series A no. 103, at para. 42.
Lorna, S. (2011). *Controlling Knowledge- Freedom of Information and Privacy Protection in a networked world.* Edmonton: AU Press (p. 77).
Lusaka High Court. (1990). Arthur Wina & others v. the attorney general, HP/1878. Retrieved 2 September 2015, from http://aceproject.org/ace-en/topics/me/mea/mea01d/mobile_browsing

Luttbeg, N. R. (1988). Role of newspaper coverage and political ads in local elections. *Journalism Quarterly*, 65(4), 881–88, 897.
Martinsson, J. (2009). *The role of media literacy in the governance reform agenda*. Washington D.C.: World Bank.
McCombs, M. E., & Shaw, D. L. (1972). The agenda-setting function of mass media. *Public Opinion Quarterly*. New York, NY.
McGinniss, J. (1969). *The selling of the president 1968*. New York, NY: Trident Press.
McNair, B. (2002). *An introduction to political communication*. New York, NY: Routledge.
Mendel, T. (2000). Public service broadcasting: a comparative legal survey. Retrieved 30 August 2015, from http://www.unesco.org/webworld/publications/mendel/inter_standards.html
Miller, T. (1993). *The well-tempered self: Citizenship, culture, and the postmodern subject*. Baltimore, MA & London: The Johns Hopkins University Press.
Minow, N., Martin, J. B., & Mitchell, L. M. (1973). *Presidential television*. New York, NY: Basic Books.
Mohapatra, A. (2013). Lokpal and the role of media in propping up anticorruption movement in India. *IJSSR*, 2(3, March), 42–53.
Mohr, C. (1976). 'Carter, on Morals, talks with candor', *The New York Times*. Retrieved 10 August 2015, from http://events.nytimes.com/learning/general/specials/elections/1976/featured_article2.html.
Morrison, T. (Ed.). (1991). *Race-ing justice, engendering power: Essays on Anita Hill, Clarence Thomas and the construction of social reality*. New York, NY: Pantheon.
Muniandy, L. (2013). The impact of social media in social and political aspects in Malaysia: An overview. *International Journal of Humanities and Social Science*, 3(11), 71–76.
Murphy, P. D. (2007). Media and democracy in the age of globalization. *Suny Press*. Retrieved 29 August 2015, from http://www.sunypress.edu/pdf/61516.pdf
Nation Master. (2013). China media stats. Retrieved 27 August 2015, from http://www.nationmaster.com/country-info/profiles/China/Media
Nimmo, D. (1970). *The political persuaders*. Englewood Cliffs, NJ: Prentice Hall.
Nimmo, D., & Sanders, K. R. (Eds). (1981). *Handbook of political communication*. Beverly Hills, CA: SAGE Publications.
Norris, P. (2004). Global political communication: Good governance, human development and mass communication. In F. Esser, & B. Pfetsch (Eds), *Comparing political communication: Theories, cases and challenges*. Cambridge: Cambridge University Press.
Nyakweya, R. (2013). *Role of social media in enhancing public diplomacy*. Nairobi: University of Nairobi.
Nyange P. S. (2009). *The role of international media on third world countries' electoral process*. Nairobi: University of Nairobi.
Obot, C. (2013). Mass media electioneering campaigns and Nigeria voters' decision during 2011 general elections. *Journal of Politics and Law*, 6(1), 173–85.
OECD. (2000). *No longer business as usual*. Paris: OECD Publications.
Ong, M. (2012). *Keeping elections clean: TI-Malaysia launches election integrity pledge*. Transparency International. Retrieved 27 August 2015, from http://blog.transparency.org/2012/06/`9/keeping-elections-clean-ti-malaysia-launches-election-integrity-pledge/
OSCE. (2001). Review of the legal framework for media coverage of elections in the Republic of Kazakhstan. Retrieved 10 September 2015, from http://www.osce.org/odihr/elections/kazakhstan/14794
Oshagan, H. (1988, 2–5 July). *Looking at voting as a decisional process: What factors determine initial preference?* Paper presented at the Annual Meeting of the Association for Education in Journalism and Mass Communication, 71st, Portland, OR.

Parida, S. K., & Das, A. (2014). Social media in relation to politics in Odisha, India: An overview. *International Journal of Interdisciplinary and Multidisciplinary Studies*, 1(2), 45–47.
Patterson, T. E., & McClure, R. D. (1976). *The unseeing eye: The myth of television power in national politics.* New York, NY: Putnam.
Patterson, R. (1980). The mass media election. New York: Praeger Publishers.
Perry, D. K. (2002). *Theory and research in mass communication: Contexts and consequences.* New York: Routledge.
'Political Opinion Polls', 2009. *Spotlight* (1). Oireachtas Library and Research Service.
Rajagopal, A. (2004). *Politics after television: Religious nationalism and the reshaping of the Indian public.* Cambridge, UK & New York, NY: Cambridge University Press.
Rajput, H. (2014, January). Social media and politics in India: a study of twitter usage among Indian political leaders. *Asian Journal of Multidisciplinary Studies*, 2(1), 63–69.
Robinson, M. J. (1976). Public affairs television and the growth of political malaise: The case of the 'selling of the Pentagon'. *American Political Science Review*, 70(2), 409–32. Baltimore, MD.
Rosenberg, W. L., & Elliott, W. R. (1989). Comparison of media use by reporters and public during newspaper strike. *Journalism Quarterly*, 66(1), 18–30.
Sabato, L. J. (1981). *The rise of political consultants: new ways of winning elections.* New York, NY: Basic Books.
Sailor, M. (2012). Five ways TV has influenced presidential elections. Retrieved 2 September 2015, from http://people.howstuffworks.com/culture-traditions/tv-and-culture/5-ways-tv-has-influenced-presidential-elections5.htm
Satpathi, S., & Roy, O. (2011, June). The impact of electronic media on the modern Indian voter: A study of post liberalization era. *Global Media Journal Indian Edition*, Summer Issue (June 2011).
Scammell, M., & Langer, A. I. (2007). Political advertising: Why it is so boring. Retrieved 23 August 2015, from http://eprints.lse.ac.uk/2540
Schlesinger, A. M., & Bruns, R. (Eds). (1975). *Congress investigates: A documented history, 1792–1974.* New York, NY: Chelsea House.
Schwartz, T. (1984). *Media: The second god.* New York, NY: Anchor Press.
Semetko, H. A., Blumler, J. G., Gurevitch, M., & Weaver, D. (1991). The formation of campaign agendas: A comparative analysis of party and media roles in recent American and British elections. Hillsdale, NJ: Lawrence Erlbaum.
Sen, A. (1999). *Development and freedom.* New York, NY: Anchor Books.
Shaw P. (2005). Radio in India: Problems of public broadcasting and hope. *Media Asia and Asian Communication Quarterly*, 32(4), 234–39.
Shuman, S. I. (1956). *Broadcasting and telecasting of judicial and legislative proceedings.* Ann Arbor, MI: University of Michigan Legislative Research Center.
Smith, R. H. (2011). *Media ownership and regulation in Australia.* Centre for Policy Development issue brief. Retrieved 29 August 2015, from http://cpd.org.au/wp-content/uploads/2011/11/Centre_for_Policy_Development_Issue_Brief.pdf
Spotlight. (2009). Political opinion polls. *Spotlight*, (1). Retrieved 15 September 2015, from http://www.oireachtas.ie/parliament/media/housesoftheoireachtas/libraryresearch/spotlights/Polling_web.pdf
Steeper, F. T. (1978). Public response to Gerald Ford's statements on Eastern Europe in the second debate. In, G. F. Bishop, R. G. Meadow, & M. Jackson-Beeck (Eds), *The presidential debates: Media, electoral, and policy perspectives* (p. 81). New York, NY: Praeger.

Storck, M. (2011). *The role of social media in political mobilization: A case study of the January 2011 Egyptian uprisings* (Dissertation). University of St Andrews, Scotland.
Straight, M. (1954). *Trial by television*. Boston, MA: The Beacon Press.
Swanson, D. L. (2004). Transnational trends in political communication: Conventional views and new realities. In F. Esser & B. Pfetsch (Eds), *Comparing political communication: Theories, cases and challenges*. Cambridge: Cambridge University Press.
Swedish Govt. (2012). 'Press support, government offices of Sweden website'. Retrieved 12 August 2015, from http://www.sweden.gov.se/sb/d/14476
Tabassum, S. (2009). Media role in democracy. Retrieved 27 July 2015, from https://sadianasr.wordpress.com/2009/11/17/medias-role-in-democracy/
The Guardian. (2012). Worries about vote-buying despite Mexican reform. *The Guardian*. Retrieved 27 August 2015, from http://www.guardian.co.uk/world/feedarticle/10314939
The Hindu. (2009, 4 March). Congress gets 'Jai Ho'. *The Hindu*. Retrieved 21 August 2015, from http: // www.hindu.com / 2009/03/04 /stories /2009030460191000.htm
The Pew Research Centre. (2008). Internet overtakes newspapers as news outlet. The Pew Research Centre. Retrieved 23 August 2015, from http://www.people-press.org/2008/12/23/internet-overtakes-newspapers-as-news-outlet/
UN Human Rights Committee. (2011). Retrieved 29 August 2015, from http://www.article19.org/resources.php/resource/2631/en/un:-article-19-welcomes-general-comment-on-freedom-of-expression
UN. (1948). Universal declaration of human rights. Retrieved 30 August 2015, from https://www.article19.org/data/files/pdfs/analysis/wireless-communications.pdf
———. (1976). International covenant on civil and political rights. Retrieved 4 September 2015, from http://www.ohchr.org/en/professionalinterest/pages/ccpr.aspx
———. (1992). *Report of the UN Technical team on the conduct of a free and fair referendum on the issue of one party/ multiparty system in Malawi*. Retrieved 12 September 2015, from https://aceproject.org/ace-en/topics/me/mea/mec04/mec04a08#ref1
UNESCO. (2006). *A media policy for Iraq*. UK: UNESCO.
———. (2015). 'Public service broadcasting', Retrieved 12 August 2015, from http://www.unesco.org/new/en/communication-and-information/media-development/public-service-broadcasting/browse/15/
United Nations Human Rights. (2011). 'UN HRC adopted document on freedom of expression'. Retrieved 12 August 2015, from http://humanrightshouse.org/Articles/16813.html.
UNTAC. (1992). Media guidelines for Cambodia. UNTAC. Retrieved 2 September 2015, from http://aceproject.org/ace-en/topics/me/mea/mea01g/mobile_browsing
Ushahidi. (2012). ' Haiti and the power of crowd sourcing'. Retrieved 28 August 2015, from http://ushahidi.com
Vancil, D. L., & Pendell, S. D. (1987). The myth of viewer-listener disagreement in the first Kennedy-Nixon debate. *Central States Speech Journal*, 38(1), 16–27.
Walker, J. R. (1990). Developing a new political reality: Political information and the 1988 southern regional primary. *Southern Communication Journal*, 55(4), 421–35.
Wani, G., & Alone, N. (2014). A survey on impact of social media on election system. *Indian Journal of Computer Science and Information Technologies*, 5(6), 7363–7366. ISSN: 0975-9646.
West, D. (1993). Air Wars. Washington, D.C.: Congressional Quarterly Press.
Zora, P., & Woreck, D. (2006). HRW documents repression in Kashmir. Concurrent.org. Retrieved 21 August 2015, from http://www.countercurrents.org/kashmir-hrw011206.htm

Index

Aam Aadmi Party (AAP), 89, 178, 181, 195, 198
Advani, L.K., 180, 182
advertisements, 99, 199
 advantages of, 101
 awareness about political candidates, 101
 censor campaign, 56
 paid political, 162
 political, 63, 86, 96, 103–105, 158
 viral, 43
advertising, 16, 29, 84, 102
 and politics of political parties, 188–189
 cake, 58
 commercial, 27, 154
 government, 183
 gurus, 45
 paid, 55, 81
 paid political, 15, 84
 political, 26, 55, 62, 100, 109, 158
 revenue, 24
African Charter on Human and Peoples' Right, 131
African National Congress (ANC), 172
agenda setting, 102–103
aggressive commercialization, 1
Al Jazeera, 59
Al Jazeera English, 40, 41
Ambani, Mukesh, 28
American Convention on Human Rights, 131, 148
AM radio, 33
Arab Social Media Report (2011), 170
Arab Spring, 39–41
audience analysis, 26
Australia, cross-media ownership law in, 56
Ayodhya case, 180
Ayyub, Rana, 193

Bahujan Samaj Party (BSP), 192
Balsara, Sam, 45

Banerjee, Mamata, 186
Baruah, Dev Kant, 186
Bellary illegal mining scam (2011), 194
Ben Ali, Zine el-Abidine, 40
Benegal, Shyam, 121
Bharatiya Janata Party (BJP), 44, 89, 178, 186, 193
 victory in UP elections of 2017, 192
Bikitsha, Nikiwe, 173
BlackBerry Messenger, 41
bloggers
 Canada, prohibition from reporting results, 161–163
 United States law on governing, 162
blogs, 37, 41
Bofors scandal, 188
British Broadcasting Corporation (BBC), 24, 27, 59, 159
 privatization of, 58
British National Party (BNP), 164
British War Cabinet (1944), 117
broadcast, 30, 61, 66, 118, 120, 157
 additional programming, 81
 licensing, 56
 market, 63
 media, 23, 73, 83, 153, 168
 music, 59
 private media, 159
 regulator, 88
 regulators, functions of, 76
 stations, 7
broadcasters, 27, 53, 56, 82
 aim of, 80
 independent and private national, 24
 multinational, 59
 national public, 30
 Nepal rural, 17
 private, 29
 publicly owned or funded, 83
 regulation of, 75

responsibilities during election time, 25
  state, 15
Broadcasters Liaison Group (BLG), 142
broadcasting, 149, 202
  digital, 35
  frequencies, 24
  license, 31
  regulation of, 75–77
  stations, 31, 132, 157
Broadcasting Standards Commission, 164
Bucaram, Abdala, 9
Bush, George W., 109, 111, 125, 161

Cable News Network (CNN), 59
Cable-Satellite Public Affairs Network
  (C-SPAN and C-SPAN II)
  network, 114, 118
cable television, 59, 98, 125
Cameron, David, 43
campaigns, election, 13, 85
  in India for 2014 general elections, 88–90
  media as platform, 14–15
  Narendra Modi, 45
  new media as, 43
candidate(s), 16, 61, 93–95
  and voters, interaction between, 98
  electorate information, 15
  media as platform for, 18
  media use for public interaction, 13
  nomination, 8
  women, 20
Carter, Jimmy, 93, 113, 123
CBS Corporation, 28
Charter of Rights and Freedom,
  Canada, 163
Chavan, Ashok, 16
  paid news case, 174
checker speech, 110
Chikmagalur by election of 1978, 183–184
Chomsky, Noam, 1, 180, 198
Churchill, Winston, 117
Citizen Control, 39
citizen journalism, 13, 19
Clarín, 57
Clear Channel company, 28
Clinton, Bill, 111
CNBC 18, 28
CNBC Awaaz, 28

CNBC-TV18, 191
CNN-IBN, 28
commercial radio license, 56
community, 2
community broadcasting, 31, 76
community media, 31
community radio stations, 30
Conference on Security and Cooperation in
  Europe (CSCE), 131
*Congress ka Haath, Aam Aadmi ke
  Saath* (Congress' loyalty rests with
  the common man) slogan, 188
Congress party, 89, 90, 179, 182, 187, 188,
  195, 196
contemporary media, 23
Convention on the Elimination of All
  Forms of Racial Discrimination
  (CERD), 148
corruption, 4, 59, 68, 193, 196
  exposure by media, 105
  in judiciary, 108
  in public life, 9
  political, 61
coverage in media, types of
  direct access programmes, 82
  news and current affairs, 80–81
  special information programmes, 81
coverage packages, 181
current affairs, 81
cyber-rallies, 18

defamation, 68, 71, 77, 132, 135, 141, 146
de Mello, Fernando Collor, 8
democratic elections, essence of, 61
Desh Bachao slogan, 185–186
digital broadcasting, 35
direct access broadcasting, 153
direct access programmes, 82, 83, 87, 88
direct TV politics, 118
Doordarshan, 188
Douglas, Stephen, 122
Dutt, Barkha, 191

editorial autonomy, 63
editorial bias, 63
editorial freedom, 28
editorial opinions, 83
educational role of media, 19–20

Egypt, new media and election transparency, 169–171
Eisenhower, Dwight, 121
Election commission
    Gambia, communications plan, 165–166
Election commission
    regulation on media, responsibility of, 143
Election Commission (EC), 13
election(s), 8
    campaigns in India, 88–90
    complaints procedure technique, 144
    coverage, 33
    freedom of political debate during, 60–61
    general elections in India (2014), 44
    guidelines for media during, 60–62
    implementation mechanism of media during, 141
    importance of, 52
    in French (2012), 48
    in Russia (2012), 56
    in UK 2010, 43
    media during, restrictions on, 137–139
    media ownership and, 56
    media pluralism during, 55
    media professionals safety during, 140
    media role during, 12–14
    news for media, 16
    opinion polls, regulation on, 145
    political speech, restrictions on, 137
    public media role during, 86–87
    right to access, 150–152
    self-regulation by media during, 142
    State of Uttar Pradesh vs Raj Narain, 173–174
    televised debate, role of, 101
    US presidential, 16
    violence, 39
Elections media commission, 143
electoral commissions, 43, 140, 142
electoral democracy, 12, 170
electoral fraud, 8, 15, 38
electoral politics, 16, 23, 95
electronic media, 36, 64, 96, 109, 125, 155
El Mercurio newspaper, 29
Ennahda party, 40
Estrada, Joseph, 9
ETV channels, 29
euphoria press, 6
European Commission of Human Rights, 135
European Convention on Human Rights, 131
European Court of Human Rights, 60, 69, 72, 129, 132, 133
exit polls, 63, 85, 126

Facebook, 19, 23, 37, 41, 43, 89, 90, 195, 197
    election, 43
FM radio, 2, 17, 33
Ford, Gerald, 113, 123
freedom of expression, 24, 25, 31, 47, 52, 53, 88
    and media role, 68–70
    and political parties, 71
    during elections, 69–70
    fundamental human right, 65
    negative and positive obligations, 66
    news media and, 71
    restrictions on, 68
    right to express itself, 66
    universal recognition to, 66
freedom of political debate, 60–61
freedom of political discussion, 133
freedom of speech, 48, 49, 60
    during elections, 165
    restrictions on, 50
free or non-captured media, 104
free press, 4, 105, 108
Fujimori, Alberto, 9
funding, media
    community media, 30–31
    party and politician owned media, 31–32
    private media, 27–30
    public media, 26–28

Gaddafi, Muammar, 42
Gandhi, Indira, 188
    campaign strategy, 185
    National Emergency in 1975 and press censorship, 181–183
Gandhi, Rahul, 90
Gandhi, Rajiv, 188
Gandhi, Sonia, 186

Garibi hatao slogan, 186–187
gender discrimination, 22
gender relations and role of media, 20–22
Georgia, media monitoring in, 171–172
Global Media Monitoring Project (GMMP), 22, 172
Globo, 57
Gobodo-Madikizela, Phumla, 173
good media practices, 7–11
The Guardian online, 192

Halberstam, David, 95
hate speech, 148–150
　in United Kingdom, laws governing, 165
Hazare, Anna, 195
Herman, Edward S., 180
Hill, Anita, 119
Hindi-Chini Bhai-Bhai (Indians and Chinese are brothers) slogan, 186
Human Rights Committee (HRC), 134
Hussein, Abid, 54

incumbent governments, 137
Independent Electoral Commission (IEC), 143
　Gambia, 165
Independent Media Commission (IMC), South Africa, 143
Indian Express, 192
India Shining campaign, 186, 189–190
Indonesia, euphoria press revolution, 6
information
　gatekeepers, 25
　importance of, 8
　on public domain, importance of, 11
Information Technology Act, 2000, Section 66-A of
　and court rationale, 50–51
　challenge, 49
Instagram, 23
Institute of War and Peace Reporting (IWPR), 168
Inter-American Commission on Human Rights, 129
Inter-American Court of Human Rights, 69, 132
Intergovernmental Council of the International Programme for the Development of Communication (IPDC), 64
International Committee for the Red Cross, 140
International Covenant on Civil and Political Rights (ICCPR), 53, 65, 70, 130, 200
　Article 19(3) of, 67
　Article 19 of, 133, 137, 147
　Article 20 of, 137, 147
　goals and objectives of, 130
　obligation to states, 69
international law on elections and media, 132
International Telecommunications Union, 34, 35
Internet, 18, 19, 23, 37, 47
　challenge broadcasting monopolies, 59
　media ownership, 59
Internet and Mobile Association of India (IAMAI), 89
investigative reporting, 2
　dangers of, 10
　impact of, 10
Iris Knowledge Foundation, 89
Italy, law to access media, 161

Jai Jawan, Jai Kisan slogan, 185, 186
Jai Shree Ram slogan, 193
Janata Party, 184
'*Janta Maaf Nahi Karegi*' slogan, 45
Jefferson, Thomas, 3
Johnson, Lyndon, 111
Joshi, Prasoon, 45
journalism, 18
　canons of, 63
　for peace, 2
　independent and investigative, 74
　investigative, 108
journalists, 7, 64, 90
　accuracy and impartiality in reporting, 207–208
　code of conduct during elections, 206
　cooperative media regulation, 202
　ethical obligations, 208
　ethical standards faced during elections, 204–205
　fear among politicians, 6

legal provisions during election
coverage, 206
objectivity challenge faced by, 201–204
operate pool system, 151
press restrictions, legality of, 201
pressure during elections, 199
protection of sources, 201
regulation of, 77–79
rights and responsibilities of, 9, 71, 200
safety of, 74–75, 201
judiciary role during elections, 142–143

Kalifulla, Fakkir Mohammed Ibrahim
(Justice), 173
Karnataka assembly elections 2013,
192–194
Kejriwal, Arvind, 90, 181, 195
Kennedy, John F., 101, 109
coverage of assassination, 110
Khan, Azam, 192
Kinhalkar, Madhav, 174
Kumar, Ananth, 193

landscape, media
factors determining, 24
Lankesh Patrike, 10
La Republique des Pyrennees newspaper,
145
Le Parisien newspaper, 145
Lincoln, Abraham, 122
Lok Sabha, 119, 120
Lok Sabha TV (LSTV), 119
London Weekend Television, 164

Maa, Maati, Manush (Mother, motherland
and people) slogan, 186
Malema, Julius, 173
*Manufacturing Consent: The Political
Economy of the Mass* Media,
180
mass media, 1, 48, 52, 61, 69, 91, 96, 102,
105, 115, 121, 125, 160
campaigns, 15
challenges to, 8
freedom of express and information,
132
in democratic process, role, 104
influence on human life, 160

in political campaigns, role, 91
monitoring during election periods, 14
private, 28
technological advances in, 53
use of internet and new media
platforms by, 59
Mayawati, 191, 192
media
as a campaign platform for political
parties and candidates, 14–15
as medium between administrators and
citizens, 4
as peace and consensus builder, 11–12
as voice of marginalized sections, 5
at national level, 23
constraints, 7
content, 7
coverage, concern of, 13
democratic role of, 53
exposure, 8
fixation, 180
freedom, European court on, 52
free, importance of, 177
functions of, 107
houses, obligations for, 61
in conflict situations, 12
in democracy, significance of, 178
institution for prevention and
investigation of violations of
political parties, 8
liability, limitations of, 135–136
literacy, 32–33
mapping, 23
monopolies, 54
network regulating bodies, 88–89
outlets, 61
owners, 7
peace building and social consensus,
role in, 1–2
professionalism, 28, 90
professionals, safety during elections,
139–140
public cynicism due to, 1
reports, candidates right to defend
against, 136
role as fourth estate, 1
role in 2014 general election of India,
178

role in democracy, 3–5
role of, 53–54, 62
to consider public interest, 160
trial by, 2
usage as proxies by political groups, 2
Media Experts Commission (MEC), Bosnia-Herzegovina, 143
Media Monitoring Project of Zimbabwe (MMPZ), 166, 167
micro-blogs, 37
mobile phones, 37
Modi, Narendra, 89, 178, 180, 192, 195
    and social media, 45
    obsession during 2014 general elections, 190–191
Mubarak, Hosni, 41
multiparty democracy, 4

Naidu, Katta Subramanya, 194
National Democratic Alliance (NDA), 189
    India Shining campaign, failure of, 189–190
National Food Security Act (NFSA), 179
National Public Radio (NPR), US, 27
NATO, 42
NBC Universal, 28
NDTV, 191
Network 18 Group, 28
new media, 37–38
    as a forum for dialogue, 45–46
    as campaign platform, 43–44
    as fourth estate, 37–39
    as public educator, 43
    regulation of, 46–48
news, 81
    balance and impartiality in, 82–84
    blackouts, 145
    programmes, 10, 124
news media, 12, 38, 70, 71, 97
    bias, 203
    coverage of politics, 112
    personnel, 113
newspapers, 4, 7, 10, 15, 37, 73, 91, 92, 103, 110, 121, 136, 149, 192
    cost of, 16
    in mature democracies, 30
    liberal, 203
    private, 29
    public, 88
    secondary, subsidies to, 58
    stories, 99
    stories and advertisements, public awareness through, 99
    traditional media, 18
New Vision newspaper, Uganda, 28
Nigeria, media ownership impact on, 167–169
Nigerian Election News Report (NENR), 168
Nijjar, Surinder Singh (Justice), 173
Nirbhaya gang rape in New Delhi, 195
Nixon, Richard, 110
non-media conglomerates, 30

Obama, Barack, 43, 194
online communities, 30
online media, 17, 30, 43, 48
online signature campaigns, 18
Operation Kamala by BJP, 193
opinion polls
    conduct of, 85
    importance of, 84
    interpreting, 85–86
Organization for Security and Cooperation in Europe (OSCE), 171
Organization of African Unity, 118
Organization of American States, 74
Organization on Security and Cooperation in Europe, 74
ownership of media, 7, 54–56
    global, 56–60

paid news, 16, 174, 181
paid political advertising, 56, 84, 156
    in Canada, regulations on, 164
Pandey, Piyush, 45
Party Election Broadcasts, 142
party owned media, 31–32
peace journalism, 12
Perez, Carlos Andres, 8
Perot, Ross, 111
Pew Research Center study, 25
photo identity card, 150
Pillay, Navi, 47
Playboy magazine, 93
pluralism, media, 55, 56, 63, 73, 135
    threats to, 53

political advertising, 26, 108–109
  American-style, 115
  origin of, 188
political campaigns
  and media coverage, 100
  and social responsibility of media, 102–108
  candidates controversies during, 93–95
  coverage of, 93–94
  electoral debates on, 95–96
  mass media role in, 91–93
  news media role in, evaluation of, 99–102
political candidates, 29, 56, 101, 113, 149, 156, 204
political corruption, 61
political markets, 107
political participation in electoral process, 79
  right to, 80
political parties, 8, 13, 19, 32, 52, 70
  and freedom of express, 71
  and newspaper, 31
  favour to men over women, 20
  media coverage to, 61
  use of mass media by, 15
Political Research Quarterly, 59
political slogans, 184–187
political speech, restrictions during elections, 137
political violence, 19
politician owned media, 32
politicians
  criticism of, 137
  TRP and saleability of, 191–192
Prasar Bharati, 120
press, 1, 3
  free and fair, 9
  freedom, 10
print media, 35–37
  licensing system for, 77
  regulation of, 76–77
  technical registration of, 77
private broadcasters, 29, 55, 58, 59, 73, 82, 83
private broadcasting, 24, 58
private media, 28–30
  associated with military dictatorship, 58

  in South America, 24
  operation of, 28
  provisions for, 151–159
  responsibilities during elections, 139–141
private newspapers, 29
private print media, 29
professionalism, media, 12, 32, 63, 204, 207
profiteering, 1
public broadcasters, 59
  publicly-funded entities, 86
public broadcasting, 28, 58, 63, 87, 155
public forum, media as a, 15–19
public media
  in emerging democracies, 58
  provisions for, 151–159
  responsibilities during elections, 139–141
  role during elections, 86–87
public newspapers, 88
public service broadcasters, 81, 159, 173
public service broadcasting networks, 13
public service broadcasting (PSB), 28, 55
  definition of, 27
  establishment of, 28
  functions of, 27
  principles of, 27
  public broadcaster statutory independence in South Africa, 28

radio, 2, 13, 15, 26, 33, 34, 76, 91
  networks, 16
Radio Sagarmatha (FM Radio), 17
Radio Swargadwari, 17
Rajya Sabha, 120
Rajya Sabha TV (RSTV), 120, 121
Reddy, Janardhana, 193
Reddy, Karunakara, 193
Reddy, Somashekara, 193
regulation
  media, 72–73
  of broadcasting, 75–77
  of journalists, 77–79
  of print media, 76–77
Reliance Industries Ltd (RIL), 28
Representation of the People Act of 1951, 175
right to effective remedy, 138
Romney, Mitt, 194

Rove, Karl, 125
Rupert Murdoch's News Corp, 28
Rwanda conflict, 12

Samajwadi Party (SP), 192
Samvidhan mini-series (Shyam Benegal), 121
satellite communication, 23
satellite television, 59
Scheer, Robert, 93
second-tier media firms, 57
Sen, Amartya, 4
sensationalism, 1
separate print, 30
Seshan, T. N. electoral reforms during regime of, 176
Setty, S. N. Krishnaiah, 194
Shah, Amit, 192, 193
Sharma, Rajat, 190
Shastri, Lal Bahadur, 186
Shinawatra, Thaksin, 9
short message service (SMS), 38
Shreya Singhal case, 49
Sina Weibo, 37
Singh, Giriraj, 192
Singh, Kalyan, 193
social media, 13, 19, 37, 39, 89
  in Indian politics, role of, 194–196
  in Lok Sabha elections of 2014, impact, 196–198
  role of uprisings, 42
  services, 23
  used to overhaul hate speech, 39
South Africa, gender parity in elections, 171–173
Southern 'Super Tuesday', 99
Special Broadcasting Service (SBS), Australia, 27
Special Economic Zones (SEZs), 187
special information programmes, 81, 87
Special Investigation Team (SIT), 180
Sriramulu, B., 193
Star News Corporation, 24
Suharto dictatorship, in Indonesia, 58

Tehelka magazine, 10
telecommunications, 76
  markets, explosion in 1990s, 57
telecom services, 23

Televisa, 57
television, 26, 34, 76, 91
  advertising, 16, 111, 157
  and governing process, 115
  and international political processes, 114–115
  and political campaigns, 110–112
  and politics, perspectives on, 115–116
  broadcasters, 13
  categorization of ownership, 35
  coverage of parliamentary bodies, 115–119
  digital programming, 35
  elections, impact on, 120–124
  Indian parliament proceedings in, 119–121
  Indian voters, impact on, 124–128
  news coverage of political campaigns, 111–113
  private channels, 63
  satellite, penetration in Egypt, 35
  terrestrial programming, 35
television media and elections, role of television, 34–36
Tempo magazine, 18
Tharoor, Shashi, 195
Thatcher, Margaret, 118
The Guardian, 41
The New York Times, 41
Thomas, Clarence, 119
Time Warner, 28
traditional media, 36, 37, 48
  watchdog role, 39
traditional media and elections, radio role, 34
transparency, 7, 8, 27, 38, 130
  guarantees, 4
  impact on elections, 152
  media, 19
  of electoral process, 12
Transparency International (TI), 39
Tunisian Revolution (or Jasmine Revolution), 40
Tweeter Election 2014, 90
Twitter, 19, 23, 37, 39, 41, 43, 90, 195, 197

UN Human Development Index, 190
UN Human Rights Committee, 70, 129

UN Inter-Agency Meeting (first), 65
United National Movement, 171
United Nations Development Programme (UNDP), 4–5
United Nations General Assembly, 65
United Nations Human Rights Committee (UNHRC)
    freedom of expression, 53
United Nations Transitional Authorities, Cambodia, 135
United Progressive Alliance (UPA), 44, 178
    Garibi hatao slogan, 186–187
Universal Declaration of Human Rights, 65, 129
UN Plan of Action on the Safety of Journalists, 64
UN Special Rapporteur for Freedom of Expression, 21, 53, 134, 140, 148
UN Special Rapporteur for Freedom of Opinion and Expression, 129, 135, 136
UN Special Rapporteur for Freedom Opinion and Expression, 54
UN Technical Team on the Malawi referendum of 1993, 133
Urs, Devraj, 184
US Communications Act (1934), 56
U-Shahid, activist organization, 170
Ushahidi cloud-sourcing software, 39
US Inter-Parliamentary Union, 22
Uttar Pradesh assembly elections 2017, 192–193

Vajpayee, Atal Bihari, 186
Viacom, 28
virtual communities, 30
Voice of America, 24
voters, 12, 13, 16, 17, 20, 71
    access to election information, 56
    education, 21
    education videos, 43
    importance of vote, information about, 62
    individual characteristics of, 102
    media as basic source of information, 61
    media as platform for, 19
    right to freedom of information, 72
    television impact on, 124–128

Walt Disney, 24, 28
Wilkie, Wendell, 122
women participation in political process, 21
World Bank, media monopolies, dominance of, 7

Yedyurappa, B. S., 193
YouTube, 37, 43

Zimbabwe, 39
    biased coverage during elections, 165–167
Zimbabwe Broadcasting Corporation (ZBC), 167
Zuma, Jacob, 172

About the Author

Bheemaiah Krishnan Ravi is Professor in the Department of Communication, Bangalore University, Karnataka, India. He has 28 years of teaching and research experience. He has written in several international research journals and has published five books. Professor Ravi specializes in the following subject areas: Indian media industry, development communication, political communication and film studies. He has several television programmes and radio productions to his credit. During 2002–2006, he was a member of the Karnataka State Commission for Backward Classes. Before he started his academic career, he spent a decade as a journalist. Presently he is serving as the Registrar of Bangalore University.